Publications in Librarianship no. 57

Colleges, Code, and Copyright

The Impact of Digital Networks and Technological
Controls on Copyright and the Dissemination
of Information in Higher Education

Center for Intellectual Property
University of Maryland University College

Association of College and Research Libraries
A Division of the American Library Association
Chicago 2005

The paper used in this publication meets the minimum requirements of American National Standard for Information Sciences–Permanence of Paper for Printed Library Materials, ANSI Z39.48-1992. ∞

Library of Congress Cataloging-in-Publication Data
Colleges, code, and copyright : the impact of digital networks and technological controls on copyright and the dissemination of knowledge in higher education.
    p. cm.   (ACRL publications in librarianship ; no. 57)
  "Papers of the annual symposium hosted by the Center for Intellectual Property, University of Maryland University College, Adelphi, Maryland, June 10-11, 2004."
  Includes bibliographical references and index.
  ISBN 0-8389-8322-7 (alk. paper)
  1. Copyright United States Congresses. 2. Scholarly publishing United States Congresses. 3. Academic libraries Law and legislation United States Congresses. I. Center for Intellectual Property. II. Series.

  Z674.A75 no. 57
  [KF2994.A2]
  346.7304'82 dc22
                                    2005008033

Printed on recycled paper.

Printed in the United States of America.

09 08 07 06 05   5 4 3 2 1

Table of Contents

Preface

Digital information and digital networks are changing how universities access, share, and use information for scholarship, teaching, and learning. The fundamental shift to using digital information to educate students and in sharing resources has caused sweeping changes in how many believe digital information should be accessed and protected. The Center for Intellectual Property at the University of Maryland, University College, seeks to explore changes in how information is protected and disseminated in the digital environment. To achieve that end, the center educates, conducts research, and develops resources on the impact of intellectual property law and policy on higher education and the digital environment.

As part of its ongoing educational programming, in June 2004, the center conducted a national symposium that included a call for papers. The symposium was entitled "Colleges, Code, and Copyright: The Impact of Digital Networks and Technological Controls on Copyright and the Dissemination of Information in Higher Education." Its goal was to assemble stakeholders to discuss the technological, legal, and practical issues that influence the dissemination of information on campus and the protection of intellectual property.

The symposium offered thematic tracks on a wide range of topics, such as the intersection of copyright and higher education, the state of scholarly publishing, current copyright legislation, peer-to-peer file sharing, and best practices in digital rights management. The papers in this monograph reflect the various topics discussed at the symposium on a stage figuratively set by Dr. Clifford Lynch, Executive Director of Coalition for Networked Information and the center's 2004–2006 Intellectual Property Scholar, in his keynote address.

Acknowledgments

The Center for Intellectual Property would like to express its sincere gratitude to the following individuals who made presentations during the symposium: Kenneth Crews, Indiana University School of Law-Indianapolis; Gail Dykstra, University of Washington; Bryan Pfaffenberger, University of Virginia; Brian Crawford, John Wiley & Sons, Inc; Joan Lippincott, Coalition for Networked Information (CNI); Karla Hahn, University of Maryland Libraries; M. J. Tooey, University of Maryland, College Park; Lee Strickland, University of Maryland, College Park; David Galper, Ruckus Network; David Green, MPAA; Matt Jackson, Pennsylvania State University; Mark Luker, EDUCAUSE; Miriam Nisbet, American Library Association; Kenneth Salomon, Dow, Lohnes, & Albertson, PLLC; Gigi Sohn, Public Knowledge; John Vaughn, Association of American Universities; Rick Johnson, Scholarly Publishing and Academic Resources Coalition; Jo Ann Oravec, University of Wisconsin; Rodney Petersen, EDUCAUSE; Kristin Diamond, University of Colorado; David Lombard Harrison, University of North Carolina; Farid Ahmed, Catholic University of America; and Keith Winstein, Massachusetts Institute of Technology.

This volume has been reviewed in draft form by individuals chosen for their diverse perspectives and technical expertise. The purpose of this independent review is to provide the authors with critical comments to ensure that the publication meets acceptable publication standards. We wish to thank Dr. Theodore Stone, executive director of the Center for the Virtual University at the University of Maryland, University College, and Dr. Lynch for reviewing the symposium papers. The individual authors maintain responsibility for the final content of the papers.

Finally, the Center for Intellectual Property would like to acknowledge the efforts of the following CIP staff and consultants: Kimberly Kelley, who moderated several panel discussions and served as a subject expert for participant selection; Kimberly Bonner, who served as project director for the symposium and the proceedings publication; Maria Lee, who assisted with coordination of logistical arrangements; Michael VanderHeijden, who researched and secured background readings, managed participant registrations, and provided support for the paper review process; Olga François, who managed the call for papers, the paper reviews, as well as marketing and advertising; and Andy Joyce, Christian Guirreri, and Daniel Wendling, who provided multimedia support.

Chapter 1

Keynote Address: Digital Rights Management Systems and Scholarship[1]

Clifford Lynch

I'm going to talk about digital rights management (DRM) and talk specifically from the perspective of higher education. So much of the policy discussion surrounding DRM is predicated on the assumptions and values of the consumer marketplace, and on developments such as peer-to-peer file sharing that are perceived to alter the economics of that marketplace. I believe that there's actually a great deal of value in asking specific questions about digital rights management in the settings of scholarship, teaching and learning, and higher education broadly. How does DRM fit in with the values, behaviors, and activities that characterize scholarship as opposed to the needs and desires of the various players in the broader consumer world? Asking this helps to illuminate two distinct areas. The first is the potential consequences and collateral damage that public policy decisions about the consumer marketplace may have on the worlds of scholarship, higher education, and cultural memory. The second is to help clarify the agenda that higher education might want to pursue for the development and deployment of DRM for its own purpose and within its own sphere. Let me simply note at the outset that I'm not an attorney and I'm not giving legal advice here. My focus is really on the implications of this set of developments at the nexus of technology and law.

1

I'm going to start with a little discussion of this horrible term *DRM* (digital rights management), where it comes from and the various things it means to different people. Part of this is to make sure that we are all understanding the grab bag of things that are subsumed under the DRM umbrella, some helpful and some frightening. From there, I'll move on to look at how these various technologies align with or against academic values and practices. One of the particular things I want to touch on toward the end of my talk is the fact that there doesn't seem to be in the higher education community a consensus about the positions the academy and the cultural heritage sectors should be taking regarding the support and deployment of DRM; I want to look at a few of the areas of disagreement. I would invite you to consider these questions as I talk.

My work takes me to a lot of places where the research world intersects with more operational systems and infrastructure deployment in higher education. And one of the things that I hear from some technologists that I talk to in these settings is, "Why don't we do a DRM project in higher education?" They want my thoughts on how such a project might be structured and focused. They want to know whether I think it's a good idea and whether I (and the organization I represent, the Coalition for Networked Information) would support such a project.

We need to collectively be prepared to answer questions like these. I'll share some of my answers and my thinking, and I hope that it will be helpful in refining your own. And I hope, too, that at the end of the talk we'll have time to compare notes on our answers.

Oddly enough, many of the technologies around DRM, because they are so difficult and complicated and arcane, are irresistibly seductive to a certain class of computer scientists, engineers, and related technologists. (I can say this, I'm a computer scientist myself.) Indeed, it's not at all clear that major parts of the DRM problem actually *have* sensible engineering solutions under any sort of reasonable deployment assumptions, which only makes it more challenging. And many engineers who find the technology fascinating are simultaneously and variously bemused, puzzled, appalled, or revolted by the applications to which people want to put it. On my really bad days, I'm reminded of accounts I've read about the same kind of weird fascination and simultaneous repulsion that the physics community had about the engineering not so much of the atomic (fission) bomb but, later, of the hydrogen (fusion) bomb. As a piece of engineering, the H-bomb was so elegant, some of them said, that *they had to build it*, even though they were horrified by the consequences and effects of the weapon.

Because DRM systems and technologies can define, implement, and enforce policies, DRM system and technology designers and other proponents will often argue that they are, in fact, policy neutral and that it is up to the individual content owners to determine what kinds of policies are to be associated with their content. This is a dodge; at some level, code is policy—and the kinds of policies that we can and cannot encode and accommodate in a given DRM system (the choices available to content holders), as well as the extent to which they also honor or ignore legal and social precedents and expectations surrounding content use, means that DRM systems design can imply centrally important policy choices. We need to talk about what sorts of policies are important to accommodate from the perspective of scholarship and education.

So, let me begin with this awful term *digital rights management,* or DRM for short. I have not gone through the painful process of trying to figure out exactly where and when this terminology originated (this would be a useful thing for someone to do and I wish someone would). I can tell you a fair amount about where some of the underlying ideas seem to have originated. There is a long prehistory, mostly involving technologies to protect computer software and prevent copying of such software. This was usually just called software copy protection. Mark Stefik (at Xerox Palo Alto Research Center, now just Palo Alto Research Center, or PARC) formulated and articulated a number of the key ideas that underpin broad-purpose DRM in the early to mid-1990s. He portrayed a closed system operating in a world of commerce and exchange in "digital objects" in which the objects came with a set of properties that said what you could do with them. Examples of properties are: Could you print it? How many copies could you print? How long could you use it before it went away? The system would enforce the properties; of course, when you went outside the system, all bets were off, and one property was whether an object could be exported outside the boundaries of the system. I don't think, at least in the early days, Stefik used the term *digital rights management.* He was really, in many ways, more concerned, not so much with talking about enforcing rights, but with talking about the properties that digital objects have within a certain system context or inside a certain system perimeter and how this could facilitate commerce. In fact, he used language about "trusted systems" (and did a very nice article of the same name for *Scientific American*), a very important idea and we'll come back to that. Let me just note here that when we move from talking about "properties of objects" to "rights," we suddenly drag in a whole legal and public policy dimension that didn't seem to be a central part of Stefik's original thinking.

You should read Stefik's work, by the way. He couches much of his discussion in the context of enabling e-commerce in digital content; one of his key essays is titled "Letting Loose the Light: Igniting Commerce in Electronic Publication." His work speaks mainly about enabling new marketplaces and market uses, and it has a very positive rhetoric, a very different feel than most discussions today of DRM (whether by rabid DRM proponents or opponents), which seems to be about new systems that are designed to do ever less than the older systems they replace, about tracking and control and restrictions and stopping consumer criminals. Stefik is a thoughtful and balanced thinker on these topics; he has written two very fine books on these topics: *Internet Dreams: Archetypes, Myths and Metaphors* (1996), and *The Internet Edge: Social, Technical and Legal Challenges for a Networked World* (1999).

Stefik's work was at the core of the patents and technologies that Xerox moved into the ContentGuard joint venture with Microsoft and [which] are the foundation for standards like XRML and the systems that implement it. And there were other important players who developed major technology bases and patent positions, notably Intertrust (now owned jointly by Sony and Phillips).

Anyway, at some point, probably in the early 1990s, I'm guessing, along came this awful term *digital rights management.* It means very different things to different people. Some people would have you believe that content owners are entitled to special rights and protections in the digital environment and that these DRM technologies are there to protect and enforce those rights. Indeed, they'll suggest that there need to be stronger laws and more aggressive law enforcement to make the world safer for these DRM technologies and special rights, to make these DRM technologies stronger and more robust. These propositions seem to have little basis in fact, law, or social precedence, though this hasn't stopped some DRM proponents from trying to turn these fantasies into law.

Let's start by unpacking digital rights management as rhetoric from a factual and critical perspective before we get into the technologies. In the first place, the phrase definitely gets an oxymoron award because there really aren't any "digital rights," as I said earlier. There are rights in certain kinds of intellectual property (for example, under copyright law), and those rights exist whether the content is on paper or in digital form. There are, to be sure, all kinds of issues (many of which are being explored in other presentations at this conference) that arise when content moves to digital form about how the traditional rights and limitations that have governed our use of intellectual property transfer to the digital environment; but the notion that somehow there are "special digital rights" has very little basis in fact. Digital rights management not only gets recognition as an oxymoron, but it gets an Orwell award because it's really not about digital rights, it's about control and restriction and management in the sense of making sure you don't do things, mostly, and that in any event what you are doing can be appropriately monitored. Indeed, many people now expand the acronym DRM as "digital restrictions management" rather than "digital rights management," and this is, to be sure, more accurate. It probably would have been a better world if we had started from the departure point of digital restrictions management because it greatly tones down the legal and moral appeals and rhetoric and concentrates on the engineering problem without the argument that it's engineering in the service of upholding the God-given rights of the rights holders.

There actually are, I believe, things that legitimately show up in the management of rights in a digital environment that aren't Orwellian, but the way DRM is framed does have that tone to it sometimes. Note that the term *Orwellian* is often reserved mainly for the actions of politicians and demagogues, for state action; in DRM, we find also the cynicism of Orwell gone commercial, the sort of organizational PR-speak that uses phrases like "to serve you better" when what they are doing is reducing or eliminating services.

On to the technologies. There is not a particularly clean, clear definition that I've been able to find of what DRM really means; in my view, roughly, DRM is a group of technologies concerned with the documentation of rights, permissions, and policies associated with digital objects and services, and control and management of the use of digital content and services consistent with those rights, permissions, and policies. This is vague and very general. So to get specific, let's talk briefly about some of the actually deployed technologies that fall under the DRM rubric.

The first technology is a very familiar one. It's about access control. Obviously, if you have content that is restricted under license to a specific community of users, then you need to, according to the terms of that license, control who gets to look at or otherwise use that content. That's a very familiar scenario, reaching back to the dawn of time in computer systems, practically, and one that certainly our academic libraries have been working with since the 1980s at least, dealing with institutionally site-licensed material. We now have rather elaborate systems in place at most of our colleges and universities to deal with access management, with authentication and authorization, with deciding who is who and who is a member of the university community. And, indeed, over the past ten years or so, we have invested heavily in these access management systems. We have developed, for example, some fairly difficult and delicate compromises around privacy versus accountability, some balances between anonymity and access control. The library world, in particular, has had to sort through things where they really *don't* want to know who you are. They just want to know you're a member of the appropriate community. In higher education we really don't want to track, on an individual basis, who's reading what in our libraries, by and large. On the other hand, we need enough accountability in these systems so that if you are seeing a signature of behavior that is pretty obviously in contravention to license agreements (for example, someone is logging on from the U.S. and Japan simultaneously for eighteen hours a day or someone just downloaded copies of eleven thousand journal articles), the institution can track down what's going on and deal with it. So, access management is certainly part of the management of various kinds of licensed and owned content in the digital world. It's a very familiar one.

Many people would argue that while access management is a form of DRM, it really doesn't go far enough. The real essence of DRM, as it's portrayed by the consumer electronics folks and by the content industries (i.e., sound recordings, movies, etc.), is not just about access management, it's about downstream control. It's about the idea that once you've gotten access to it, there is some continuing control over what you can do with it. It might be that your access to it evaporates after thirty days. It may be that you can't make a copy of it. It may be that you can't transfer it off the specific machine onto which you've downloaded it. It may be that only when the moon is in certain phases and you're putting quarters in the slot are you allowed to look at it. It may be that you can only read it twice. You can only play it fifteen times and then it evaporates or becomes locked. Every time you want to look at something, that something "calls home" to find out if it should show itself to you again or if it should self-destruct. There is no end to the ingenuity of the constraints and controls one can imagine, and you can clearly see why this is interesting to the content industries. It is interesting because it deals with the things that they call piracy, some of which really are and some of which seem to me to be reasonable use of something that you've acquired. It also can be used to shut down a lot of pesky business models that the content industries have found very annoying, but that are quite legal. And, of course, at least in theory, it opens up the possibility of new revenue streams (at least to the extent that consumers will put up with being charged over and over again for the same content).

One of the foundational ideas of copyright is the doctrine of first sale. Basically, the idea is that once you acquire a copy of something in the marketplace, the rights holder doesn't have any real downstream control over what you do with that copy, except for those constraints on copying that are provided by copyright law. You can loan it to somebody. You can burn it. You can use it as landfill. You can put it in your attic and pass it down to your grandchildren. You can annotate it. You can't copy it, necessarily. That is specifically prohibited, but downstream use isn't controlled otherwise. This means that all kinds of things can take place, like loaning recordings to a friend, used book sales, resale of textbooks, used music sales—all these things that let two people enjoy a book, for example, without the rights holder getting revenue from the second use. (In some cases, some of these activities are controlled in some other countries under their copyright laws.)

Library circulation is another important activity that is enabled by first sale. When you think about the practice of circulating libraries, "first sale" is fundamentally what makes that work. And first sale is important for more than just circulation, it also is an essential part of allowing any interested cultural heritage organizations, or indeed individuals, without any other special mandate, such as copyright deposit laws, to collect and maintain records of our intellectual and cultural discourse. First sale is a cornerstone of the way we have thought about intellectual property in the U.S. and is an essential enabler of our ability to preserve it for future publics.

When you start talking about the kind of downstream controls that the content industries dream of and champion, this goes far beyond stopping piracy. It changes the way individuals and society are able to use digital content in absolutely fundamental ways. And it allows content owners to reach into private spaces and behaviors in ways that they have never been able to previously.

Another wonderful piece of rhetoric you hear is "new business models." New business models, to be sure, include being responsive to the idea that consumers might want to rent access to large libraries of music (or other digital content) rather than purchase them. This is actually an attractive economic proposition for a substantial number of consumers. I think that it's great to have more alternatives. But the talk of new business models also often carries the implication that we will get rid of older business models, particularly those that have aspects that the content owners don't like, and never mind the broader consequences. This leads to a world where the proposition to the consumer that being able to do anything other than rent access to digital content within a highly constrained and controlled technical framework is a great privilege and one that can only be granted if the content is wrapped in very strong and controlling technological DRM. And don't think I'm just making these scenarios up to scare you. It's very interesting to hear DRM technology purveyors talk about their products when they talk primarily to the content community. I remember very vividly, for example, when the first generation of e-book readers came out, hearing those people make the pitch to the publishers that if you go with e-books on this platform, you can at long last capture the revenue that is being "stolen" from you by used book sales.

The enforcement and downstream control technologies are complicated and controversial, and as I've already said, there's reason to debate how well they work under reasonable environmental and contextual assumptions. I'll have more to say about that later, but let me first finish the survey of technologies that are typically discussed under the DRM rubric.

There's another set of technologies, which are often also called DRM technologies, but that have a very different character. They are about tracking and accountability rather than enforcement. These have to do with certain kinds of watermarking, for example. Here's the general scenario for these technologies: every time that you sell a copy or license a chunk of digital content to someone, anytime you hand a copy of some protected thing to somebody, you basically put a serial number on it and embed that serial number in a way that it can't be disentangled from the object itself. If you later discover that a copy of your thing is sitting on a public Web site or being passed around in one of the file-sharing systems, then you can look at it computationally, extract this watermark, and do two things. First, you can determine if this is, in fact, a licensed or restricted or otherwise owned piece of material and then, secondly (at least in some implementations), whose copy it is. This lets you, as a content owner, both identify things that are circulating inappropriately (through highly automated mechanisms) and demand that they be removed; you can also potentially go after the people who released them into these venues. In fact, you also see a certain amount of this being done without necessarily serializing the copies; basically, just making it easy to computationally determine whether someone asserts an ownership or rights claim over an object is a lot simpler and still very useful. A common application is tracking images on the net. A company called Digimark, for example, lets you embed a watermark in images. Then there are spiders that go around the Web to sites with a lot of images on them, basically checking to see if these objects are there. The spiders report back, the results are consolidated, and out comes a report from which content owners can generate takedown notices, cease and desist letters, or take another course of action if they so wish.

Note that watermarks can also, at least in theory, be used to provide instructions to technical enforcement mechanisms as well as tracking systems; for example, a copy program might refuse to copy things that did or did not have a certain watermark. In that sense, watermarks can be viewed as an especially tight way of binding metadata and content. There are other approaches here for binding content and metadata (so called "secure containers" or IBM's Cryptolopes).

There are various schemes that attach metadata to digital content that declare what rights and permissions and ownership are associated with that content and what various enforcement systems should and should not do with the content. This would include things such as the Creative Commons licenses, the various rights and restrictions definitions languages (e.g., ODRML, XRML), and an array of metadata schemes and standards that allow the documentation of ownership, provenance, and rights (Dublin Core, PREMIS, METS, and the work of MPEG 21 are a few relevant examples). The important point I want to stress here is that in order to be useful and valuable, metadata need not be tightly coupled to a technical enforcement scheme; an indicator that a content object may be freely used for nonprofit purposes is very helpful, but very hard to enforce technically.

And this brings me to the last things that I want to talk about under the DRM umbrella, which often aren't thought of as technologies but are important to remember. They are basically policies and enforcement mechanisms around policies. Back in the old days, when we dealt in physical objects, we actually had rights management and enforcement through a set of such things as the legal system and, to a lesser extent, the law enforcement apparatus that hung off the legal system (think civil and criminal law). The actual rights and usage policies were most often shaped by public policy (first sale, for example) rather than custom-tailored and imposed by the content owner. Even today, this legal enforcement system is important because if you look at how we, in fact, enforce licenses today within higher education, mostly it's not technological. Certainly, for example, we do little with downstream technical controls. Mostly, it's a matter of community education and institutional and public policy. So I don't think we should overlook that in our portfolio of conversations about DRM. There are alternatives to technological enforcement.

One question that often comes up is whether DRM works and, if so, how well. The review of the grab bag of things that are characterized as DRM should convince you that how well it works depends crucially on what you are trying to do with it. Of course, some people are most concerned with the enforcement side, and here it's hardest to give conclusive answers other than to say that many smart people believe that, on a technical level, the enforcement mechanisms will inevitably have flaws as long as people use digital content on general-purpose computers and retain control of those computers. (As I'll describe later, one approach to addressing these concerns is to simply forbid people to have computers that they can control.)

I do want to note that even pathetically weak enforcement technology is now being backed up by increasingly draconian laws; circumventing a DRM enforcement system will likely soon carry penalties on a par with major violent crimes at the rate we are going. These legal backups are also causing a huge flurry of other bad consequences, many of which I'd like to believe are unintended. You'll hear examples of this in other presentations at this symposium.

One of the key issues that I want to focus on is the idea of *perimeters* in DRM enforcement (or, if you prefer, the scope of a trusted system). Let me give you a couple examples of simple, early DRM that mostly worked. There have been various panics over the years about consumer electronics appliances that let you make copies. Certainly, the film and television industries panicked over the VCR and tried to ban it. And we've had legislation, for example, in digital audiotape (a product that never really took off in the U.S. market), that basically says that if you build digital audiotape recorders, you can't make second-generation copies. It was essentially mandated that any consumer-market machine that was built had circuitry in it to prevent you from doing this. There is a similar discussion going on now about digital television and something called the broadcast flag, which would signal various recording devices to refuse to record or copy content with this flag turned on. Basically, the general idea is that government would forbid the manufacture or import of any device that records and doesn't pay attention to this flag. Unfortunately, because of the convergence of computers and consumer electronics that's now far along (and was only at best a prediction about the future when the digital audiotape legislation happened), this means basically regulating and crippling computer software and hardware in order to protect these broadcasts, a quandary that will come up again as we look at other DRM proposals.

For digital audiotape, or any other sort of traditional stand-alone consumer electronics device, this kind of DRM is pretty effective: someone can't get around this protection unless they have the skills to build their own recorder to modify an existing commercial recorder (which probably involves some hardware tinkering) or can get one in the grey or black market that doesn't have the protection in it. Somebody probably can't put a copying-enabler patch program on the net so that this one piece of software let loose in the world allows people to circumvent or disable restrictions in hundreds of thousands of devices. The copy protection in these devices is at least partially in hardware, and often their software isn't designed to be easily modified by users. So, circumventing the DRM takes possibly specialized tools and considerably more skill than simply downloading and running a program.

There's another interesting case study in this arena that's probably worth a quick detour. Did you know that when they designed the DVD player, the folks who hold the patents on this technology basically decided to divide the world into six regions having to do with where they thought they wanted to sequence the release of movies? So, in fact, all DVD disks come with a region code. Now, it can be set to play in any region, but often it's not, particularly for movies. And all DVD players, whether stand-alone consumer electronics devices or DVD players built into computers, come with a region code built into them. A DVD will only play if the code on the disk is consistent with the code in the player. (Let me just be clear here: there are also video encoding issues, NTSC vs. PAL vs. SECAM and all that, but these are quite different and distinct from region coding.) So, for example, if you go to Singapore or

London and buy a DVD, you may very well discover when you get home that it won't play on your U.S. DVD player because the regions are inconsistent. This was part of Hollywood's strategy for controlling the movement of content from place to place because they often release first-run movies here and then they release them later in Europe, so they don't want any of these annoying people picking them up here and taking them over to Europe. Just stop and think about this for a moment and compare it to the way things worked with books and sound recordings historically, where people could fairly easily import innovative artistic and intellectual works from one nation to another, at least among democracies.

Now, it became very popular to hack your DVD player to circumvent this system of control; it seemed to people that they really ought to be able (legally and legitimately) to purchase a disk in London and play it in San Francisco. There were little software patches you could get, particularly for DVD players, which were attached to personal computers and driven by personal computer software. Well, guess what? After a couple of years of this, the patent holders basically told the industry that was building these DVD players under patent, "Thou shalt put the regional checking in hardware," so that it can't be changed easily and "you will take various provisions to only let them reset it a couple of times, maximum." So, essentially, they started building region coding more deeply into hardware and firmware making it harder for consumers to hack it.

Why am I talking about this? Because periodically we hear now these policy proposals that say because of the convergence of computer electronics and computing, what we need to do is pass laws to restrict the hardware and software that make up the computing environment, following in the footsteps of the old consumer electronics model. The argument is that we need to have a government mandate that says, "Thou shalt not manufacture or sell computers without hard-to-circumvent facilities in the computers that recognize some kind of DRM tagging and honors the restrictions expressed in that tagging to prevent acts like copying or playing more times than you are authorized."

There have been several legislative proposals in this area. Senator Hollings, for example, introduced a bill that proposed to do exactly this, an absolutely stunning thing full of unexpected consequences. I can't possibly, in the time allotted me this morning, do justice to these legislative proposals by saying enough bad things about them. Consider just a few points. First, computers aren't just on your desk. There are more computers embedded in air conditioners and cars and HVAC systems, medical devices, singing greeting cards, and other places than in all of the "computers" on our desktops and in our computer rooms. All of these would presumably have to be controlled. We are talking government intrusion and regulation, and interference with innovation on a scale that is almost impossible to imagine, though it doesn't seem to stop either some members of the Congress or regulators like the Federal Communications Commission (with the broadcast flag regulation) from seriously trying their best to imagine it.

Another important problem worth mentioning, of course, is that the computer industry, contrary to what some lawmakers and regulators may believe, actually is a global industry; and if you said that you can only manufacture and sell "retarded" computers in the United States, do you really think that would help the position of the U.S. information technology (IT) industry in a highly competitive global marketplace? Of course, the proponents of this kind of approach counter this by saying that they just have to put international agreements in place and, in essence, regulate and control the worldwide IT industry. The notion that one could enforce this globally is a little breathtaking to me.

These kinds of legislative and regulatory proposals are about establishing the perimeters of a system that knows about and can enforce DRM, and they are very critical. The more ubiquitous, the more mandated and global that implementation is, the scarier it gets. And the more damaging it gets. I would hate to see the U.S. or the worldwide information technologies destroyed, or innovation in information technology basically shut down in order to ensure maximal profits to some sectors of the content industries. (Of course, I would hate to see these things happen in order to ensure that governments have the ability to conveniently, comprehensively, cheaply, and ubiquitously do secret monitoring of computer use, but these kinds of proposals have been coming forward for decades, and continue to be popular as well.)

One can imagine certain very constrained trusted systems that may feel more comfortable and constructive. Let me give you an example. Libraries have been addressing the question, Can we do circulation of e-books? This is kind of neat. There are no recall notices. A library just loans the e-book; and it turns itself off at a certain time; and then the library can immediately circulate it again to another user. Saves a lot of trouble with all these fines and recall notices and things like that. If the context in which you are doing this is circulation in a library, you can reasonably assume a couple of things. You know the library holds a master of that book, either in digital or printed form, so it's not going to just vanish from the face of the earth at the whim of the rights holder. You know that the people who are choosing to borrow it from the library might equally well choose to purchase it and get their own permanent copy; the rights holder is not using an exclusively rental-only model with all that that implies for the cultural record. While there are going to be some records of use, at least temporarily, libraries are enormously scrupulous about protecting the privacy of their patrons. If you believe a few things like that, that circulation scenario sounds pretty benign.

On the other hand, if you say, "We are going to legislatively create a world where basically we can disseminate information and then cause it to vanish at a specific time or, indeed, at our whim from all the records of our society so that it only exists in people's memory," that is very scary. That does not sound to me like a future—not in a society that has any kind of accountability or long-term memory built into it.

The last general comment about DRM: I described what I think is the implausibility of mandating DRM in every computer, everywhere. It's hard to believe that the entertainment industry, for example, could get enough control of Congress to pass something this misguided, at least I'd like to believe this. Various legislators may introduce bills, but really moving forward on it, voting it into law, it's a little hard for me to believe that they'd do that. Keep in mind that the IT industries, while not traditionally as effective at lobbying Congress as the entertainment industries (particularly now that TV networks are conglomerated with the music and film industries), do represent a very significant part of our gross national product.

However, and here's where I would get very scared, there's a growing awareness that we have a big computer security problem in our society. As consumers, we basically don't know how to secure computers; we can't or won't build secure computers; we can't trust our computers, which are under constant siege by criminals, hackers, and terrorists. As organizations, we can't control our confidential documents and data. And there's now a set of initiatives under discussion about technologies with names like "trusted computing" or "trustworthy computing." Basically, systems with a secure mode of various kinds that recognize and act upon certain tags that are attached to objects in ways that cannot be disabled. These technologies are being promoted today, mostly as protecting the cyber infrastructure and protecting against information warfare terrorist attacks and things like that—and, of course, hackers and criminals. There's considerable truth in this. Some of these technologies may actually be useful for that, though they aren't, in my view, panaceas, magic bullets, or comprehensive solutions.

You will hear, if you haven't already, about two other closely related framings of this set of ideas. One is about the control of confidential documents. This nasty thing keeps happening to organizations: documents slip out, often providing evidence of assorted kinds of malfeasance and bad behavior, and it seems no matter what those organizations do, these pesky embarrassing docu-

ments and other digital objects just keep getting loose. If we really had good
document security, I should be able to make sure that only people who are
currently affiliated with my organization and who are on the list of good guys
could read those documents, and that when they leave, the documents they
might have taken with them should evaporate, right? That's a very popular
idea in many corporate settings. This is about good management and good
security and good information security. And, of course, this helps protect sensitive government documents, too, needless to say. And sensitive consumer
credit data. Here's another piece of it: we're talking about things like moving to electronic medical records, and you'd all like your medical records to
stay private, right? You're all worried about information on your computer
getting loose. Now, if we have good security on our computers, if they were
"trustworthy," this wouldn't be a problem. You could tag your medical records
as "private" and the computer would honor that. Only you and your doctor
and, of course, your insurance company and your bank and all of the people
that they want to give them to could see them and you would feel much better. Well, if we actually go ahead with some of this trusted systems security
stuff, we're potentially going to get a relatively ubiquitous DRM infrastructure as an unexpected by-product. So, I would remind you that there is a
coupling here between some of the discussions of possibly mandating certain
standards or technologies for computer *security* and the possible concomitant
enactment of very broad DRM enforcement perimeters that is not getting a
lot of attention. It's something of which you should be very aware.

I've got a lot more that I want to cover this morning, so I'd better keep
moving. Let's talk more specifically about DRM and the academy. Let me
just selectively remind you of a few points about copyright and DRM in
higher education. First, one of the things that scholars rely on very heavily is
the notion of fair use. Without getting very technical or legalistic about it,
let me just remind you that fair use is basically framed as a defense against an
accusation of copyright infringement. In making that defense and evaluating
that defense in a court, you look at a number of complicated and somewhat
subjective factors, including the purpose of the copying, the extent of the
copying, the economic impact of the copying. These are things that I don't
know how to program a computer to do, and I don't know of anyone else
who knows how to do it either. When you look at the kinds of constraints
that DRM knows how to enforce, these constraints are all about counting
and about time and about repetition and about number of bytes copied, they
are not about purpose. "Well, are you doing this for a parody?" I don't know
how to write a computer program that reads minds and figures out whether someone is copying this with the intent of producing parody or, indeed,

whether a court, in evaluating the user's claim to be making a parody, would, in fact, concur it's a legitimate parody. My view on this is that the whole notion of fair use, which is so important in the academy (and, it should be said, to society as a whole, very much beyond the academy), is, at some level, fundamentally inconsistent with at least some of these downstream enforcement technologies. A lot of people who promote these technologies will say, "Well, we'll let you read up to three pages and that will take care of fair use." Or, "We'll let you print up to two pages a week without paying." That may be a very good thing for the content provider or the technology provider to enable, but it's not fair use. Fair use inherently doesn't require the consent or cooperation of the rights holder. What's sometimes characterized incorrectly as fair-use features in DRM technology actually are other sorts of surrogate things that may provide nice amenities, but, at least in my view, I feel are not a direct replacement for fair use. They just happen to be the kinds of things you can do computationally that look vaguely similar to some popular and commonplace activities that are permitted under fair use.

I do not have time to do any more than mention the issue that if you physically or technically cannot copy something, there's not much point talking about fair use, which is a way to justify the making and use of a copy in specific contexts. This is a problem in a world of DRM, particularly for complex multimedia content that's hard to simply read and transcribe. Sometimes this issue gets framed as asking whether we need an affirmative right to make fair uses.

Next, let me note that the academy has a set of DRM-related issues that aren't so much about fair use of other people's material but, because so many in the academy are content creators themselves, are about controlling the use of one's own materials by others in ways that are consistent with academic values and objectives. If you look at the type of controls that people in higher education want to put on materials, here are some of the most common ones:

- I would like to be acknowledged as the author of this work. But please, read it and pass it along to others to read; quote from it; translate it; build upon it.
- While I would like this work to be read and shared widely, I would like to ensure that the integrity of this work isn't subverted in some fashion. Maybe it's only to be reproduced in toto, if it's reproduced.
- Do whatever you want with this work for educational or research purposes, but if you are going to market it, then you need to talk to me about it.

None of these kinds of things, with the possible exception of reproducing in toto and author attribution, are things that DRM systems can do. A computer can no more determine that you are making copies for educational use than it can that you're making a copy for parody. These are just not things that at least today's computer can do.

If we are going to put technical controls on content but also honor a range of uses that are characterized by the purpose of that use, be it fair use under law or educational use under specific permission associated with a piece of content, we face another set of issues that I think are interesting and that resonate particularly with questions about copyright education and accountability in the academy.

Let me do a thought experiment with you and let's see how you feel about it. I just told you an untruth a minute or two ago, which is that I don't know how to program a DRM system that supports fair use. Actually, I do; and let me describe it to you and let me see how you feel about it. The way it works is it does its DRM control thing, but it also puts a button on the screen that says, "I hereby declare fair use," and when you click this button the DRM system rolls over and dies and hands you the unconstrained digital object to do what you will with it. If you are mostly concerned with protecting content, you probably won't be enthused about this proposed DRM system. If the most important thing to you is supporting fair use, I think you'd agree that this meets the requirements fairly well. Now let's alter this imaginary system slightly and see how you feel about it. Keep in mind that we *do* try to teach people about fair use in the academy and we try to teach them that all use is *not* fair use, that just because you are a professor doesn't mean that you can copy everything whenever you feel like it and it's somehow fair use. Now supposing that in our imaginary DRM system when you hit that fair-use button, it puts up a little declaration that said "I hereby declare I'm making fair use of this" and then asks you to put your name in and send a copy of that signed declaration off to the rights holder. Sort of fair use with accountability. How do you feel about that? Is that a good compromise? We could build something like this for "noncomputably verifiable" uses like fair use or educational use. That would change the accountability–privacy mixture in a way that we haven't looked at before. We need to explore this more carefully. Being thoughtful about this is very much a part of our values in the academy.

Let me just make two other points about DRM and higher education and how it fits with academic values. The first is that, at least to the best of my knowledge, the publishers—even the commercial publishers—that support scholarship and deal in scholarly books and journals really aren't talking much about DRM enforcement technologies. I'm hearing very little demand from those sources for this sort of downstream DRM. Mostly, what those folks are worried about is access control and about technologies and procedures that can help them and the institutions that license their content deal with gross license term violations such as massive downloading. I think this situation reflects a lot of the common values that we all share about the purposes of management of scholarly publication, and I think it's significant. To me, it bodes well about the future of scholarly discourse and the likelihood that DRM technologies won't cause too much trouble in this area.

The second of my two points is more troublesome. One of the things that gets very scary is the fact that the raw material of future scholarship includes a lot of things that go out into the commercial marketplace and those are things that our research libraries need to capture and preserve and make available for future scholarship. We've still got to face these DRM issues around these works of culture that we're going to want as raw material for ongoing scholarship. We have a huge problem here. The academy and our cultural memory institutions have some special needs that are not well recognized or well honored in the current debates about DRM for this material in consumer markets. Our society may pay dearly for this in the long term. I've written about this extensively elsewhere. I feel very strongly about this point and could go on at length, but I will not belabor it here, as this talk is intended to be a broad survey of these issues. But I would urge that it not be overlooked.

So, let's talk, finally, about some of the elements of the consensus that are in place and some of the elements of the consensus that are missing as we look at what we might do with the grab bag of DRM technologies in a higher education setting.

First, one of the things that is clearly very crucial is the question of identifying and describing rights for digital objects. Notice I said "identifying and describing"; I didn't say anything about "enforcement" here. Indeed, as I've already discussed, we have major technical problems trying to figure out how to enforce what are likely to be some of the most common usage permissions, such as those involving "research or educational use." We have enormous amounts of digital content. Some of it we acquire under license. Some of it we just pick up off the net. A lot of it we create ourselves in various settings within the academy, and we're increasingly realizing that we're going to want to preserve, share, and reuse this. We're going to want to re-purpose it. The net, digital libraries, and other technologies allow us to share and distribute our content much more widely than we have in the past. We have to develop systems that let us keep track of who owns the rights, what rights our institutions have in things, what rights are automatically available to anyone, who to contact to clear additional rights. We need to do this to the extent possible in ways that are machine parsible, machine representable, so that we can apply automatic discovery and retrieval and organizational and management tools, so, for example, you don't necessarily have to print this out and talk to general counsel object by object when you are trying to migrate two million objects from one format to another in a digital repository. It just doesn't work! Scale and managing scale means we've got to represent rights and permissions electronically for these digital objects. I point you to the work with the Creative Commons licenses, which get into exactly these kinds of declarative things, although I'd also note that the Creative Commons licenses don't necessarily deal with who to contact for more (at least not yet). They basically let you say things like, "This is free for educational use." Creative Commons doesn't necessarily say who holds the other rights.

I would point out that when we point out who holds the other rights, just putting in a text field that says "Cliff Lynch" in a world where copyright is life of the author plus seventy-five years is not very helpful. We're dealing with time spans now that are really a problem, and if you look at the experience that people are having with clearing rights, for example, to scan old books, most of the cost isn't paying people for those rights. Often they'll just give them to you. It's *finding* the people with the rights, such as the descendents and heirs of the original author. We're going to need to start thinking about integrating our declarations about ownership with broader identity management infrastructure. Obviously, we need to do this respecting consent and privacy, but often, at least again in the academic world, rights holders want to be found. Indeed, we should talk about whether there are obligations or ethical reasons for academic authors to make it possible for people to find them in a world of very lengthy copyright (this is a fascinating and complex issue that I do not have time to explore today even superficially). Note that if a university is capable of keeping track of people so that it can ask them for money as alumni, if it's capable of tracking them so that it can give them pension money as retirees, why can't we tie that infrastructure and investment to the owner names associated with objects that higher education institutions maintain, again with some kind of opt-in consent? That's a service that's really consistent with our academic values and practices.

Finally, I think we need to think carefully about whether we want some of these limited perimeter kinds of DRM environments within higher education settings. I already described the one about circulating e-books, for example; most of the e-book applications using readers where you download the e-book have taken place in public library settings, to the best of my knowledge. Academic libraries have preferred the more familiar site license model for reasons that seem reasonable to me, but we might explore the relevance of these models for certain kinds of circulation and perhaps e-reserves. Let me give you another one that is very interesting. There is a piece of legislation called the TEACH Act that was passed a couple of years ago. Again, without getting into a lot of detail that we don't have time for here, one of the ways I think about the TEACH Act is that it says if you are willing to set up a controlled technological perimeter that you might think of as delineating sort of the boundaries in space and time of a virtual classroom, within that protected perimeter, you can do a number of things. You have a number of specific new copyright exemptions that allow you to use content in that virtual classroom. Now, that's a sort of a legislative invitation to think about: Are those exemptions worth the trouble and complexity of setting up that controlled perimeter, or do we not want to bother? Can we set up such a perimeter? Do we have the technologies, and are they deployed and supported by the necessary infrastructure at our institutions? How strong does the perimeter have to be? And I think right now a lot of institutions are sitting on the fence about this issue. They're sort of looking at it and saying, "Well, this is pretty complicated; do I really want to go there or not?" But the TEACH Act does provide another and rather different example of a place where these kinds of limited perimeter environments are relevant.

It's appalling to me to think about building a higher education world where some sort of mandated control is integrated into every thermostat and every laptop and every projector and every other device with a computer in it. I think it's repugnant and frightening and, thankfully, in my view utterly impractical. I have to believe that this kind of world is, in fact, deeply inconsistent with the traditional values of the academy and that the academy would resist its construction. But at the same time we do need to think about limited-perimeter trusted systems, and if and when we want them. I will say that when we think about limited-perimeter systems, we better be very clear why we are doing them and what we hope to accomplish, our expectations about the strength of the perimeter and whether we are realistic in those expectations, and about how we'll ensure that we can still honor academic and cultural memory needs and uses of content broadly even if they may be constrained within the perimeter's boundaries.

I've covered a lot of ground here, and I'm out of time. I hope I've at least given you some feeling for the various definitions, interpretations, and framings of DRM; and I hope I've given you another context to think about DRM besides the context that we keep hearing again and again of consumer rights, control of copying, of music piracy, and related questions—a kind of broader context that takes into account and looks at the sort of real practices and values that happen within our higher education setting. And I hope this will provide at least a point of departure for some further discussion about how this class of technologies is and is not consistent with the advancement of those academic values and objectives.

Thanks. I look forward to your questions and comments.

Note

1. This is a considerably edited version of a transcription of my keynote address; as such, it maintains much of the character of a talk rather than a formal paper. I do want to note that in this editing, it was interesting to discover how memory plays tricks, especially about when various events happened. In my talk, I dated early work on DRM, such as the efforts of Mark Stefik, to the mid- to late 1980s or early 1990s, but in pulling out Stefik's work to check the title, it's clear that mid-1990s is probably more accurate. It seems that although consumer electronics copy protection and also software copy protection technologies were certainly familiar ideas by the 1970s, the debate about DRM really starts in the early to mid-1990s. As I say in the talk, it would be very useful for someone to establish and publish a good timetable of developments, particularly because visible developments in the literature (such as Stefik's work) are paralleled by a set of much-less-visible developments in the world of patent filings.

Chapter 2

The TEACH Act: Issues, Challenges, and Options

Donna L. Ferullo, J.D.

Abstract

In November 2002, a new law entitled the Technology, Education and Copyright Harmonization Act (TEACH) was enacted. TEACH rewrites the distance education exemption to the copyright law. This new amendment not only drastically changes the distance education landscape, but also has implications for the use of digital components to traditional classroom teaching. TEACH challenges colleges and universities to step up to the copyright plate and brings to the forefront many copyright concerns on college campuses. This new amendment to the copyright law also places numerous requirements on faculty, information technology staff, students, and higher education institutions as a whole. This paper explores the implications and impact of TEACH at both the macro and micro levels.

The Technology, Education, and Copyright Harmonization Act, more commonly known as the TEACH Act, was enacted in November 2002.[1] TEACH is a total revision of the distance education exemption, Section 110(2), of the U.S. Copyright Act. There are many advantages to this new legislation, but there are also many challenges for universities and their faculty should they choose to utilize this exemption. It is a complex piece of legislation that shares the burden, benefits, and responsibilities of copyright awareness, compliance, and infringement across all levels of the university.

Educators realized fairly early on that the distance education exemption to the 1976 copyright law was not very helpful in the digital age. The exemption was structured for a broadcast television/cable network–type of transmission and reception. It was the technology in use at that time and was considered to be the most efficient way to deliver education at a distance. In addition to limiting the types of transmission, this exemption also restricted the categories of works that could be transmitted. This section to the copyright law did not adequately meet the instructor's needs in providing education to a diverse group of students. More and more tools were available that allowed instructors to provide courses in an innovative and creative manner, but the digital technology outpaced the law. The old legislation did not envision the ever-evolving virtual classroom.

The lack of a sufficient distance education exemption prompted many faculty, including librarians, to voice their concerns to Congress. In 1998, Congress found a way to formally introduce the topic of distance education and digital technology by including in a piece of legislation entitled the Digital Millennium Copyright Act (DMCA)[2] a section that required the Register of the United States Copyright Office to prepare a report on copyright and digital distance education to submit to them. The report[3] was completed and submitted to Congress in May 1999.

No substantive action was taken on the report's recommendations until March 2001 when Senators Leahy and Hatch introduced the TEACH Act into the Senate. The legislation passed the Senate in June 2001 and was introduced into the House that same month. TEACH then sat in the House Judiciary Committee until July 2002 when it was unanimously approved and sent to the full house for a vote. In the end, the TEACH Act was incorporated into a Department of Justice Appropriations Authorizations bill, HR2215, which was approved by Congress and sent to the president for his signature in November 2002.

The TEACH legislation that was first introduced into the Senate and ultimately passed into law was the result of a collaboration among all the stakeholders (i.e., faculty, librarians, publishers, and other copyright holders). They spent many months crafting legislation that would hopefully address the concerns that had been identified over the years and had been articulated in the register's report to Congress. Not everyone agreed with every aspect of TEACH, but they did come to a consensus, recognizing that although it was not perfect, they could live with it. The language was carefully crafted by the group so that there could be a basic agreement among all concerned parties. Both the House and the Senate realized the importance of retaining the original language and did not materially alter the original draft. However, now comes the challenge in not just how to implement it, but also how to interpret various provisions of the new law.

Basic Copyright Law

Copyright was first recognized in the United States in the Constitution,[4] and the current U.S. Copyright Act[5] was enacted in 1976. There have been many amendments to the law in order to update various sections of it, but the majority or body of the law is still from the 1976 act. It is important to remember what the world was like in 1976 because the law reflects the technology and educational models that were in use at that time.

Copyright law is about balancing the rights of copyright holders against the rights of the public to use the copyright protected works without seeking permission or paying royalties. Copyright holders have exclusive rights to their work, such as distribution, reproduction, public performance and display, and the creation of derivative works.[6] It is the exemptions and limitations on the copyright holder's exclusive rights that allow for the balance that was envisioned by Congress to be achieved. The exemptions and limitations are critical to education.

Copyright protects many types of creative works as long as they have some originality and are fixed in a tangible medium of expression. Since 1998, copyrighted works are protected for the life of the author plus seventy years.[7] In 1988, the United States became a signatory to the Berne Convention, which is an international treaty on the protection of literary and artistic works.[8] One of the concessions that the United States made in order to comply with the treaty was to abolish the requirement that copyrighted works have a notice on them (i.e., the copyright symbol, year of publication, and name of copyright holder). This lack of notice has resulted in some confusion among the public. With the advent of the Internet and the availability of a vast amount of information with sometimes no indication as to who owns the copyright to the work, many think that the work can then be freely used. Free access does not equal free use. The only works that can be freely used are those in the public domain. Unfortunately, there is no database of all public-domain materials to assist a user in determining whether or not a work is still protected by the copyright law. Only works that have been published prior to 1923 and works by U.S. government employees that are created within the scope of their employment are more than likely in the public domain.

The digital revolution has made copyright infringement easier than ever before. It also strengthens the importance of both the education exemption and the fair-use defense. It is in the best interest of the user of copyrighted works to understand and be able to articulate their exemption of choice because they generally cannot maintain their anonymity in a digital world. Digital fingerprints, in most cases, can be easily traced and identified. The current climate is zero tolerance for digital piracy. It is therefore important that those utilizing TEACH are fully cognizant of the scope of the legislation and the responsibilities not only they assume, but their institution does as well.

The Old versus the New

The education exemption is section 110 of the U.S. Copyright Act. It is divided into two parts: (1) addresses the use of copyrighted works in face-to-face or what is known as traditional classroom teaching; and (2) is the distance education exemption, which is now known as TEACH. The distance education moniker to Section 110(2) is somewhat of a misnomer because this section also applies to traditional courses that include digital components. It is not unusual in current educational models to combine a traditional classroom and a virtual one. It is important for institutions and their faculty to be aware that TEACH reaches beyond the traditional distance education boundaries.

The 1976 distance education exemption was limited to synchronous education. It was quite restrictive given the reality of today's virtual classroom. The transmission was to be received in a classroom or similar place devoted to instruction, and the recipients of such transmission were limited to people with disabilities or people who had special circumstances that prevented their attendance in a classroom. The TEACH Act totally did away with those restrictions so that asynchronous education can take place, instruction and access at anytime and from anywhere. It is important to also remember that TEACH is only applicable to digital transmissions.

The new law retains the categorization of works into displays and performances. However, the types and amounts of works included in those categories that can be transmitted have been changed. As in the 1976 law, the transmission of performances of nondramatic literary and musical works is still allowed. TEACH also added another section that allows performances of reasonable and limited portions of dramatic literary and musical works and audiovisual works.[9] The addition of audiovisual works and dramatic works was considered a gigantic step forward in closing the gap between the traditional classroom and the virtual classroom. Although TEACH does not give specifics as to how much is a reasonable and limited portion, there certainly was some discussion as to the parameters. The analysis in the Senate Report identifies the criteria as to what constitutes a reasonable and limited portion: the instructor or student must assess the nature of the market for the type of work and must look at the pedagogical purpose of the performance, and the performance must be comparable to what typically takes place in a live classroom setting.[10]

Although the performance section was expanded, a new restriction was added to the display section.[11] The reasonable and limited portion now also extends to displays, which is more restrictive than the old distance education exemption. All displays must be analogous to what takes place in a live classroom setting. The rationale behind the restriction of displays is that the likelihood of displaying an entire text under the old exemption was minimal, but now in today's digital world, it is far easier to display and transmit perfect copies of complete works.

The TEACH exemption then added some categories that can be used in distance education but, in keeping with the concern of content holders, also narrowed the amount of what can be displayed. However, before TEACH can be invoked, there are many requirements that first must be satisfied.

TEACH Act Requirements

The TEACH Act exemption does not come without some requirements. I have labeled it the four step plan. If an institution cannot pass the first step, there's no point in continuing on to the next steps. Each step builds upon the other. It appears to me that the drafters of TEACH saw this as an opportunity not only to update the law on digital distance education, but also to require the institutions to increase the visibility of copyright at many different levels on their campuses. The trend in copyright law appears to hold institutions more accountable in educating their community on copyright and compliance issues.

First Step. Institutional Requirements

1. The first hurdle is the institutional requirements. The 1976 exemption applied only to nonprofit educational institutions. However, the TEACH Act also requires that they now must be accredited.[12] Institutions that provide postsecondary education must be accredited by a regional or national accrediting agency recognized by the Council on Higher Education Association or the United States Department of Education. TEACH is also applicable to all K–12 schools provided they are recognized by their state through either certification or licensing procedures. For-profit, nonaccredited institutions are not eligible to claim TEACH as an exemption.

2. Institutions are required to have copyright policies in place.[13] The language of the legislation does not specify or recommend what should be included in such a policy. Institutions certainly then have the flexibility to draft a policy that will be a good fit for their needs and culture. The institution must have such a policy before it can claim the benefit of TEACH. Inherent in this requirement is that institutions must address copyright on a campus level and acknowledge that they do have a responsibility to not only the university community, but to owners of copyright protected material as well. Drafting a new policy or revising a current one is usually a challenge at most universities. However, this TEACH requirement is also an excellent opportunity for many different parts of the university to come together and address the issues at a macro level instead of only at the micro level. Many times, the onus has been on libraries or information technology departments to handle copyright issues. This new requirement, though, elevates the importance of having all the players in a university understand the impact of copyright to a variety of constituencies.

3. In addition to having a copyright policy in place, institutions must provide informational materials that promote compliance with the U.S. Copyright Law to faculty, relevant staff, and students.[14] The legislation is quite specific that only "relevant staff" needs to receive the informational materials. It is more than likely a recognition that there are campus employees, such as dining services or physical facilities maintenance staff, who will not be handling copyright issues as part of their employment. Again, there is no guidance from the legislation or the legislative history that provides more definitive information on what should be included in such materials. It is also silent on what medium the message should be sent that would be acceptable and in compliance with TEACH. The interpretation and implementation is left to the discretion of the institution. It is probably in the best interest of the institution to disseminate the copyright information as broadly and as comprehensively as possible. To this end, Web sites might need to be developed specifically devoted to copyright as well as tied in to "traditional" Web sites such as Dean of Students, Information Technology, and/or Human Resources. Printed information might also need to be distributed to the recipients identified by TEACH.

4. The institution must provide notice to the students that the materials used in their course may be subject to copyright protection.[15] It is important to note that the legislation recognizes that there cannot be blanket protection because there is the possibility that some public domain works may be included as part of the course content. There are certainly many ways to provide this notice to students; however, many

institutions are considering having such a notice appear every time the student accesses the course.

If the institution has all of the above requirements in place, it can proceed to the next step, which is the technological requirements.

Second Step. Technology Requirements

Information technology departments are key players in ensuring that institutions are in compliance with the new law. There are many technological requirements that institutions must have in place in order to meet this second step.

1. Institutions must implement technological measures that reasonably prevent recipients from retaining digital transmissions for longer than the class session.[16] There certainly has been much debate in the copyright community as to how long a class session is, particularly in an asynchronous environment. Some have interpreted that clause to be as narrow as for only the length of time that a student is signed on at any one time. Others are considering setting artificial limits as to the number of times someone can access the materials before one class session has expired, and others take the view that the class session is as long as the student needs it to be in order to complete the assignment. However, the language in the Senate Report is very specific in that the exemption does not include having material available for the entire duration of the course.[17]

2. TEACH requires that the transmissions be made solely to officially enrolled students, at least to the extent that is technologically feasible.[18] Course management software such as WebCT and Blackboard will more than likely play an instrumental role in assisting universities by incorporating the necessary technology to comply with this specific new requirement as well as some of the other requirements. This section is a major recognition by Congress that learning takes place in a variety of ways, at different times, and in many different places.

3. Copies of digital works cannot be maintained on the system in a manner that is ordinarily accessible to the intended recipients for longer than reasonably necessary to facilitate the transmission.[19] It appears that the work can be stored on the network when the course is not being taught, as long as not everyone has access to it. It is reasonable to expect that the instructor and the information technology department personnel have access to it, but not just anyone who has Web access. TEACH also clarifies that transient or temporary copies that are automatically made as part of the digital process for distance education will not be considered an infringement of copyright.

4. Information technology departments must also attempt to implement technology that reasonably prevents the recipients from further distributing the copyrighted works.[20] Controlling the redistribution of the works can be problematic given that perfect technology does not exist. However, the drafters of the legislation wisely realized that there is no perfect system and all that should be expected is a reasonable effort. Because there is currently no technology that can easily prevent the redistribution, some institutions are considering adding another statement to the opening screen of the course along with the copyright notice, informing students that redistributing the copyright protected materials is prohibited. This section highlights the concern of content holders who fear that students will download perfect copies of works and distribute them all over the world, free of charge, thus negatively impacting the copyright owner's profits.

Third Step. Instructor Requirements

Most of the instructor requirements refer to performances and displays. Also, there is in many ways a great deal of repetitiveness in the requirements. This section really highlights the conflict the drafters of the legislation had as well as either the reluctance to truly recognize the distinguishing aspects of a virtual classroom or just lack of knowledge as to how much technology has transformed how education is delivered. To this end, the use of digital works must be analogous to what takes place in a live classroom.

1. The performance or display must be directly related and of material assistance to the teaching content.[21] Any digital work used should truly be needed as part of the course content. There is much concern that instructors would use more of a work than they normally would in a traditional classroom because it is so easy to transmit large amounts of digital works in a relatively short period of time and the clarity of the work is generally excellent.

2. The performance or display must be an integral part of a class session, which is offered as a regular part of the systematic mediated instructional activities.[22] The phrase "mediated instructional activities" is defined as any digital performance or display, which must be an integral part of the class experience, must be analogous to what would take place in a live classroom setting, and must be made by, at the direction of, or under the actual supervision of the instructor. The Senate Report stresses that the intent of the legislation is not to require the physical presence of the instructor, only that the instructor is aware of what is going on and has authorized the use.[23] Again, there is the concern that the instructor should only use what is necessary for the course content and what would be used in a traditional classroom. Works that would be considered supplementary materials would not be allowed under TEACH.

3. Instructors must only use works that have been legally made and acquired.[24] No pirated works allowed. TEACH also holds the institution accountable if it knew or had reason to believe that the work being used was not a legal copy.

Fourth Step. Materials Requirements

The TEACH Act addresses what types of digital material will be allowed to be transmitted via distance education. This section was quite obviously written to protect the copyrighted works of the content holders. Most digital works are under lock and key in order to preserve the revenue stream for the publishers.

1. Digital works that have been produced or marketed primarily for mediated instructional activities are not covered under the new exemption.[25] Neither are textbooks, course packs, and any other material in any media that is typically purchased or acquired by students and that is used in one or more class sessions. If instructors wish to use such material, they apparently have two options: obtain permission or rely on fair use.

2. TEACH also amended Section 112 of the U.S. Copyright Act entitled Ephemeral Recordings. Print or analog versions of works cannot be converted to digital works except under certain conditions. If no digital version of the work is available to the institution or the digital version of the work contains technological protection measures that prevent authorized use under the copyright law, the conversion would be allowed. However, the amount that can be converted is limited to only the amount that is permitted under Section 110(2), which is generally a reasonable and limited portion. The converted amount should only be just what is needed and would have only been used in the traditional classroom.

Conclusion

There is much debate over some of the language in TEACH. Until there is litigation clarifying some of the words and phrases used, such debates will certainly continue. Institutions must decide how best to comply with the numerous requirements of TEACH or decide if the legislation is too complex to be implemented at their institutions, such as Western Washington University did in early March, 2004.[26]

TEACH is a very narrow copyright exemption to the copyright law. Even if all the institutional and technological requirements are met, there will be times when the use goes beyond the instructor or materials requirements. When such an event occurs, all is not lost. The broader fair-use doctrine, which is Section 107 of the U.S. Copyright Act, should be applied.[27] There has been some confusion that fair use could not be used in conjunction with TEACH or for distance education. However, the testimony before Congress and included in the Senate Report makes it quite clear that it was agreed upon by all parties that drafted the legislation that fair use is not intertwined with the education exemption.[28] Fair use, in addition to TEACH, is another limitation on the copyright owner's exclusive rights. The four-factor fair-use analysis may be used if the intended use of materials for a course in either a traditional classroom or a virtual classroom does not qualify for TEACH. This is a very valuable option and should be utilized as necessary.

One of the major challenges with the TEACH Act is that it more or less requires distance educators who teach in virtual classrooms to mirror traditional classroom teaching, thereby ignoring the fundamental differences between the two. However, TEACH is in many ways a step forward and provides an opportunity to include materials in distance education courses that have previously been prohibited under the education exemption. TEACH, like many amendments to the copyright law, has some gray areas, which will only be clarified by litigation and court interpretations. It does have benefits, but it also has many new responsibilities that universities must assume should they opt to utilize TEACH.

Notes

1. *Technology, Education and Copyright Harmonization Act of 2002*, 116 Stat. 1910 (2002).

2. *Digital Millennium Copyright Act of 1998*, 112 Stat. 2860 (1998).

3. Register of Copyrights, *Report on Copyright and Digital Distance Education* (Washington, D.C.: U.S. Copyright Office, 1999).

4. *U.S. Constitution, Art.* I, §8, cl. 8.

5. *Copyright Act of 1976*, 17 U.S.C. §§ 101 et seq.

6. Ibid., §106.

7. *Sonny Bono Copyright Term Extension Act of 1998*, 112 Stat. 2827 (1998).

8. *Berne Convention Implementation Act of 1988*, 102 Stat. 2853 (1988).

9. *Copyright Act of 1976*, 17 U.S.C. §§ 110 (2).

10. U.S. Congress. Senate. *Technology, Education and Copyright Harmonization Act of 2001*, 107th Cong., 1st sess., 2001. S. Rep. 031.

11. *Copyright Act of 1976*, 17 U.S.C. §§ 110 (1).

12. Ibid., §110(2), §110(2)(A).

13. Ibid., §110(2)(D)(i).

14. Ibid.

15. Ibid.

16. Ibid., §110(2)(D)(ii)(I)(aa).

17. U.S. Congress. Senate. *Technology, Education and Copyright Harmonization Act of 2001,* 107th Cong., 1st sess., 2001. S. Rep. 031.

18. *Copyright Act of 1976,* 17 U.S.C. §110(2)(C)(i).

19. Ibid., §110(2)(D)(ii)(I)(aa).

20. Ibid., §110(2)(D)(ii)(I)(bb).

21. Ibid., §110(2)(B).

22. Ibid., §110(2)(A).

23. U.S. Congress. Senate. *Technology, Education and Copyright Harmonization Act of 2001,* 107th Cong., 1st sess., 2001. S. Rep. 031.

24. Ibid., §110(2).

25. Ibid.

26. Carnevale, Dan. "Western Washington U. Will Eschew Protection of New Copyright Law," *Chronicle of Higher Education* (Mar. 5, 2004): A28.

27. *Copyright Act of 1976,* 17 U.S.C. §107.

28. U.S. Congress. Senate. *Technology, Education and Copyright Harmonization Act of 2001*, 107th Cong., 1st sess., 2001. S. Rep. 031.

Chapter 3

The Academic Mission and Copyright Law: Are These Values in Conflict?

Marcia W. Keyser

Abstract

If the academic mission of a university is to foster teaching and research, and the purpose of copyright is to "promote the sciences and useful arts," where is the conflict? It is in the day-to-day use of copyrighted materials and the growing enforcement of anti-infringement policies. When professors and students use readings, graphs, images, recordings, or publications in any format, someone is likely to be paying a copyright clearance fee. In some circumstances, such a fee is not necessary, but it is paid out of fear or misunderstanding of the law. In other circumstances, it is the result of overzealous enforcement of clearance fees or of stringent anti-infringement policies. This paper outlines several situations in which copyright enforcement has interfered with the academic mission at a typical institution of higher education. Examples include prohibited uses of articles or graphics from licensed electronic databases; overpriced course readings provided via commercial copy shops or via e-reserves; computer security research; campus film series; and some dubious educational efforts produced by copyright enforcement advocates. It concludes with a look at two potential solutions: better licensing and open-access publishing.

Some of the more extreme examples of copyright enforcement, such as the request for fees from the Girl Scouts for songs sung around a campfire[1] or lawsuits against preteenagers from public housing projects,[2] should be readily familiar. Although these are regrettable extreme actions, they take place in the day-to-day world. I would like to focus on the academic world, the world where I work every day, the world of a typical college or university campus. Let me take a moment to state that I believe in copyright. It is one of the "values" referred to in my title. It is an important component of "promoting the progress of science and the useful arts."[3] Nevertheless, there are times when the stringent enforcement of the rights of the copyright holder interferes with the application of educational fair use on a university campus.

The Academic Mission

The Academic Senate and Trustees of California State University defines the academic mission as advancing and disseminating knowledge.[4] In my own opinion, our mission is *to create intellectually engaged people*. Students are our primary goal, but we are also involved with faculty, staff, and the broader community. There is value in thinking and studying and finding out more about most issues, even when there isn't a profit. This is what we believe as academicians; it is an especially strong belief among librarians. Society benefits when a significant number of people are intellectually engaged in their lives and their communities.

Another definition of the academic mission came to me from one of the criteria provided by our accrediting board, The Higher Learning Commission:

> IV. Criterion Four: Acquisition, Discovery, and Application of Knowledge. The organization *promotes a life of learning* for its faculty, administration, staff, and students *by fostering and supporting inquiry, creativity, practice, and social responsibility in ways consistent with its mission* (emphasis added).[5]

The following section addresses the ways in which we foster and support inquiry, creativity, practice, and social responsibility. In a university, we frequently use published information from other persons in order to support such inquiry and creativity.

Everyday Use of Information at a University

In carrying out the academic mission, we will study, think about, teach with, and base research on the products of other people's study and research. Furthermore, we will want every one of our students to study, think about, and base research on the products of other people's study and research. We want ourselves and our students to be engaged in these activities. Those products of people's study and research are published as books, journal articles, e-prints, conference proceedings, Web sites, white papers, databases, statistical compilations, films, and so on.

Academicians create and publish much information, but so do corporations, the government, private foundations, or think tanks. We still need access to their results and findings. We should have ready access to the information we need to carry out our mission. This is "everyday life" at a university.

The outputs from other people's research are often assigned readings for college students. "Fair use" applies to all formats of publication. However, there are some situations in which most analyses state that a copyright clearance fee must be paid. One of these is the repeated use as a course reading, regardless of the means of distribution or format. One-time use may be fair use, but a typical interpretation of the copyright law is that second or further uses are not fair due to its impact on the market for that reading.[6]

Staff or librarians at a university commonly process the clearance fee through the Copyright Clearance Center. The widely ranging fee is usually set by a standard pattern of a set price per page multiplied by the number of students. The copyright holder sets the price per page. What it translates to, in real life, are some extraordinary clearance fees. The examples below are from classes taught during the 2003–2004 academic year at Drake University. The fees are for distribution via electronic reserves. Remember, they are for single articles out of many assigned for the course:

• A nine-page article from the Journal of Medical Philosophy for a thirty-student class: $58.05

• A fifteen-page article from the American Journal of Health System Pharmacy for a class of 107 students: $167

• An eighteen-page article from Current Gene Therapy for a class of eighteen students: $328.86.

• A twenty-six-page excerpt from a book: $62.66[7]

Lest you think it's only a problem for the sciences, the last example is from a class of nineteen students taught by a history professor.

In each case, the professor decided to use some other method of distributing that information to the students. Sometimes he summarized it verbally. Sometimes he chose another reading. Sometimes he referred it to a local copy shop. In each case, the simple act of assigning a reading and having the student read it was thoroughly complicated by a standard fee arrangement, brought about by copyright.

If the university processes the clearance fee, then (usually) the university pays the fee. And it pays not just the copyright fee itself, but the salary and time of the person processing it. Note also that although the copyright clearance center can provide quick permissions, many of the items used in a typical college-level class are not listed in its database; these items will require individually submitted and processed permissions—and fees—with many different publishers.

If a local copy shop handles the distribution, the students have to pay the clearance fee—and a hefty one. I've heard reports of course packs that cost $150. I'm sure you can think of similar examples.

Harking back to the example of songs sung around a campfire, I can accept that those campers may get by just as well—and perhaps better—singing songs from the public domain. But when professors are choosing the readings for a class, they should be able to choose the most up-to-date and relevant readings they can identify. They should consider which author has the most inspiring arguments, which piece of writing fits in with the topics of the course and the growing knowledge of the students. They should consider how well the articles or books are written. They should consider selecting readings that quote and respond to each other, and provide insight into their subject matter. The price, whether to the student or to their department, should not have to be considered (especially when other readings are free). It creates what I call the HMO Model of course readings, in which course readings are chosen by price, not by quality or appropriateness.

In almost any other walk of life, we have to consider price when making a selection. But I argue that the academic mission is higher, and more important, than the profit motive. We should not have to consider price.

A recent article in the *Chronicle of Higher Education* reported on a survey that revealed "that an exuberance about electronic resources, evident several years ago, has been replaced by a gnawing dissatisfaction with the scholarly materials available online."[8] I think that dissatisfaction stems from the fact that we can see what is possible: total information access, whatever you need, whenever you need it. But copyright restrictions are keeping it from happening.

We pay a hefty fee for the collections of periodicals in electronic format common in university libraries. The collections are neither recreational nor optional; they are necessary for scholarly research. But their content is not quite the same as the paper versions.

In many cases, images are copyrighted separately from written content; sometimes the image is not available for redistribution in a database. Consequently, we will sometimes get articles with some or all of the illustrations missing. In some scientific articles, missing a particular graph or chart can make the article unusable.

Watermarks have recently been introduced onto pages of some articles available, for a fee, online. The watermarks are present to indicate who the copyright owner is. These marks are not only bothersome, when they land behind a chart or a graph, they can make it almost illegible.

Many schools have created successful online education programs to meet the needs of their students. It does not need to be emphasized that professors wish to give their online students the same quality educational experience as their in-classroom students. However, the rights for using copyrighted content in a face-to-face classroom are much easier to define than those for the online learning environment. When electronic reserves cost too much to continue, and online journal articles may be affected by the loss of graphics or occluded by excessive watermarking, it shows a situation in which the stringent enforcement of copyright interferes with teaching our students.

A recent article in *BMC Medical Education* reports on the process used to secure copyright clearance for journal readings to support a Web-based master's program in population health evidence. Although the articles were available in subscription databases at the university library, the program co-ordinators wished to make copies of individual articles stored on a secure server so that they would be readily available to students in their Web-based program. They spent a great deal of time and money attempting to make the articles legally available and ultimately failed to secure permissions for all articles. They came to this conclusion:

> The variation in access to on-line material for educational
> purposes may introduce bias in medical education, as there
> may be a tendency for web-based courses providers and uni-
> versities to favour readily available "one-click" resources. The
> dissemination of original research may therefore be disad-
> vantaged by factors *other than its' intrinsic validity and medi-
> cal or public health relevance* [emphasis added].[9]

In the United States, the TEACH Act was created with the goal of making the use of copyrighted content in distance education easier. Even its name indicates so: it is the Technology, Education, and Copyright Harmonization Act. However, it did not completely succeed. It came with a long list of conditions that must be met before the TEACH Act can be claimed when using copyrighted materials. It requires, among other things, that the institution have a written copyright policy and an active program to educate students and faculty about copyright. Materials used in the online course must be protected in such a way as to prevent their use or distribution outside the class session, must be part of the "systematic mediated instructional activities," etc.[10] At some institutions, the decision whether to claim TEACH, to claim fair use, or to seek permission can be very difficult. Although the goal in creating the TEACH Act was good, its outcome has been more of the same: continued complications brought about by the enforcement of copyright.

Computer Security Research

The case of Ed Felten, a professor at Princeton University who accepted a challenge from a software company to test its encryption and was then sued when he planned to publish the weakness he found, is well known, and I will not go into detail about it here.[11] I would like to call attention to other computer scientists and researchers in related professions. There are many times when some reverse engineering may be needed to meet their specific needs.

The DMCA (The Digital Millennium Copyright Act) was created to protect copyrighted content when it is distributed through electronic media and protected with DRM (Digital Rights Management). It is written such that even in cases in which the DRM can be easily circumvented, it is illegal to do so. Furthermore, computer scientists and other interested persons are prevented from sharing the methods for circumventing DRM technologies. When considering simple cases such as an encrypted DVD of a popular movie, it makes sense. However, the same law applies to software sold for academic purposes. It prevents the development and distribution of tools for bypassing DRM when there is a legitimate reason to do so. Because no programmer can completely predict the needs of others, there is always the possibility that another person, using the software, may need to change some of its functions to meet their needs. Quoting from *Science*:

> *The implications of the DMCA for science are not limited to computer security and encryption researchers. Virtually all computer scientists, as well as many other scientists with some programming skills, find it necessary on occasion to reverse engineer computer programs.* Sometimes they have to bypass an authentication procedure or some other technical measure in order to find out how the program works, how to fix it, or how to adapt it in some way. The act of bypassing the authentication procedure or other technical measure, as well as the making of a tool to aid the reverse engineering process, may violate the DMCA.

> *Although the DMCA also has an exception for reverse engineer-*
> *ing of a program (*26*), it too is narrow.* It only applies if the
> sole purpose of the reverse engineering is to achieve pro-
> gram-to-program interoperability and if reverse engineering
> is necessary to do so (27). Trying to fix a bug or understand
> the underlying algorithm does not qualify. Information even
> incidentally learned in the course of a privileged reverse en-
> gineering process cannot be divulged to any other person ex-
> cept for the sole purposes of enabling program-to-program
> interoperability (28) (emphasis added).[12]

I argue that this prohibition is inhibiting further development of computer programming. Even though there is an illegal application of these tools,
reverse engineering and the bypassing of authentication measures have their
place in computer research. Furthermore, the DMCA prevents scholarship
and publications based on information gained, even incidentally, during a
reverse engineering process. I quote again from *Science*:

> Under a strict interpretation of the DMCA, a reverse engi-
> neer could not, for example, publish lawfully obtained inter-
> face information or details of the program's authentication
> technique in an academic or research paper.[13]

Access to Information by Community Members

Although the majority of the researchers using scientific or medical literature
are affiliated with a university or a hospital medical library, there are exceptions. For example, community doctors in independent practice may depend
upon a local university for access to medical literature. Gibbs, writing in *Scientific American*, describes other situations well: "a patient newly diagnosed
with leukemia, a parent concerned about a risky operation her child is facing,
a precocious high school student—whatever their motivation, ordinary citizens have for decades enjoyed free access to the latest scientific and medical
literature, so long as they could make their way to a state-funded university
library."[14] However, the digital subscriptions that many libraries now have
often come with "strict licensing provisions that prohibit librarians from allowing public access."[15]

Why is this a problem? It is a problem because we want to maintain a
community of individuals who are intellectually engaged in their lives. It is a
problem because when a person wants to investigate an issue in-depth, they
are often referred to the nearest academic library. In many communities,

that is the only potential source of serious scholarly publications. Further, in the print versions that we have traditionally collected, such access was not a problem.

For multiple semesters, Drake University hosted a Sunday Foreign Film Series. It featured films that were well known in their own countries, but rarely shown in the United States. The series attracted a group of around fifty regulars, while some films attracted up to 150 people. All showings were free.[16]

Then, in the fall of 2003, Dr. Susan Hanson (one of the organizers) received a phone call from a staff member of New Yorker Films, a distribution company. He had come across Drake's film series announcement while surfing the Web and noticed that several films distributed by New Yorker Films were on the list. The staff member made no attempt to collect a fee for previous showings. He did want to make sure that we understood the law and that New Yorker Films would expect Drake to pay the normal performance fee if we showed any of their films in the future.

Because the normal fee for performance rights typically runs several hundred dollars for full-length feature films, this is prohibitive for us. And hence, the Sunday Foreign Film Series came to an end.

The distributor can claim this fee because the films were not being shown to registered students in a university class. Educational fair use can be claimed in such cases. However, this series was open to the general public, for no charge.

You tell me: Is it beneficial to have international films available for students, faculty, and some community members to see? Many people will come when it is convenient, when they do not have to sign up ahead of time, or worry about a test. Films like these can stimulate conversation, thinking, and intellectual engagement. They can provide a different point of view. According to Dr. Hanson, "This is one of those circumstances in which copyright simply ought not to apply."[17]

Yes, the organizers can do some research and select films that include public performance rights in their purchase fee. There are companies that provide this sort of film. But that adds a burden to them—and to the librarians that help him do this research—*and severely limits* the overall selection of available films.

Duplicating Copyrighted Material for Staff Development

Have you ever read an article and felt that your colleagues should read it too? Did you attach a copy to an e-mail and send it out, or have the department secretary make copies and put them in everybody's mailbox? Oops! That's in violation of copyright. Even educational fair use doesn't cover "professional development." The "students" in such cases must be enrolled students in a formal college course.

> Sharing and discussing new research is a common part of academic life. Our libraries pay for thousands of full-text articles each year; distribution for professional development seems like a reasonable use.[18]

To my knowledge, no university has been caught on this offense. However, corporations have been—and on more than one occasion.[19] I suspect that it is only a matter of time before we see this sort of action on a college campus.

Potential Conflict of Interest

The current controversies about the use of copyrighted materials have resulted in several outside organizations purporting to educate students and faculty about copyright. Examples include the MPAA (Motion Picture Association of America[20]), the RIAA (Recording Industry Association of America[21]), the National Association of College Stores,[22] and others.[23] The educational materials provided by these organizations do not give proper consideration to the right of fair use and downplay the difficulty of processing permissions. Sometimes these organizations contact students or faculty directly, or hand out materials at conventions and other gatherings. When the organizations creating the educational materials stand to profit from clearance fees (or the processing of them), I consider that a conflict of interest.

A related situation occurs when advertisements from commercial copyright clearance centers imply that permission is needed for any copies made. These advertisements can confuse individuals who are not aware of their rights.

Solutions

Some partial solutions to the conflicts I describe lie in better licensing agreements for electronic information, and in the open-access movement. As librarians and other university purchasers subscribe to online information, they are becoming more and more savvy about the intricacies of licensing agreements and more and more willing to argue for an agreement that permits typical academic uses of the material. Further, some have created task forces specifically for this issue.[24]

The second partial solution lies in the open-access movement. Proponents of open access, such as SPARC, have already created and put into operation viable business models for journals that allow their content to be available online, without fee.[25] Another model, the Institutional Repository, is also being developed.[26] Materials published via either method are protected—by copyright—from misappropriation, but they are freely available for use by anyone who might need them. I look forward to a future in which all scholarly output is easily identified, located, and accessed—for the benefit of us all.

Notes

1. Lisa Bannon, "Birds Sing, But Campers Can't—Unless They Pay Up," *Star Tribune,* 1996.

2. Johnie Roberts, Barney Gimbel, and Sarah Childress, "Out of Tune" *Newsweek* 142, no. 12 (2003): 42. *Academic Search Premier.* EBSCO. June 1, 2004.

3. U.S. Constitution.

4. Academic Senate and Trustees of California State University, Task Force on Intellectual Property. *Intellectual Property, Fair Use, and the Unbundling of Ownership Rights: Furthering the Mission of Public Higher Education.* March 2003. Accessed February 2004. <http://www.calstate.edu/AcadSen/Records/ Report/Intellectual_Prop_Final.pdf>

5. The Higher Learning Commission, *Accreditation of Higher Education Institutions: An Overview, 2003 Edition* (Chicago: The Higher Learning Commission, 2003).

6. Georgia Harper, "The UT System Crash Course in Copyright." Available online from http://www.utsystem.edu/ogc/intellectualproperty/cprtindx.htm [cited 7 March 2003].

7. Copyright Clearance Center. 2004. Available online from http://www.copyright.com/.

8. Harper, "The UT System Crash Course in Copyright"; Vincent Kiernan, "Professors Are Unhappy with Limitations of Online Resources, Survey Finds." *Chronicle of Higher Education* L, no. 33 (2004),

9. Michele Langlois, et al., "Restrictions Impeding Web-based Courses: A Survey of Publisher's Variation in Authorizing Access to High Quality On-line Literature." Available online from http://www.biomedcentral.com/.

10. *The TEACH Toolkit: An Online Resource for Understanding Copyright and Distance Education.* 2004. Available online from http://www.lib.ncsu.edu/scc/legislative/teachkit/.

11. Pamela Samuelson, "Anticircumvention Rules: Threat to Science," *Science* 293, no. 5537 (2001): 2028–31.

12. Ibid.

13. Ibid.

14.   W. W. Gibbs, "Public Not Welcome," *Scientific American* 289, no. 3 (2003): 24.

15.   Ibid.

16.   David Skidmore, 2003. Drake University Sunday Foreign Film Series.

17.   Susan Hansen, 2004. Drake University Sunday Foreign Film Series.

18.   Copyright Committee of Washburn University. 2004. Available online from http://www.washburn.edu/copyright/ [cited 2 November 2003].

19.   Krissah Williams, "Legg Mason Told to Pay Newsletter," *Washington Post*, October 7, 2003, E01.

20.   Motion Picture Association of America. "Respect Copyrights." Available online from http://www.copyright.org/home.htm [cited 29 April 2004].

21.   Recording Industry Association of America. "Copyright Laws." 2003. Available online from http://www.riaa.com/issues/copyright/laws.asp [cited 29 April 2004].

22.   The National Association of College Stores. "Why Coursepack Materials Disguised as Classroom Handouts Need to Have Permissions." Available online from http://www.nacs.org/public/copyright/handouts.asp [cited 3 March 2003].

23.   Association of American Publishers, Inc., National Association of College Stores, Inc., and Software & Information Industry Association, Inc. 2003. "Questions & Answers on Copyright for the Campus Community." AAP; NACS; SIIA.

24.   Harper, "Licensing Resources." 2001. Available online from http://www.ut-system.edu/ogc/intellectualproperty/licrsrcs.htm [cited 28 April 2004].

25.   Budapest Open Access Initiative. "Open Access Journal Business Guides." 2004. Available online from http://www.soros.org/openaccess/oajguides/index.shtml [cited 29 April 2004].

26.   Raym Crow. "SPARC Institutional Repository Checklist and Resource Guide." 2002. Available online from http://www.arl.org.sparc.IR/IR_Guide.html [cited 29 April 2004].

Chapter 4

A Humanist's Perspective on Digital Scholarship and Publishing

Allyson Polsky McCabe

Abstract

This paper explores the role that digital publishing may play in the humanities in the twenty-first century. Although the publication of academic books by junior faculty is typically considered a prerequisite for tenure consideration (and indeed increasingly a criterion for tenure-track job candidates), university presses have been forced to cut back on the number of titles they can accept for publication due to budgetary constraints. This situation not only presents a significant professional risk for graduate students and junior faculty, but also threatens the profession as a whole, higher education generally, and the larger public who benefits from the widest dissemination of ideas. The protection of intellectual property rights is a particularly strong concern for humanities scholars, and this paper addresses the current state, and ongoing development, of tools to guard against copyright infringement.

Introduction: Complex Issues, No Simple Solutions

Lately, there has been a lot of buzz in the academy about the so-called crisis in scholarly publishing, yet the problem is oversimplified and thus not well understood. In this discussion, I will explain why the scholarly publishing problem, pervasive as it is, cannot be boiled down to the simple fact that at the same time that colleges and universities are facing enormous budget cuts, the volume and price of information is going up. By addressing how the sciences and humanities experience this crunch differently, I hope to shed light on the need for a multilayered approach that involves unprecedented cross-institutional collaborations among administrators, faculties, publishers, librarians, and technologists.

Understanding the Roots of the Scientific Publishing Crisis

To understand what makes collaborative solutions difficult, but absolutely necessary, I will begin by considering some key differences between the sciences and the humanities. Because the scope of my paper necessitates a brief discussion of the sciences, I will refer to an ARL-cosponsored roundtable that effectively identifies the current scientific publishing crisis as a consequence of outsourcing to commercial publishers that first took hold in the mid-twentieth century.[1] According to their report, the shift to commercial publishing gained momentum as relatively well-funded universities grew in number, size, and prestige and as research output began to exceed the preexisting academic publishing apparatus. Further, as colleges and universities experienced rapid expansion, so, too, did the number of campus libraries, thus enabling the formation of stable markets for scientific research. Both conditions made scientific publishing appear potentially lucrative to the commercial publishing houses.

The report holds that in the initial phases of this transition, science faculty welcomed the opportunity to hand over unwanted production and distribution tasks to publishers while they retained authorial and editorial control. In this respect, the relationship was mutually beneficial. However, the growing market for scientific literature led to a conflict of values and eventually to an unequal distribution of power. A prime reason is that as a condition of their partnership with the presses, faculty authors routinely handed over their copyrights, a concession that made it difficult for faculty and institutions to retain control over the research "products" being sold by the presses. As a consequence, authors lost control of what was done or could be done with their published work. Moreover, as the commercial presses have become increasingly consolidated, their financial and legal edge over academic institutions and faculty has given them an exceptionally favorable bargaining position that is arguably unfair.[2] Whereas there were thirteen major publishers in science, medicine, and technology in 1998, by the end of 2002 the number had decreased to only seven.[3]

To put this problem in further perspective, note that scientific journal publishing is now a $3.5 billion industry.[4] This is in large part due to the fact that as the primary conduit for scholarly communication in the sciences, the commercial presses have enjoyed an enormous amount of control over pricing structures. They have diminished competition by bundling electronic content and offering it at high prices through multiyear licensing agreements that have forced libraries to cancel holdings from smaller presses.[5] Much has been written about problems with this kind of journal aggregation—the so-called big deal contracts—and one notorious scientific publishing leader, Reed Elsevier, has even required "no-cancellations" contracts with its university licensees that would leave them vulnerable to unlimited fee increases.[6] If anyone doubts that pricing is out of control, consider that a pricing study conducted in 2002 by *Library Journal* indicated that subscription prices for journals in science, medicine, and technology were ten to twenty times higher than those of humanities journals.[7] Prices have escalated to the point that the cost of a single scientific journal subscription can now exceed $20,000 per year.[8]

Scientific researchers have recently attempted to fight back against this exploitation by creating their own online open-access research distribution channels (e.g., arXiv.org at Cornell) and journal archives (e.g., HighWire, a project of Stanford University Libraries), free online journals (e.g., Public Library of Science, or PloS) and development-stage commercial projects (e.g., BioMed Central). In place of subscription fees, open-access channels typically charge authors page fees (in the range of $500 to $1,500 per article in the case of PloS) to help cover production costs. These fees can often be absorbed by scientists' research grants, and a limited number of waivers are available to scientists whose papers are accepted but do not have adequate funding to cover publication costs. Although charging authors to publish their work is a foreign concept to humanists who do not enjoy anywhere near the same degree of institutional or external research support, it is important to point out that both BioMed Central and PloS currently operate at a loss.[9] Therefore, it appears that the main motivation for adopting the open-access approach is not financial benefit but, rather, enhanced editorial control and unfettered information exchange.

Although open-access projects in the sciences have enjoyed considerable interest and an impressive degree of early critical success, it is important to point out that not everyone is on board. Nonprofit publishers, for example, sometimes side with their commercial counterparts because their own revenues (for infrastructure, grants, scholarships, etc.) depend on institutional subscription fees. Further, as mentioned above, not all authors will be able to shoulder the new fees, and not all open-access journals will prove financially viable in the long term. Indeed, PloS is currently assisted by a $9 million start up grant that it received in 2002 from the Gordon and Betty Moore Foundation.

Further problems emerge when one considers that a possible result of the open-access publishing model may be that costs are not eliminated, but merely shifted, and in the transition period, academic institutions may have to cover both subscriptions and authors' fees. Moreover, some scientists fear that new open-access journals will flood the market, making it difficult to determine which will enjoy lasting prestige. Publishing in an unestablished journal that may fold is a risky proposition for an up-and-coming research scientist, and even though senior scientists are generally comfortable working with electronic media, they may consider the new online journals to be lacking in tangibility, permanence, quality, and authority. Although the future of open access remains to be seen, at least scientists are confronting the issues and trying new approaches. In the humanities, this has been less the case.

Understanding the Roots of the Humanities Publishing Crisis

To understand the complex reasons for this reticence and how the crisis in academic publishing has affected the humanities, we first need to understand why humanities scholars publish and why they are reluctant to acknowledge threats to the continued viability of this enterprise. I acknowledge that my following comments may appear strident, and I recognize that there is some truth in the observation that we are often the harshest critics of own our cultures. However, I hold that candor is a necessary component of any successful plan to address a pervasive and intensifying problem.

In the humanities, the monograph is considered king despite the fact that a "best-seller" typically means sales in the low to mid-hundreds of copies (usually to libraries and colleagues). Unlike commercial authors, humanists don't hope to draw large audiences for their specialized studies and don't necessarily see publishing as having a direct personal or institutional financial benefit. Similarly, because humanities books attract a limited market and have rarely been lucrative, they have not been attractive to commercial publishers. By and large, these books are still produced and distributed by academic publishing houses, and thus there is no perceived "evil corporate empire" for scholars to get fired up about.

Like scientists, humanists publish to achieve professional visibility, to advance knowledge in their field, and to create a permanent record of their research endeavors. Unlike scientists, however, many humanists still operate in a nineteenth-century paradigm when it comes to the connoisseurship of ideas. Perhaps this is in part because it takes, on average, nearly a decade to complete a Ph.D. and nearly half that time to write a monograph.[10] Books are viewed as precious objects in which knowledge has been carefully collected and fermented; books and the libraries that archive them are viewed with a kind of mysticism and religiosity.

Humanists generally prefer browsing primary source materials, and rare or unique holdings are typically privileged in relation to holdings that are easily reproducible and distributable.[11] Further, humanists are more concerned with qualitative questions of meaning and interpretation than quantitative data generation and analysis; thus, the cliché that the library is the humanist's laboratory does ring true. We have a strong emotional as well as professional investment in physical artifacts, including books themselves.[12] The intellectual lineage of English is based strongly on citation—generations of scholars writing books about books—yet the economic realities of publishing nowadays have called into question the very legitimacy of humanistic inquiry.

The crisis that humanists now face is increased pressure to publish books as a condition not only for tenure and promotion, but also for *hiring*, at precisely the time when the budgets of nonprofit university presses have been slashed and editorial positions in certain subfields have been totally eliminated.[13] Academic publishers have been forced to severely limit the number of titles they can accept for publication, and many young scholars believe that the only way a book can be published is if its author is a celebrity or the manuscript is marketable as a textbook (e.g., for freshman composition).

This view is supported by frequent reports, both published and anecdotal, that several university presses have turned to "market analyses" to determine whether a manuscript should be submitted for review, and some have even responded to submission inquires by English professors by bluntly stating that they categorically reject publication inquiries from certain fields.[14] For example, faculty members have received notices from the presses indicating that "[they] no longer publish literary criticism," in spite of the fact that this area is considered by scholars to be central to the discipline of English.[15]

Libraries have historically been the largest market for scholarly monographs; however, as the ARL Materials Budget Surveys reflect, acquisitions have decreased steadily over the past decade.[16] In the current climate, even if a scholar is lucky enough to have her specialized scholarly manuscript published by a university press, the potential audience for her work may be adversely affected by the high costs of scientific journal subscriptions, which eat up library acquisitions budgets. In this unfortunate way, the sciences' publishing problem indirectly has had a negative impact on the humanities' publishing problem. This situation, coupled with the widespread view that the sciences receive preferential treatment because they bring substantially more grants and profits to the university, does not make scientists and humanists natural allies, but at best strange bedfellows. Solutions that work for one group won't necessarily work for the other.

In recent years, humanists and their scholarly societies have become well aware of the impact on the profession of the disappearing monograph, but there is still no consensus about how to address it. The preference for monographs is so great among humanists that the former president of the MLA, Stephen Greenblatt, suggested in an open letter to members of the organization in 2002 that, "if institutions [read: tenure committees] insist on the need for books [from tenure-seeking candidates], perhaps they should provide a first-book subvention, comparable to (though vastly less expensive than) the start-up subvention for scientists."[17] However, if institutions can't or won't adequately support the university presses, what makes Greenblatt and others believe that they will fund the publication of books by junior humanities faculty with subventions in the range of several thousand dollars? Isn't there already the perception that the junior sabbatical—time off from teaching to research and write the monograph—is the "free ride"? And will universities also be willing to offer such support to their graduate students or adjunct faculty to jump-start their careers in a foreboding job market?

Although it is not possible for me to exhaustively address the wide range of problems with Greenblatt's proposed subvention solution to the monograph crisis, I want to acknowledge the possibility that it raises (or exposes) very serious inequities that must be addressed as part of any long-term strategy for sustaining venues for scholarly communication.[18] To give you just a glimpse of the issues, consider that if a prospective junior faculty author submits his manuscript to a university press along with a subvention, this may not signal that his book is better than one by an author without a subvention, merely that his home institution has more money than the other author's school. There is a risk that subventions will be viewed as a kind of payola, making a mockery of the whole enterprise of academic publishing in the humanities. This is the last thing that humanists need.

Some, including publishers, have suggested shifting the focus of scholarly communication to publishing in journals; however, this venue holds less appeal for humanists than it does for scientists for a number of reasons.[19] First among them is the culture of humanities research itself. Speedy dissemination is not a top priority for humanists and not just when it comes to monographs: it can take a year or more from the submission of a journal article for it to appear in print.

Perhaps this is because humanists rely less on journal literature than monographs for scholarly communication; even though the rejection rate is an amazing 70 to 90 percent, journal articles are often considered "drafts" of anticipated monograph chapters.[20] Advancing unproven theories and ideas or claiming discoveries before one's colleagues do is not of high professional value and the impact of humanities research is rarely, if ever, instantaneous or direct, especially if it is innovative. Although the situation is worse for junior scholars, even articles published by established authors may be met with resistance if they challenge disciplinary orthodoxy.[21]

Further, albeit not nearly at the rate of science journals, librarians note that humanities journals prices are also rising, which could prove problematic in the near future. Humanists are unlikely to view these cost concerns as serious enough to warrant such interventions as taking journals exclusively online and, even if they reduce costs to some degree, many question how such venues would be financed. Humanities research generates only "cultural capital" for its authors, and the university presses and the scholarly societies typically publish the journals. Humanities authors typically earn lower salaries than their counterparts in the sciences, rarely receive sizable grants, and cannot afford to pay hundreds or even thousands of dollars to publish their work. There is also no for-profit industry as in the sciences that can offset the costs of producing journals through the generation of advertising revenue.

Journals also hold less appeal because the humanities disciplines are relatively fragmented. No single journal dominates all of the humanities disciplines, much less a single discipline within the humanities. In English, for example, there are many specialized journals in various subfields (e.g., poetry, cultural studies, romance literature, etc.). Although a small number of "superstars" manage to penetrate several specialties or even disciplines, faculty members generally rely on departmental colleagues to know what is happening in a field other than their own and consider the university press–published monograph the gold standard for judging the "seriousness" of a colleague's (or prospective colleague's) scholarship.

Additional Barriers

Putting aside these obstacles for the moment, even those humanists who are interested in exploring alternative venues for scholarship and publishing in the digital world often find that information technology support is deficient and the learning curve is steep. These are also among the reasons why humanities faculty members typically rely on technology only for text editing, citation management, and e-mail communications.[22] Further, many humanists prefer "off-the-shelf" technology research aids and want academic librarians to act as "mediators" of digital information.[23] On the whole, humanists are less knowledgeable (and enthusiastic) about digital publishing and use online sources less than scientists.[24] Senior humanities scholars who are less familiar or comfortable with technology may not be capable of producing or qualified to review digital or multimedia texts. Many hold the limited conceptualization that digital scholarship and publishing means producing and reading endless pages of text on a computer screen, and they rightfully react to this prospect with sheer horror.

The strong professional resistance I have described is often accompanied by the belief, whether naïve or willful, among some scholars that, in the end, traditional publishing models will endure and quality will prevail. Some senior scholars, who came of professional age before academic publishing and the humanities job market dried up, even believe that the increased competition for book contracts will positively motivate younger scholars' achievement. Of course, many men and women of letters who hold this view have not experienced the publishing crisis directly: they have either achieved professional prominence long ago and are proven "sellers" or they have not published at all as posttenure members of the faculty. They are only too happy to support the view held by some of their junior colleagues that abstaining from publishing themselves will create more opportunities for others.[25]

These humanists perceive digital publishing as a threat to existing professional, organizational, and disciplinary cultures when the true threat is the collapse of the old academic infrastructure that once supported humanities research. They are concerned about the quality of e-texts, which they consider to be lacking in permanence and authority, and they fail to understand that the old "publish or perish" rule affects the stability not only of individual careers, but also of whole departments and fields of inquiry. Rather than seeing digital scholarship and publishing as faddish, humanities faculty must consider them as part of a potential solution that can help the humanities disciplines grow in promising, if unexpected, ways and meet institutional demands to stay fresh and relevant.

To encourage humanities faculty to explore digital scholarship and publishing, at base we must address their widely held concerns about intellectual property and electronic and open source models. The concept of individual authorship is highly prized, and plagiarism is a major concern for humanities faculty who worry that the easy copy-and-paste quality of online texts makes it too easy to pass off someone else's research as one's own. Reluctance to publish in digital environments is thus related to the worry that researchers will lose authorial control over their own work, its reproduction and dissemination. It is, however, ironic that many humanists who express these concerns have no problem making up their own course packets to be produced and sold to their students by the local copy shop without copyright authorization.

I believe that a balance must be struck between maintaining authorship rights and increasing access to materials for promoting knowledge and learning. There may be cases when transferring certain rights is appropriate and even professionally advantageous (e.g., when enhanced dissemination leads to greater visibility). As encryption methods and password-protected access systems continue to evolve, information technologists can better partner with faculty to design effective strategies for protecting data. We should also bear in mind that electronic publishing and open access are not all-or-nothing propositions, and determining who will control the licensing for online texts must be part of an open negotiation process in which all participants are able to make informed and unconstrained decisions.

Promising Directions

Perhaps I have made too grim a forecast about the future of digital scholarship and publishing in the humanities. Despite the considerable obstacles I have discussed, there are a significant number of promising collaborative digital projects under way. For example, in the past decade, we have seen the launch of new online journal collections, like Project MUSE and JSTOR, that are strong in the humanities. Interdisciplinary institutional research portals have been developed, such as the digital history centers at George Mason University and the University of Virginia, that include humanities research. In the disciplines of history and literature, Oxford and Cambridge University Presses have digitized their backlists, which are experimentally mounted at the University of Pennsylvania to track usage; the American Council of Learned Societies has posted nearly 1,000 history books online; and the History Cooperative has launched online editions of a dozen journals.[26] Online publishing has also been initiated by projects like Romantic Circles at the University of Maryland, the NINES Project at the University of Virginia, and the Scholarly Publishing and Academic Resources Coalition (SPARC).

In terms of potential futures for the monograph, library press cooperatives, such as Penn State's multimedia and digital publishing initiative and EPIC at Columbia University Press, which publishes prize-winning history dissertations in an electronic multimedia format, are springing up at more and more institutions.[27] Projects such as these, which need broader publicity and support, offer not only potential solutions to the crisis in scholarly publishing, but, more important, foster a culture of innovation, potentially breathing new life into the humanities by raising crucial questions about how we currently define and can redefine authorship, readership, narrative structure, the role of images and sound in relation to the word, archival architecture, and the integration of research and pedagogical tools, just to name a few.[28]

Recently, Jennifer Crewe, editorial director of the Columbia University Press, has also offered a provocative challenge to the Modern Language Association (MLA) to assume a more active role in establishing and maintaining new electronic venues for the monograph.[29] Among a series of articles on scholarly publishing in the 2004 issue of *Profession*, the MLA's annual professional publication, Crewe throws down the gauntlet by inviting the formation of unprecedented partnerships in which the organization would host a Web site on which a consortium of university presses could mount their active lists. Access to the materials posted on the site could be arranged via library subscriptions at an attractively negotiated rate, and the usage figures for particular books could be easily collected. Because the presses would maintain their role as selectors, editors, and designers of the monographs, hiring and tenure committees would likely view these books as legitimate. Although start-up costs for such a project would require substantial grant funding, long-term costs could be successfully offset by requiring the MLA to pass on some of its subscription revenues to the presses in the form of royalties, and individual books could be sold from the site in either an electronic format or via print on demand.

I believe that by building team-based relationships among humanities scholars, university presses, academic libraries, and other specialists in information resource and digital policy management, we are capable of developing successful alternative scholarship models and publishing venues. The architecture of these digital resources must, however, ensure that the same rigorous standards are upheld for e-texts as those that are currently used for traditional scholarly publishing. They must also address design, implementation, and utilization issues that are particular to peer-to-peer file-sharing communities, such as how to guard against unauthorized copying, modification, and redistribution. Humanities faculty must be assured that new scholarship and publishing channels are intended to supplement, but not replace, existing models and the validity of those traditional models must be affirmed. The guide for choosing a research dissemination mode must consider what is most effective for conveying ideas, not simply what is the most economically efficient.

Finally, I believe that new digital ventures will have the best chance of succeeding when they are organized cross-institutionally rather than under the control of a single institution or department; in other words, they must be voluntarily designed and managed by and for those vital communities that are formed by shared intellectual interests. These communities have always been "virtual" and "imagined" inasmuch as ever-expanding technologies from the copy machine to the Internet and beyond have created the conditions that enable the growth and multiplication of new knowledge networks that extend beyond physical or institutional borders. To summarize my view about digital scholarship and publishing in the humanities:

- Faculty must be educated about scholarly communication issues and treated as partners in all discussions about prospective solutions.
- Faculty must be offered encouragement, training, and support to explore new venues.
- Faculty must feel that technology use is a choice.
- Faculty must consider electronic publications as evidence of legitimate scholarly productivity in hiring and tenure decisions.
- Senior faculty should be encouraged to publish in and otherwise support these venues to help elevate their status.
- Junior faculty, part-time faculty, and graduate students must be supported in their professional development and should be encouraged to explore new venues.
- Intellectual property issues must be addressed by all stakeholders.
- Professional standards must be upheld in the creation and management of new venues, and indexing and archiving also must be central concerns.
- A selective cross-institutional peer-reviewed process must be in place for new venues.
- Digital resources and venues should be widely publicized with training and support.

Conclusion

In closing, I believe that scientists and humanists need not exclusively characterize the situation in scholarly publishing as a crisis. Indeed, it represents an exciting challenge to how we currently organize information in academic institutions and an opportunity to improve both our disciplinary and interdisciplinary scholarly approaches and resources. Evolving technologies will foster unprecedented access to information and ideas and stimulate the generation of new concepts and ways of thinking, but only if we know how to develop, manage, and teach others how to work with these tools properly. For me, what is exciting about this challenge is envisioning how various professions might forge a collective effort to produce, manage, and disseminate ideas. Effective long-term solutions require sustained and systemic teamwork among multiple stakeholders.

Therefore, administrators, faculty, publishers, librarians, and technologists need to establish a new kind of dialogue. We have much to learn from each other not only about our respective methods and modes of inquiry, but also about how we view the creation and management of knowledge and information. Although it is clear that our multiple perspectives are not identical, we may find that they are complementary. Our conversations may help us to design integrated approaches to preserve our knowledge bases and, ultimately, to anticipate and prevent future scholarly communications crises, rather than responding to them reactively.

Notes

1.   Association of Research Libraries, Association of American Universities, and the Pew Higher Education Roundtable, cosponsors, "To Publish and Perish," *Policy Perspectives Special Issue* 7, no. 4 (Mar. 1998). Available online from http://www.arl. org/scomm/pew/pewrept.html [accessed 15 March 2004]; see also Jean-Claude Guedon, "In Oldenburg's Long Shadow: Librarians, Research Scientists, Publishers, and the Control of Scientific Publishing," *ARL Proceedings* 138 (May 2001). Available online from http://www.arl.org/proceedings/138/guedon.html [accessed 3 January 2005].

2.   Mark J. McCabe and Theodore T. Bergstrom, "And Then There Was One: Industry Consolidation in Journal Publishing and What It Means for Libraries," SPARC/ARL Forum held at ALA Midwinter meeting in Philadelphia, January 25, 2003; Mary H. Munroe, "The Academic Publishing Industry: A Story of Merger and Acquisition," prepared for ARL and the Information Access Alliance. Available online from http://www.niulib.niu.edu/publishers/.

3.   ARL Office of Scholarly Communication, "Framing the Issues: Open Access," September 20, 2004. Available online from http://www.arl.org/scomm/open_ access/framing.html [accessed 5 January 2005].

4.   ARL, AAU, and Pew Higher Education Roundtable, "To Publish and Perish"; Lila Guterman, "The Promise and Peril of 'Open Access,'" *Chronicle of Higher Education* (Jan. 30, 2004). Available online from http://chronicle.com/weekly/v50/ i21/21a01001.htm [accessed 29 April 2004].

5.   ARL, "Framing the Issues."

6.   Kenneth Frazier, "The Librarians' Dilemma: Contemplating the Costs of the 'Big Deal,'" *D-Lib Magazine* 7, no. 3 (Mar. 2001). Available online from http:// www.dlib.org/dlib/march01/frazier/03frazier.html [accessed 29 April 2004]; Cindy Yee, "Open Access Journals Debated," *Chronicle Online: The Independent Daily at Duke University* (Feb. 4, 2004). Available online from http://www.chronicle.duke. edu/vnews/display.v/ART/2004/02/04/4020e8b9af79a [accessed 29 April 2004].

7.   Lee Van Orsdell and Kathleen Born, "Periodicals Price Survey 2002: Doing the Digital Flip," *Library Journal* (Apr. 15, 2002). Available online from http://www. libraryjournal.com/article/CA206383?display=searchResults&stt=001&text=period icals+price+survey [accessed 3 January 2005].

8.   Guterman, "The Promise and Peril of 'Open Access.'"

9.   Yee, "Open Access Journals Debated."

10.   Louis Menand, cited in Richard Byrne, "Scholars Mull Their Separation from the Mainstream," *Chronicle of Higher Education* (Jan. 7, 2005). Available online from http://chronicle.com/weekly/v51/i18/18a03101.htm [accessed 3 January 2005].

11.   Stephen E. Wiberley Jr., "Habits of Humanists: Scholarly Behavior and New Information Technologies," *Library Hi Tech* 9, no. 1 (1991): 17–21; Stephen E. Wiberley Jr. and William G. Jones, "Time and Technology: A Decade-long Look at Humanists' Use of Electronic Information Technology," *College & Research Libraries* 61 (2000): 421–31; Wendy Duff and Catherine Johnson, "Accidentally Found on Purpose: Information-seeking Behavior of Historians in Archives," *Library Quarterly* 72, no. 4: 472–96.

12.   Wiberly and Jones, "Time and Technology."

13.   Stephen Greenblatt, "A Special Letter from Stephen Greenblatt," Modern Language Association. Available online from http://www.mla.org/resources/documents/rep_scholarly_pub/scholarly_pub [accessed 30 January 2003].

14.   MLA Ad Hoc Committee on the Future of Scholarly Publishing, "The Future of Scholarly Publishing," in *Profession 2002* (New York: MLA, 2002), 172–86.

15.   Carey Nelson and Stephen Watt, *Academic Keywords: A Devil's Dictionary for Higher Education* (New York: Routledge, 1999), 226.

16.   ARL, "Library Material Budget Survey." Available online from http://www.arl.org/scomm/1mbs/index.html.

17.   Greenblatt, "A Special Letter from Stephen Greenblatt."

18.   Carlos J. Alonso, "Intervention at the ACLS," 2003. Available online from www.acls.org/03am/alonso.pdf [accessed 5 September 2004].

19.   Lindsay Waters, "A Modest Proposal for Preventing the Books of the Members of the MLA from Becoming a Burden to Their Authors," *PMLA* 115 (2000): 315–17.

20.   Peter Suber, "Promoting Open Access in the Humanities." Available online from http://www.earlham.edu/~peters/writing/apa.htm [accessed 3 January 2005].

21.   Byrne, "Scholars Mull Their Separation from the Mainstream"; Marjorie Garber, "Why Can't Scholars Write Their Second Books First?" *Chronicle of Higher Education* (Oct. 15, 2004). Available online from http://chronicle.com/weekly/v51/i08/08b02001.htm [accessed 15 October 2004].

22.   Stanley N. Katz, "Why Technology Matters: The Humanities in the 21st Century." A Wisbey Lecture, King's College, University of London, Oct. 16, 2003.

23.   Virginia Massey-Burzio, "The Rush to Technology: A View from the Humanists," *Library Trends* 47, no. 4 (1999).

24.   Katz, "Why Technology Matters."

25.   Cathy N. Davidson, "In Search of Solutions for Scholarly Publishing" (Live Colloquy). *Chronicle of Higher Education* (Oct. 2, 2003). Available online from

http://chroncle.com/colloquylive/2003/10/publishing [accessed 20 July 2004].

26. Katz, "Why Technology Matters."

27. Kate Wittenberg, "Scholarly Editing in the Digital Age," *Chronicle of Higher Education* (Jan. 20, 2003). Available online from http://chronicle.com/weekly/v49/i41/41b01201.htm [accessed 29 April 2004].

28. Ibid.

29. Jennifer Crewe, "Our Business Is Your Business," in *Profession 2004* (New York: Modern Language Association, 2004), 25–31.

Chapter 5

Why Can't I Manage Academic Papers Like MP3s? The Evolution and Intent of Metadata Standards

James Howison and Abby Goodrum

Abstract

This paper considers the deceptively simple question, Why can't downloaded academic papers be managed in the simple and effective manner in which digital music files are managed? We make the case that the answer is different treatments of metadata. Two key differences are identified: first, digital music metadata is standardized and moves with the content file whereas academic metadata is not and does not; and second, digital music metadata lookup services are collaborative and automate the movement from a digital file to the appropriate metadata whereas academic metadata services do not.

To understand why these differences exist, we examine the divergent evolution of metadata standards for digital music and academic papers. It is observed that the processes differ in interesting ways according to their intent. Specifically, music metadata was developed primarily for personal file management whereas the focus of academic metadata has been on information retrieval.

We argue that lessons from MP3 metadata can assist individual academics facing their growing personal document management challenges. Our focus, therefore, is not on metadata for the academic publishing industry or institutional resource sharing; rather, it is limited to the personal libraries growing on our hard drives. This bottom-up approach to document management combined with p2p distribution radically altered the music landscape. Might such an approach have a similar impact on academic publishing? This paper outlines plans for improving the personal management of academic papers—doing academic metadata and file management the MP3 way—and considers the likelihood of success.

Managing Music and Managing Electronic Papers

There is a striking difference in the ease and success with which people manage digital music compared to digital academic papers.

Managing Digital Music

Today's computers are filled with digital music, and regular users are more than capable of meeting the exhortation to "Rip, Mix and Burn."[1] They are able to bring music onto their computers, organize and file it for personal access, mix it into many combinations, and burn it off to music CDs and digital music players. Users are proficient at managing substantial libraries of digital audio, even on the anemic interfaces afforded by today's digital music players. Figure 1 shows the work flow for personal digital music management.

A range of programs is available to assist the user throughout this cycle, many provided by the computer or operating system builders in an acknowledgment that managing personal libraries of audio is one of the factors driving the purchase of new computers. Programs like WinAmp and iTunes accept ripped CDs or files downloaded from online services, be they record industry endorsed or peer-to-peer sharing networks. In most cases, the music is quickly and transparently stored on disk and presented to the user to be mixed and played by artist, album, genre, or even beats per minute. Unlimited numbers of play lists provide personalized 'views' into the libraries. In addition to these "kitchen-sink" music programs, there is an entire ecology of stand-alone rip, mix, and burners, including the various peer-to-peer applications such as KaZaa and the venerable Napster (still kicking in the form of the OpenNapster networks). Through these networks, as well as LANs, burnt CDs, and "good old-fashioned dragging from a friend's computer," these audio files are easily shared. In fact, the controversy driven by this sharing reflects the sheer ease with which it occurs.

We venture to say that managing digital music provides probably the best personal information management experience available to individuals today, certainly exceeding managing e-mail, word-processing files, digital photographs, and, central to this paper, personal collections of academic papers.

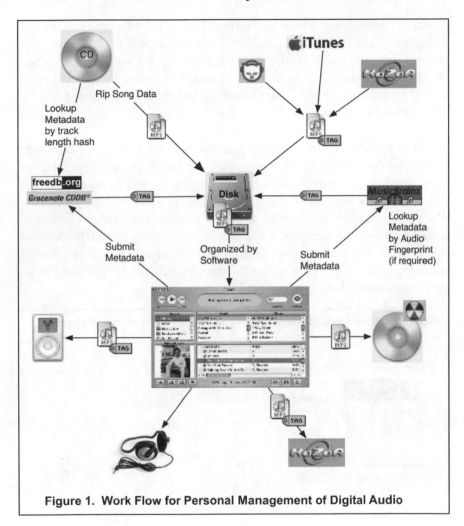

Figure 1. Work Flow for Personal Management of Digital Audio

Managing Academic Papers

In fact, the contrast between the management of digital music and academic papers is jarring. First, managing academic papers is a much more uneven experience that is far from standardized. It ranges from manual "fumbling" through to the quite sophisticated, if users employ citation managers such as Endnote or the variety of Bibtex management systems. Yet, even the most sophisticated users experience difficulty in managing their digital academic files.

Academic work flow can be modeled, somewhat whimsically, as its own "Rip, Mix and Burn." Papers are "ripped" from a variety of sources, mixed (and progressively remixed) into annotated bibliographies, reading lists and eventually new papers, which are "burned" out, with their reference lists, to disks, paper, and PDFs, which are then circulated back to the academic community through e-mail, Web sites, and, hopefully for authors, conferences and journals. Figure 2 is an attempt to model the work flow of obtaining digital papers, and figure 3 attempts to model the use of digital papers in creating new academic works.[2]

Our research into the personal digital management habits of academics is still in process: we are conducting interviews and a survey to document these practices. However, for the purposes of this paper we offer scenarios that, although currently without empirical support, will be recognizable to most academics whether it reflect their habits or those of their colleagues. The process regularly begins with a citation garnered from either a colleague, a reading list or bibliography, a database or, very often, the reference list of other papers. It is unlikely that the citation is in a structured database format, indeed quite often it is on paper or the digital paper of a PDF realized in the particular citation format of the publication.

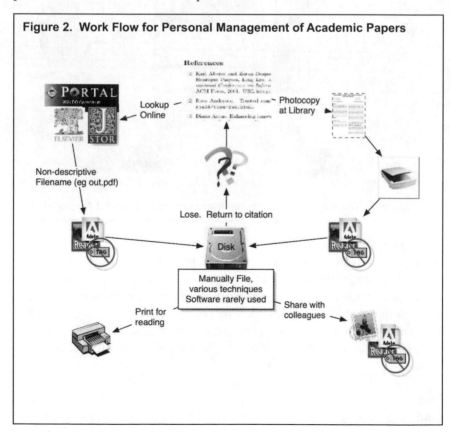

Figure 2. Work Flow for Personal Management of Academic Papers

Given just a citation most academics are quite adept at accessing academic papers from online journals, downloading, viewing, and printing them. These printed papers might well then become the primary object, placed in piles by project and eventually filled in cabinets lining office walls, adding them to an existing system of photocopied papers obtained over a career.

Those academics who do choose to keep papers in digital form typically do so without the assistance of a document management system other than that provided by the hierarchical file system of the operating system itself. These might be filed by project or, more rarely we suspect, by author or personal genre taxonomy. In any case, so crude are the personal management techniques that it is often easier to store only the citation and return to the online databases when the paper is again desired, despite that often being a technical violation of the terms of use.[3]

The use of papers during "mixing" (writing) might involve the use of a quotation that has to be typed from the paper copy into the document-processing system being used or copied (often with frustrating idiosyncrasies) from a PDF. Finally, the reference list has to be prepared listing the sources used by the authors in their "remix." Figure 3 is an attempt to model this work flow. For those not using a citation manager, this process can be quite frustrating and was described by one respondent as "fumbling."

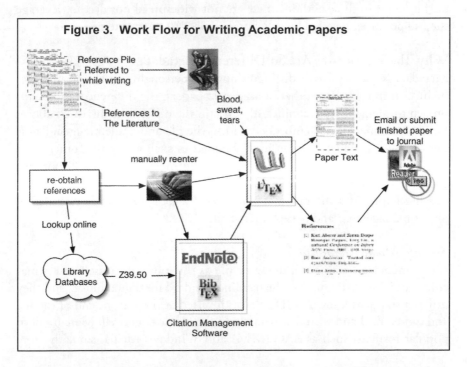

Figure 3. Work Flow for Writing Academic Papers

Reference Pile
Referred to
while writing

References to
The Literature

Blood,
sweat,
tears

Email or submit
finished paper
to journal

manually reenter

Paper Text

re-obtain
references

Lookup online

Library
Databases   — Z39.50 →

EndNote

Bib TeX

References

Citation Management
Software

Frustratingly, even having the original paper, in either digital or paper format, often is not sufficient to prepare the full citation. Rather earlier "remixes" (reference lists) are a common source of citations, manually transformed from the original published format into the intended outlet's required citation format.

Thankfully, a range of citation managers is available in addition to graduate students! Programmatic citation managers such as Endnote or Bibdesk, a Bibtex manager,[4] integrate with the writing environment, such as Word or LATEX, allowing the insertion of citation macros that are then used by the systems to prepare inline citations and reference lists in the specified format.

Although convenient and powerful, these systems stop short of the positive experience of managing digital music. The most frustrating thing about the academic work flow is that when the paper is shared, for example, by e-mail or, hopefully, published in a journal, the entire process is repeated. The document access and citation effort expended by one author is almost completely unavailable to subsequent authors. The fact that my neighbor has recently found, photocopied, and stored an article from our library is no help to my information needs, nor is their often-Herculean citation formatting. To be sure, there are localized practices that facilitate shared repositories or citation exchange (Endnote and Bibtex files can be e-mailed or downloaded), but, it seems to these authors, these are not widespread nor do they leverage the full potential revealed by collaborative peer-to-peer systems.

Why These Processes Are So Different: Metadata

Metadata is the key factor distinguishing the personal information management of music files from that of academic papers: the differences in the approach to metadata can significantly explain the differences discussed above. First, music metadata is embedded within the file and academic metadata is not. Second, metadata for music is obtained in such a way that other users can leverage the efforts of others by accessing metadata from collaborative databases; this is not the case with academic metadata. Metadata is important because it provides the raw materials used by tools to provide easy digital object management and personal retrieval.

Storing Music Metadata

Music metadata is stored in the same file as the music data itself and is machine-readable. MP3 files are the baseline standard for digital music, and they utilize a standard known as ID3 that is inserted at the start or end of the file and can be read and written separately to the music data itself. More modern popular formats, such as AAC (MP4) and Windows Media, similarly store their metadata in the file, using a file "wrapper" able to handle many digital objects in the one file. MP3 ID3 tags are discussed in detail below.

With this metadata, the management tools are able to provide many different views of the personal library and to store and name the digital files in a logical manner under user control. There is no requirement for separate metadata databases.

The advantages of storing metadata with the digital object are twofold. First, embedding ensures that the metadata travels with the file content. Simply moving a file on a local disk does not separate or invalidate the metadata. More important, moving the file across devices retains the metadata, thus downloaded music files often come complete with metadata. Similarly, when files are moved to digital music players, the metadata is available to facilitate collection browsing. Without metadata, these devices would be very hard to use.

The second advantage of embedded metadata is that the objects are never separated; if one is available, the other is also available. They are thus far more readily available and less likely to get out of synch. This is particularly important for versioning (e.g., when dealing with remixes or covers).

Storing Academic Metadata

By contrast, academic citation metadata is managed as a separate object. This is true of paper management as well as even the most sophisticated citation management tools available. There are a wide variety of formats for storing citation data, but they are all used to create some type of database, from flat text or word files, to XML to SQL backends and proprietary binary formats. At best, these formats permit pointers to the actual digital object that they describe, for example, providing a local file pointer, a digital object identifier (DOI), or a URL that points back to the publisher's canonical location for the object. They stop short of inserting the metadata directly into the PDF file.

Figure 4   Bibdesk Stores a Reference to the File, But the File Does Not Store the Full Metadata or Even a Reference to It.

Local-Url	file://localhost/Users/james/Documents/University/Syracuse/Research

Obtaining Metadata

Despite the advantages of embedded metadata for music, there are two situations in which metadata is separated from the song content and must be added: when ripping from audio CDs or when downloading inadequately tagged files from p2p sharing networks. Happily, there are automated techniques available for lookup in both cases.

The audio CD format does not contain textual metadata. Users of standalone CD players will attest that all that is available is the number of tracks, and their length, not the artist, album, or song title. Yet, when a CD is inserted into a networked computer using any decent management software, full metadata appears in the player, listing the song titles, artist name, and album just as outlined on the CD liner. This metadata can be edited (to, for example, alter the genre) and can be retained through the ripping process and inserted in the digital tags.

This metadata is obtained through a network lookup that sends a hash of the file lengths to a server and receives machine-readable metadata in return.[5] The hash of an individual file length is not necessarily unique, but that combined with the order of files on a CD (all provided in a CDs table of contents) provides a unique enough hash so that the CD can be identified with sufficient accuracy.[6, 7] The network services that provide this metadata are the CDDB (now know as Gracenote) and FreeDB. They utilize a standard protocol, also known as the CDDB protocol, to perform the hashes and file lookups (although Gracenote has transitioned to the nonstandard CDDBv2). The evolution of these services is discussed in detail below.

Downloading music does not provide such a consistent experience. Most files on p2p networks have metadata embedded in the file, but a great many do not or have inaccurate or useless metadata (it is not uncommon to see the name of the person that ripped or shared the file in the metadata tag e.g. "ripped by l33tboy"). So haphazard is the provision of metadata that this has become a point of commercial differentiation for the legal download services claim accuracy and completeness and typically includes at least the album cover that good music players can display.

Even when a music file is downloaded or ripped from a CD without metadata, there are network lookup services that can automate its discovery. These are relatively new and utilize the actual musical qualities of the songs to generate a hash for lookup, rather than the track length and order. They are therefore very flexible when dealing with the inevitable differences between tracks ripped by different encoders or with different lengths, although the trade-off is that there are many more near collisions and thus more user selection interaction required. The best known is probably MusicBrainz. MusicBrainz can be run over a collection of digital music files and, provided the track is in the database, will return a number of suggestions for the track and add the appropriate metadata to the music file. The tagger runs over a digital music collection and conducts an exchange of metadata, adding metadata from the server to tracks without it and uploading metadata from tracks on the local computer that are not yet present on the server. MusicBrainz does not store the actual recordings. Figure 5 compares these two music metadata processes and emphasizes their collaborative nature.

Obtaining Academic Metadata

Academic metadata is obtained in a variety of ways, yet even the most sophisticated methods stop short of the level of automation and convenience reached by digital music. For those not using citation management software, the process is a manual one of reentering citations in the required format. This is often done through "reference list raiding," is subject to copying errors, and is extremely tedious.

Thankfully, there are ways to access machine-readable citation data other than through manual entry. Citation managers can connect to, and search and import metadata from, bibliographic databases that support the Z39.50 protocol. Efforts are under way to provide Z39.50 access through a stan-

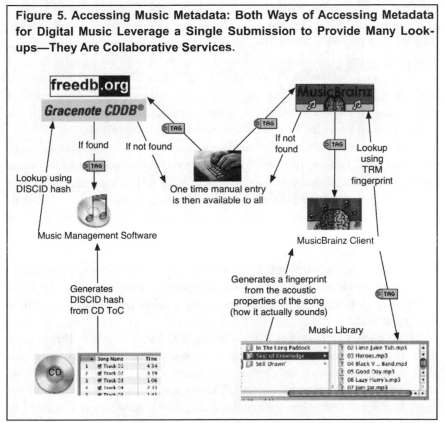

Figure 5. Accessing Music Metadata: Both Ways of Accessing Metadata for Digital Music Leverage a Single Submission to Provide Many Lookups—They Are Collaborative Services.

dardized programming interface known as ZOOM. Vendors such as OCLC, Ovid, and NISC offer a direct-export feature that allows you to automatically transfer your saved citations to your citation management software. The metadata available for searching is sparse, however; and in most instances, the connection must be handled through an institutional account or proxy server. For those databases that are not Z39.50 compliant or for complex searching, one searches using the native database search functions, then downloads the data to a text file and imports that file into citation management software using an appropriate filter configured for each database/vendor, if one is available.

Some online resources providing access to academic papers do carry the citation metadata with their referent papers as either text or exportable files from the vendor's bibliographic database. Many, however, do not provide any formatted or machine-readable metadata along with their PDF images. In fact, most online services do not even use a usefully descriptive file name, often defaulting to "out.pdf" or what is presumably an internal database number, but of no use to the user like "4456.pdf." The full text of a paper is downloaded as a PDF from one resource, and the citation metadata is downloaded into citation management software from another resource. The changing nature of scholarly publishing in some disciplines has also led to a more informal, nonarchival publishing model by individual and institutional authors in HTML, PDF, Latex, or Postscript formats on the Web. In most of these cases, citations and other important metadata are not carried with the papers or even provided from a linked bibliographic repository.

These more sophisticated systems still involve substantial manual work on behalf of the researcher. The "keys," like title and author, used for lookup are part of the citation themselves and there is no widely used automatic way to move a downloaded PDF from the digital object to the metadata. That is, little that is analogous to the DISCID hash or the acoustic hashes used by MusicBrainz. Instead, search is limited to a search key, like title, extracted by individuals—and this process is repeated by each individual who wishes to access the metadata. Although machine-addressable repositories of metadata do exist, the lookup process is not automated, nor does it leverage the work of others in linking a paper with its metadata or allow end users to contribute missing metadata.

One partial exception is Autonomous Citation Indexing.[8] This process uses AI techniques to probe the content of a digital file for its own citation metadata, scanning for elements such as authors and titles, drawing on similarities in document formatting. This system has been used to build the "grey-literature" computer science database, CiteSeer, which is discussed in more detail below. Autonomous Citation Indexing by itself does not, however, leverage the necessary manual corrections and additions from outside the document made by other academics in the course of their writing work, although CiteSeer has built a partial solution (discussed below).

The academic metadata lookup process, therefore, lacks the strong connection between content and metadata that facilitates the effectiveness of the digital music process. Because metadata is managed as a separate digital object, obtaining it is an interactive process that requires separate user involvement and searching skills. This separation is also a source of uncertainty about the version correlation that is the bane of electronically received academic works.

The availability of metadata is the factor that facilitates successful management of digital resources. It is easier to accomplish the obtaining and managing of metadata for digital music because of the combination of storing metadata with the file and the availability of collaborative services that support retrieval of metadata given the digital object.

By contrast, academic metadata is stored outside the file and the movement from paper or file to machine-readable metadata is not supported by an automated system. Therefore, citation management is largely a difficult and repetitive process that fails to leverage the efforts of others.

There are, however, the beginnings of a better way of doing things, and this paper attempts to draw the threads together. First, however, we outline our main contention: an explanation of the reasons for these differences can be found in a comparison of the intent and evolution of these two different metadata schemes.

How Did It Come to This? The Intent and Evolution of Metadata Standards

Music metadata was designed for personal file management and with the expectation that users would first have the object (CD, file) and then seek the metadata. Academic metadata was designed for information retrieval and archiving and with the expectation that users would first have the metadata and use it to access the object. These different intents largely explain the situation we face today.

Evolution of the ID3 Tag

The ID3 metadata tag was born as a standard for personal information management and only later became used for information retrieval.

The development of the standard was motivated by the frustration of users seeking to manage the MP3 files they were creating. The MP3 data format, as designed by the Frauenhofer Institute, originally had a limited scheme that only facilitated the storing of information that was publisher relevant (e.g., copyright, copy/master bit, and a one-bit field called "private" that was for application-specific use). These facilities, although seen as useful from the publisher's perspective, did not facilitate personal information management. Indeed, the design of the MP3 header format was influenced by the requirement that it be suitable for broadcasting, rather than local play or management.[9, 10]

In 1996, this difficulty led Eric Kemp (alias NamkraD) to develop simultaneously the ID3v1 standard and a tagging program that read and wrote the tags called "Studio3."[11] The program was for personal file management. The ID3v1 standard provided the basics of metadata and facilitated the organization and "mixing" of music files. We interviewed Martin Nilsson, who was to develop the second version of ID3, who stated that when he first encountered MP3, tagging "was [a way] of keeping things neat and 'sophisticated." He added that tagging wasn't used in early MP3 retrieval systems, "I do know that MP3Get [a campus searching program used by the ID3v2 developers] didn't have any metadata, and it never really mattered in practice."[12]

The ID3v1 standard was limited in ways that frustrated users seeking to manage their personal music libraries. For example, the length of information that could be stored in each field was limited to 30 bytes and plain ASCII, and there was no ability to add additional fields. An important frustration was that the tag was at the end of the song, reducing its usefulness in situations where the track was being streamed (because the tag would arrive last). These difficulties lead Martin Nilsson to design a new version of the tag that is known as ID3v2 and is still in use today.[13] ID3v2 was rapidly adopted by the booming digital music industry (including developers of software and companies trying to become publishers of digital music). The first formal release of the tagging standard was at the MP3 conference organized by Michael Robertson's mp3.com.[14] The ID3v2 developer's attendance at the conference was sponsored by mp3.com and e-music.com

To this day, the ID3v2 standard is only an "informal" standard; it has not been adopted as an official standard of any standards organization, although experience from its development has been applied to the MPEG-7 efforts. Nilsson argues that it was not required as the adoption was sufficient and the process time-consuming: "I did a 'soft start' with the MP3 content type RFC (now RFC 3003), and it took such an enormous effort to get that document in place that I thought that it really wouldn't be worth the effort to get ID3v2 into an RFC. It was already well known."[15] A now-expired Internet draft (precursor to an RFC), draft-nilsson-id3-oo.txt, was written in December

2000, and the official spec is hosted on http://www.id3.org. This is in striking contrast to the heavy standardization effort familiar to those engaged with academic metadata.

There are three striking elements in the evolution of the metadata standard for digital music. First, the standards were developed by end users seeking to facilitate personal uses of the music files they were creating. Second, the standard was created at the same time as its implementation and was designed to meet just those goals required at the time. Third, the standard was propagated freely and without serious efforts to achieve an official status for the standard.

Compared to the evolution of metadata standards for academic papers, outlined below, the ID3 tag had a simple intent, had significant 'first mover advantage'—there was no competing standard—and was in a field that lacked an obvious standards forum. The open culture of sharing, which exists in the online music community, promoted interoperability and there were no incentives to "reinvent the wheel."

The Evolution of Collaborative Metadata Services

Inserting a CD into a computer in the mid-1990s wasn't very different from using a CD player. In particular, it was likely that only the track numbers and lengths were available to the user and that track selection occurred by manually cross-referencing the physical liner notes. The situation is different today because of collaborative work by Internet users that resulted in a service called CDDB (the Internet Compact Disc DataBase).

In a story that recalls the history of the Domain Name System, the CDDB has its origins in a text file that resided locally on a user's computer in which metadata that had been manually entered by users was stored. Also stored was a hash that allowed the player to remember if a CD had been seen before and to associate the appropriate metadata. By 1996, the Internet had facilitated trading and combination of these individually entered files so that the file grew so much that it began to exceed the ability of Windows players to use it.[16] The solution was the development of a client/server database hosted at cddb.com. The protocol developed for this database allowed both the retrieval and, crucially, the submission of CD metadata by individuals.

The database grew quickly through these individual submissions, providing a valuable service to the digital music community. It was peer-to-peer in that the service facilitated the transfer of digital information entered by one user to many others. However, the CDDB actually stored copies of the object being shared, the metadata, on a centralized server; by contrast, Napster, which also utilized a centralized server, did not store the actual object, just a reference to which user's hard drive it could be obtained from. Like other centralized collaborative systems, however, the CDDB was vulnerable to attack. Yet, unlike the legal attack on Napster, this attack came from "inside" when the CDDB was commercialized by the owners of the server who took out a patent on the system and announced their intention to begin to charge the authors of software (as opposed to the users) for their software's access to the database.

Unsurprisingly, this action caused an uproar on behalf of the users who had voluntarily contributed the contents of the database and who had expected reciprocation in exchange. FreeDB is the open-source alternative developed as an alternative to the CDDB service.

However, CDDB had a strong head start and its strategy of charging small fees to the authors of music management software has proved to be the foundation of a reasonably successful business. They renamed themselves Gracenote and developed a patented new protocol, CDDBv2, which effectively locked free players out of the community-contributed database. Gracenote did, however, face the prospect of weeding out "junk" or misspelled data from its system.

The focus of CDDB reflected the state of digital music in 1996. It is a system that is tightly coupled with CDs themselves and was initially developed without an expectation that the songs would necessarily be "ripped" from the CDs. The system did not require a tagging format; the metadata was stored separately from the file. Tagging was left to the MP3 upstarts led by Eric Kemp and, eventually, Martin Nilsson. In fact, the CDDB was not interested in an engagement with the mp3 tagging efforts: Nilsson paraphrases their response as "We don't want to be associated with MP3, since record companies think of it as illegal."

The rapid growth of digitized music and the p2p file-sharing applications outpaced the ability of music users to maintain accurate metadata. Enormous downloaded collections were without useful metadata for personal management other than file names or have polluted metadata. Recently, other services have emerged to make the link between music files and the metadata needed to manage them in large collections and on digital music players, like the iPod. These services cannot rely on the firm publisher–determined CD publishing format of track length and order because files are individualized and ripped in ways that alter their length.

The alternative strategy now adopted is more sophisticated. It relies on acoustic fingerprinting algorithms that create a hash of the way the music actually sounds. This also opens the service up to music never released on CDs, such as audience live recordings and underground "mash-up" remixes.

MusicBrainz also solves the "dirty" data problem through collaborative voting that reflects the community's opinion on which metadata is the most accurate and/or complete.

Digital music metadata is widely available today because collaborative services—p2p in function, if not in technical structure—allow large groups to leverage the minimal efforts of individuals in manually entering the music metadata. These services combine with the development of embedded tags that store the metadata within the file to facilitate the effective digital music experience widely enjoyed today.

Evolution of Academic Metadata Standards

Academic papers and metadata have historically been managed as separate objects. A separation of object and metadata made sense, placing the catalog cards with the book on the library shelf would not have been a sensible system. Today, however, computer systems are capable of benefiting from their combination.

Metadata in the form of indexes are as old as publishing itself, coming into their own as stand-alone entities with the rise of scholarly publishing in the eighteenth century. As publishing began to computerize its processes, abstracting services began to provide access to their publications' metadata-only digital catalogs on CD-Roms and eventually migrated to dial-up and Web-based access. It is important to note that, in most cases, access to the bibliographic record or to an abstract did not also entail access to the full text of scholarly papers. Full-text availability is still a new phenomenon in academic publishing, and many journals are still not available in full text outside print. Moreover, the publishers of bibliographic indexes, abstracts, and catalogs have not been the publishers of the journals themselves. For these reasons, academic metadata has long been provided apart from the papers themselves. The same historical circumstances explain why metadata lookup systems are not collaborative or complete: they have been used for comparative economic advantage.

Today, however, this continued separation of metadata and object is the cause of significant frustration and inhibits building effective management applications and sharing the work of linking metadata with the digital files.

It is clear that the metadata required for personal file management differs between music and academic resources. Academic metadata is more complex than music metadata. Although artist, album, title, and genre are sufficient to describe the vast majority of music, academic metadata schemes must deal with quite a number of different publication types requiring different schemas (e.g., journal articles, articles in conference proceedings, books, and book chapters to name but a few). No doubt this complexity is a factor in the lack of standardization of academic metadata formats. A recent review of academic metadata for personal bibliographic management argues, however, that "While the library standards are largely 'overkill' with respect to personal and small group management of data to produce a bibliography, many of the basic needs behind the requirements remain the same."[17] When academic metadata is considered only as those fields required by academics when preparing bibliographies, the complexity can be significantly reduced. Schemas like bibtex and refer (used by Endnote) adequately serve the needs of large communities. Finally, additional complexity has been introduced to academic metadata systems by their information retrieval focus, information that is not used in the paper-writing format.

Doing Academic PDFs the MP3 Way: A Better Way?

How, then, can the lessons of digital music management be applied to improve the practices of personal information management by academics? The two key differences identified in this paper are standardized metadata stored with the file and collaborative metadata lookups. The proposals developed here are modest and minimal, and aim at bottom-up adoption by emphasizing immediate usefulness for individuals managing their collections of digital academic papers. The authors believe that better systems for the management of academic papers would relieve some of the frustrations from the work flow outlined in figure 2 and help academics focus their energies on building knowledge rather than chasing lost papers.

Getting Metadata into PDF Files

The portable document file (PDF) is an open standard defined by Adobe and implemented in its Acrobat product line. The openness and fidelity to paper of this standard has led it to become the ubiquitous format for electronic publishing of academic papers. Free readers have been available for upwards of eight years. Adobe charges for the ability to create PDFs providing sophisticated Macros for Microsoft and their own page layout products. However, an increasing number of free and open source products also are able to produce publication-ready PDF files. For example, the L^{A}T$_E$X system, which initially produced PostScript, now typically writes straight to PDF and the Apple OS X operating system uses PDF as its screen-display description language and is able to produce a PDF from any document or screen-shot.

The PDF standard has the ability to store a predefined and limited set of metadata in the document information dictionary (DID). The DID has fields only for title, author, subject, keywords, Created on, Modified On, and Producing application. Perhaps because of these limitations, or perhaps because of limitations in production tools, these fields are extremely rarely used in the academic world. None of the academic electronic document publishers used by the authors utilizes these inadequate fields.

Adobe has produced a relatively new, open standard for storing metadata that can be used for PDFs and in a wide variety of file formats. The eXtensible Metadata Project (XMP) allows the addition of "bullets" of well-defined data in the XML-like resource description format (RDF).[18] This has excellent potential for reaching ubiquity as the cross-platform container for machine-readable metadata. Adobe has provided a software development kit, but currently it is very difficult to produce compliant XMP and add it to PDFs without using the for-pay full Adobe Acrobat Libraries. This is slowing adoption, but the open source community is committed to building tools to utilize XMP; it is a highlighted 'Tech Challenge' of the Creative Commons project.[19]

Is It Necessary to Standardize Machine-readable Metadata?

If XMP is the candidate most likely to bring together the digital academic paper with its machine-readable metadata, what format is that metadata to be in? The metadata required for personal and citation management is less complicated than that required for library use, but still more complicated than that for music. Countless hours have already been spent in committees aiming to standardized academic metadata.

Happily, it is not necessary to adopt or promulgate only one standard; indeed, the recent heated debates over the format for blog feeds (RSS versions and Atom) indicates that many variations can coexist.[20] Because the formats are both written and read by machines, and because RDF formats reference name spaces available online, variations in formats are not the great problem they once seemed. The next-generation 739.50 projects are quite liberal in the formats that they can deal with, including marcxml, mods, and dc. In fact, while this paper has highlighted the ID3v2 tagging format, quite a number of others are hidden behind the scenes, including OGG-tags and ACC-tags. In the first instance, it seems reasonable to employ RDF translations of the widely used Bibtex and Refer formats, but the authors are actively researching this topic.

Making Academic Metadata a Collaborative Practice

Our discussion of digital music emphasized the role that collaborative metadata databases, such as CDDB and MusicBrainz, play in maintaining the ease of the digital music process. We also argued that two elements needed to be resolved before the excellent start that is Z39.50 can be as useful in the management of academic digital papers. The first was a way to automate the lookup process so to easily move from the digital papers to the machine-readable metadata. The second is to leverage the efforts of one's peers to build comprehensive databases.

The more sophisticated approach of MusicBrainz and other acoustic matching services points the way forward. Recall that these services use a hash built from the acoustic properties of the digital music. Analogously, a lookup hash can be harvested from the actual content of the paper. In fact, many algorithms are available to measure the textual similarity between documents, all that is needed is to use these to match downloaded PDF files with metadata in a digital repository. These "fuzzy-matching" techniques have two added advantages over the more simplistic approach of calculating a simple hash from the PDF file (e.g., MD5). File hashes are excellent at assessing whether files are identical, but even semantically meaningless changes render vastly different hash results.

Content-based hashes do not have that limitation and can, in fact, help resolve the versioning problem. If a user has a digital copy of an earlier version of a paper, the content-matching systems should be able to match that with its more developed "kin" and return the results in publication order, thereby alerting the user to a later version that might be of great interest.

One challenge to the content-based lookup approach is that many journal services provide their PDF files as images, rather than text. For older articles that have, in fact, been scanned from paper copies, the reason is obvious. For newer articles, which are generated from the digital production files, the reason is, to these authors, obscure. The approach that seems most promising is the application of optical character recognition techniques to the image documents. It is an open research question to find content analysis algorithms that are able to make accurate matches, even in the face of the noise introduced by faulty OCR.

The second requirement is to inject collaboration into the process of citation management by allowing users to upload the metadata that they associate with a paper and to make that available for query by others. The existing metadata databases are publisher and institution bound and thus are incomplete. Worse, they are viewed as competitive assets and obstacles are placed in the way of their consolidation. Peer-to-peer collaborative uploading appears to be the most likely way to build an adequately large collection of downloadable metadata.

We are actively researching the creation of such an automated collaborative metadata service and welcome any input regarding the components outlined above.

Prospects of Success

Incentive issues must always be considered when building collaborative systems. The system would not be of great use if no one was motivated to associate metadata with a digital file and upload the hash and metadata for others to download. It is arguable that the success of digital music sharing is the result of the high and widespread demand for the product—and the time available to the, often teenaged, participants. These conditions don't hold for academic papers.

Thankfully, systems like the CDDB or the one proposed above have the characteristic that only one upload is required to make the metadata available to all. It is established that online availability increases citations to one's work, so it does not seem a stretch that easy availability of accurate metadata would also increase citations.[21] Therefore, the candidates with the greatest motivation to provide metadata will be the authors themselves. In any case, the effort of preparing metadata is performed by every academic who chooses to cite a work, and the marginal effort required to link this with the file and upload it is quite minimal—and likely to be of personal use to the up-loader next time he or she seeks to use the file. For these reasons, we do not consider there will be a lack of motivation to upload metadata to the system.

Checking this metadata for accuracy is an important task, and, again, it is one that we expect in the medium term to be primarily provided by the paper's authors. The Citeseer service provides Bibtex metadata that is in the first instance extracted using autonomous citation-indexing methods, but which is also open to community modification.[22] Anyone who has a free Citeseer user account can modify and edit the metadata available through the site.[23] This openness there has led to a clear trend of increasing accuracy and completeness of metadata on the Citeseer service, proving resilient, thus far, to pollution.

Conclusion

The personal information management of academic papers has a long way to go to approach the ease and usefulness achieved in the management of digital music. Yet, the processes are not that distinct. We have argued that two crucial differences that hold back personal information management for academics are that the metadata and content are managed as separate objects and that the metadata lookup services are not collaborative.

Management practices for digital music evolved from the need to manage growing libraries of "ripped" music; only later did metadata begin to play a role in information retrieval. In contrast, academic metadata was designed primarily for information retrieval and there has been very little focus on its use in personal information management.

We propose that two tasks are required to move toward more effective practices: using XMP to store academic metadata with the file and using content-based hashing to map between the digital files and a user-contributed metadata database.

Our next step will be to conduct an empirical investigation of the way academics obtain and manage their digital papers and citation preparation processes. We also intend to prepare a proof of concept for a collaborative metadata database that can be searched using content-based hashes.

Notes

1.   Apple Computer's controversial marketing slogan emphasizing the ease of use of its digital music.

2.   These work flow diagrams were published on the first author's blog during the writing of this paper. Happily, this prompted more sophisticated users to graph their own work flows and blog them. Links to these personal work flows, which draw on a range of Citation Management software, are available from the original blog posting via TrackBack. The post is at http://freelancepropaganda.com/;archives/000302.html.

3.   JSTOR, for example, states: "you may not download from the JSTOR archive an entire issue of a journal, significant portions of the entire run of a journal, a significant number of sequential articles, or *multiple copies of articles*" (emphasis added). "JSTOR Terms & Conditions of Use." Available online from http://www.jstor.org/about/terms.html.

4.   The first author is a sometime contributor to the Bibdesk program, which is an open-source Bibtex manager. See http://bibdesk.sf.net, orginally designed by Michael McCraken.

5.   A hash is the result of processing data through an algorithm to produce a substantially shorter string of data. Hash algorithms have the property that, given different input text, they will produce different hashes and, given the same input text, they will produce the same hash. For example, the MD5 (an algorithm) hash of this endnote is 7ff0b5ea8a57905070blafcfc0fb9d78.

6.   freedb.org. "DISCID Howto (Generating CDDB hashes)." 1999. Available online from http://www.freedb.org/modules.php?name=Sections&sop=viewarticle&artid=6.

7.   Although collisions are theoretically possible, the authors have never witnessed one. In any case, if more than one album matches, a simple interactive user selection can resolve the conflict.

8. Steve Lawrence, Kurt Bollacker, and C. Lee Giles, "Autonomous Citation Matching," in *Proceedings of the Third International Conference on Autonomous Agents,* ed. Oren Etzioni (New York: ACM Press, 1999a).

9. Bluecygnet Technologies, "MP3 Frequently Asked Questions." 2001. Available online at http://www.bluecygnet.com/amce/faq-amce.htm.

10. Alpha Internet Consulting, "Inside the MP3 Codec—MP3 Anatomy." 2000. Available online at http://www.mp3-converter.com/mp3codec/mp3_anatomy.htm.

11. Martin Nilsson, "The Short History of Tagging." 2000. Available online from http://www.id3.org/history.html.

12. ———, E-mail interview with ID3v2 developer, 2004.

13. ———, "The Short History of Tagging."

14. ———, e-mail interview.

15. Ibid.

16. MusicBrainz, "MusicBrainz Roots and History." 2004. Available online from http://www.musicbrainz.org/history.html.

17. Paul Shabajee, "Review of Personal Bibliographic Systems." 2003. Available online from http://www.ilrt.bris.ac.uk/publications/researchreport/rr1032/report_html?ilrtyear=00.

18. Adobe Systems Inc., "The Extensible Metadata Platform." 2004. Available online from http://www.adobe.com/products/xmp/ [accessed 14 December 2003].

19. Creative Commons, "Tech Challenge: Open Source Application Support for XMP." 2003. Available online from http://creativecommons.org/technology/challenges#challenge_entry_4005.

20. Clinton Ecker, "The Great Syndication Wars (RSS and Atom)." 2003. Available online from http://phaedo.cx/archives/2003/07/15/the_great_syndication_wars.html.

21. Steve Lawrence, "Online or Invisible?" *Nature* 411, no. 6837 (2001): 521.

22. Lawrence, Bollacker, and Giles, "Autonomous Citation Matching."

23. ———, "Digital Libraries and Autonomous Citation Indexing," *IEEE Computer* 32, no. 6 (1999b): 67–71.

Chapter 6

The Middle Way: The Very-low-cost Model for Scholarly Publishing

Gary Natriello and Michael Rennick

Abstract

As an alternative to high-cost commercial publishing and no-fee open-access models for the distribution of academic work, this article outlines the major elements of a low-cost, subscription-based approach to support scholarly communications. By focusing on strategies to contain costs and maximize readership, it might be possible to achieve wider distribution and lower subscription rates. Such a low-cost subscription model has the potential to make academic publishing more responsive to readers, lead to broader availability of scholarly material, and reduce incentives to violate copyright regulations.

Introduction

The world of scholarly publishing has been undergoing a number of transitions for the better part of a decade. These transitions are being driven by broader forces of globalization[1-3] and consolidation that are affecting commercial entities, including all parts of the publishing industry,[4] as well as by new technological developments in computing and communications.[5] The result has been a constellation of forces that has prompted great discontent among scholars who produce academic work and their home institutions that provide support for such work and then find themselves paying high costs to acquire it back for their library collections. Nearly unheard has been the voice of the broader public that often funds research and is typically denied access to its results in the published scientific literature.

Two options have been most prominent in the debates on the future of scholarly publishing. On the one hand, commercial publishers have argued that they provide valuable services in production and marketing that are essential to a vibrant exchange of ideas and the broader dissemination of knowledge. These publishers have maintained that they provide substantial value-added services, earlier in printing, marketing, and distribution, and, more recently in digital archiving, aggregating, and interlinking.[6] Moreover, they have claimed that delivering such services requires capital investments that justify subscription costs that have been rising faster than inflation for the past decade and more.

On the other hand, proponents of open-publishing initiatives have argued that the academic community can be mobilized to support free content distribution.[7] Efforts to deliver scholarly products without cost to readers hinge on the ability to use the Internet and Web technologies to handle the distribution of content in digital form. Digital distribution is viewed as having low marginal costs after initial editorial costs are covered, and this makes online journals particularly appealing to those who wish to expand the audience for scholarly products beyond the confines of academe.[8, 9] Within the academy, the benefits of free online subscriptions are eagerly contemplated by libraries that have been confronting serial costs that promise to continue to rise at eight to ten percent annually.[10]

In this paper, we propose a third alternative to the two current contenders for the way forward in scholarly publishing. We propose that very-low-cost (VLC) subscriptions paid by a broadened audience of institutions and individuals might offer some significant advantages for the future of scholarly publishing and, indeed, for the wider dissemination of knowledge.

What Is the Very-low-cost Model for Scholarly Publishing?

The model we envision would operate on two foundational principles. First, it would strive to minimize all costs associated with publication, including costs for content development and costs for content distribution. Second, the model would seek to acquire the broadest possible audience for the academic content in question. These two principles should allow the publishing enterprise to offer content at the lowest possible cost by spreading the minimal costs involved over the largest possible readership. It is important to understand that the VLC model will avoid the conflict between garnering support for publishing activities and permitting the greatest possible access. In the VLC model, it is the growth of access at the lowest possible cost that generates support for publishing enterprises. Key elements of the VLC model include both those designed to keep costs low and those intended to maximize readership.

Elements Designed to Minimize Costs

There are three key strategies that can be employed to control the costs of academic publishing: embedding editorial processes within ongoing academic organizations, creating a decentralized network of publishing activities, and employing low-cost technical solutions. We consider each of these in turn.

An Editorial Process Embedded in the Activities of an Ongoing Academic Organization

By connecting scholarly publishing activities to larger academic entities such as colleges and universities or research and development centers, it will be possible to create synergistic relationships in which the publishing activities can be supported by the infrastructure of the larger organization without an undue call on resources.[11,12] There are numerous examples of journals that are connected to such larger organizations. Maintaining and increasing such sponsoring relationships can be an important element in achieving VLC models for academic publishing. Such organizations include:

- Colleges and universities
- Research centers and institutes
- Graduate and professional degree programs
- Libraries
- Professional associations
- Foundations
- Research offices and departments
- Regular conferences

Educational institutions such as colleges and universities are natural sponsors of academic publishing because the scholars they employ produce much of the content of academic journals and because their libraries are among the most important subscribers supporting journals. Within colleges and universities, units such as graduate and professional degree programs may be logical sponsors of journals related to their fields of study, and libraries may be good locations for the publishing activities from units throughout the institution. Research centers and institutes may find it advantageous to publish journals in their areas of focus. In some cases, journals previously published as part of university units have been moved to commercial publishers to take advantage of more professional services and economies of scales. However, new communications technologies have created new advantages for decentralized publishing operations that may make it more feasible for organizations not in the traditional publishing business to sponsor scholarly publishing.

In addition to colleges and universities and their subunits, other organizations would seem to be good candidates as sponsors of publishing projects. These include professional associations that have sponsored traditional publications, foundations that have an interest in publishing in areas in which they have active programs, and research offices and departments of government agencies and other nonprofit organizations. Beyond enduring units, scholarly publishing may also advance the agendas of conferences and other regular events that lead to the creation of intellectual products.

None of the potential sponsoring agencies noted is particularly surprising, and it is possible to find examples of each of these types of organizations supporting academic publishing initiatives. What is new is that new technologies are making it easier for such sponsoring organizations to deliver professional-quality publications for modest costs. New technologies have lowered the cost of entry overall and allow for greater experimentation as new publications can be created to test audience interest.

A by-product of this lower cost of entry may be the appearance and subsequent disappearance of journals that are published for shorter periods of time as interests wax and wane. Although a less stable set of journals may pose some challenges for archiving and other maintenance activities, such easy-to-start and easy-to-stop publication outlets may result in a more efficient academic publishing effort overall if publishing operations more closely reflect the needs of scholars to communicate in particular areas.

A Very Decentralized Network of Publishing Activities

New communications technologies make it possible to create highly decentralized publishing activities.[13] By creating a network of a large number of de-centralized publications, it will be possible to maintain operations at a scale that is manageable for scholars for whom editorial activities will be only one of their roles while concurrently allowing for aggregation across the decentralized sources of material to create broad and deep repositories of scholarly materials.

Decentralization opportunities occur both at the level of individual publishing offices and within such offices at the level of individual staff. In the former case, editorial offices can be small and widely scattered without impeding the ability to assemble meaningful and substantial bodies of material. In the latter case, activities within editorial offices can be distributed so that segments of activities can be performed by different individuals at widely disparate locations, connected only by online tools that serve to organize and facilitate the activities of the publication. These options allow publishing initiatives to make use of editorial talent when and where it is available.

The Use of Low-cost Technical Solutions
By relying on low-cost technology to create and maintain online publishing sites, it will be possible to minimize the call on journal resources while providing convenient access to scholarly content. The recent evolution of online publishing tools has included several stages with important implications for academic publishing. At the outset of the Internet and World Wide Web boom, academic institutions were well positioned to place materials online and university Web sites were among the most popular online destinations. A relatively small number of academic publications took advantage of this stage to reach new audiences thanks to the technology skills of students and staff. This initial stage was followed by the mass movement of commercial ventures online, and with this came rising technical and aesthetic standards for online publishing that were achievable primarily through substantial investments in projects done by Web development and design firms, investments that proved beyond the reach of most scholarly publications. Toward the end of this stage, commercial publishers stepped in to claim online publishing as a special expertise and service that they could provide to their clients, including academic journals. None of these early stages proved optimal for the development of online academic publishing.

Most recently, a new wave of online publishing options has emerged to offer scholarly publications relatively low-cost, high-quality publishing platforms. Some of these have emerged from open software and shareware initiatives that offer "free" software to institutions and individuals with the requisite technical knowledge and hardware and network infrastructure.[14]

Our own efforts have been directed toward the development of a publishing platform offered on an application service provider model.[15] Academic publications subscribe to the publishing platform as a Web-based service and need no special equipment or technical staff. A related software product provides full support for editorial office operations.[16] Both products are available to individuals or institutions for a low monthly cost, and a completely functional publishing and editorial office configuration can be created for monthly costs typical of cable TV or cell phone service. Service can be started or stopped at will to allow maximum flexibility. We created this model to overcome the limitations of services offered through Web development firms, university computing facilities, and commercial publishers.

When the sponsors of academic journals have access to high-quality, low-cost online technology that they control, they can expand publishing activities as they see fit and reach new audiences. With the technology costs reduced to being irrelevant, academic publishers operating online can devote their resources to the development of high-quality content and to the building of large audiences for that content.

Elements Designed to Maximize Readership

Maximizing paid subscriptions is essential to the overall goal of maintaining low subscription costs. Four strategies can be important elements in an effort to maximize subscribers: easy indexing and archiving strategies and standards; automated subscription management tools; low-cost marketing strategies; and enhanced content services. Each deserves careful consideration.

Easy Indexing and Archiving Strategies and Standards

By developing readily available and low-cost tools for collaborative indexing and archiving, it will be possible to promote and sustain access to scholarly content. Much scholarly content is accessed in the course of searching subject area indexes. Indeed, scholarly content is perhaps most valuable to other scholars and their students when they are purposively engaged in their own work and are reviewing relevant literature. This means that reaching the traditional audiences for products of academic publishing requires a commitment to having materials fully indexed.[17]

Fortunately, there are ongoing initiatives that are working to make the indexing and archiving of scholarly materials readily available to academic publishing ventures.[18, 19] Perhaps even more important, there are emerging commercial search services that have an interest in improving access to academic content. For example, Google has recently launched a new search service that focuses on academic journal articles and other academic content, and the University of Michigan has recently announced an agreement with Yahoo to facilitate links to electronic scholarly resources through Yahoo's search service.[20,21]

Automated Subscription Management Tools

Although easy indexing options will facilitate access to individual articles relevant to readers with focused and purposive interests, and although such efforts are essential to maintaining and enhancing demand for scholarly materials offered through institutional subscriptions sold to academic and research libraries, academic publishing initiatives also have an interest in acquiring and managing individual subscriptions to entire publications. Such subscriptions, traditionally taken by individual scholars, are in decline across a range of publications as libraries move to institutional digital subscriptions available on the desktop. The potential for increasing individual subscriptions is dependent on the availability of three things: automated subscription management tools, low-cost marketing strategies, and enhanced content-related services. We consider these in order.

Automated Subscription Management Tools

In order to offer subscriptions to academic publications at very low cost, it is necessary to manage those subscriptions in the least expensive way. Commercial publishers have offered subscription management or fulfillment services as another advantage of the economies of scale available to large publishers. However, new technologies of communications and information management offer new opportunities for the decentralized management of subscriptions.

By integrating subscription management functions into network-based publishing platforms, it will be possible to reduce the costs associated with managing subscriber accounts. This will make it possible to offer very-low-cost subscriptions in a variety of configurations from pay per article, to annual subscriptions, to limited-time-access options such as semester-length subscriptions for students. Online publishing software vendors increasingly include the option of integrating subscription management and e-commerce to handle all aspects of the subscription process.

Low-cost Marketing Strategies

Early Web publishers, particularly those who were academically oriented, seemed to assume that "if you build it, they will come." However, the enormous growth in the availability of online content and destinations of all sorts means that those associated with academic publications must now actively seek readers who have an ever expanding number of choices. Marketing is an essential element of any effort to expand an audience of readers.

Fortunately, the same communications technologies that have enabled providers of scholarly content also make it possible to market to new readers at low cost. Our own experience publishing the *Teachers College Record* (www. tcrecord.org) is instructive in this regard. We began the most recent online version of the journal in 1999 with about 3,000 registered readers culled from lists of authors, reviewers, and scholars in the field of education. These registered members of the online site receive access to all articles available online. Registration requires only that a reader provide a name and an e-mail address to establish an account. Through 2004, we have not charged for online access. We rely on a weekly e-mail newsletter to announce new online content, and we provide readers with an easy utility to e-mail their colleagues to alert them to new articles appearing online. We engage in only limited advertising in print outlets related to scholarship in education. Now, four years later, our registered base of readers exceeds 100,000. This figure dwarfs our list of about 2,200 institutional subscriptions and about 500 individual subscriptions. Of course, the real test will come over the next year as we begin to offer online subscriptions to these 100,000 individuals.[22]

Enhanced Content-related Services

Efforts to acquire continuing individual subscriptions to online scholarly materials may well require development activities that go beyond the simple provision of text. These could include community-oriented activities such as discussion boards and live chats related to published scholarly materials. They could also include multimedia elements for such materials or the availability of specialized tools to work with content in particular academic special areas. Once again, to keep the costs of scholarly materials very low, any development activities would need to follow the principles outlined above, such as linking them to the ongoing activities of sponsoring organizations.

What Is "Very Low"?

Subscription Costs Substantially Lower Than Current Serial Subscriptions

By focusing on strategies to minimize costs, VLC publications can be offered for only a fraction of current serial costs. If efforts to contain costs are maintained, providers of scholarly content should have maximum flexibility to set subscription prices to achieve the largest possible audience. At this point, we do not know what subscription prices might be and any estimate would quickly become dated based on changing financial conditions and the results of early experimentation. However, to be perceived as offering significant value to those beyond a core audience, the costs of academic journals would have to approach the prices of popular magazine subscriptions on a per issue or a per page basis.

Benefits of the Very-lost-cost Publishing Model

With the current models for the support of scholarly communications in disarray, there will be benefits to any viable alternative that serves to expand and extend academic publishing. However, the VLC model we have proposed has three specific benefits worth consideration. The model should lead to the broader availability of scholarly material, serve to make academic publishing more responsive to readers, and possibly reduce incentives to violate copyright regulations. Each of these would strengthen the scholarly communication system.

Broader Availability of Scholarly Content

Because the subscription costs of VLC publications are substantially more modest than current serial subscriptions, they have the potential to reach more institutional and individual subscribers. Expanding the reach of scholarly communication can be important to extend the impact of academic work, to enhance public understanding and support for such work, and to build a base of financial support for academic publishing activities.

Responsiveness to Reader Concerns

Because the revenue base under the VLC model is derived from end users or readers, VLC publications have an inherent incentive to be responsive to the needs of readers. Several publishing models currently being considered to support scholarly communications do not contain such incentives. For example, open-access models that propose to offer free, unrestricted access contain little incentive for academic content providers to meet the needs of readers. So too, traditional models that rely on high-cost institutional subscriptions that are not paid by readers have limited incentives to favor the needs of individual readers over the needs of acquisitions librarians who actually purchase subscriptions. Models that propose to support academic publishing through fees charged to authors contain little incentive for academic publications to place the needs of readers before those of authors. Unless providers of academic publications begin to consider seriously the needs of readers, the long-term prospects for the system of scholarly communications seem limited.

Diminished Incentives to Violate Copyright Limitations

By providing high-value content services at low cost, the VLC model has the potential to reduce the incentives to violate copyright. Maintaining support for the existing intellectual property regime requires a sense of fairness shared by content providers and content consumers. The VLC model may serve this purpose well by attaching modest charges to the use of scholarly materials. This arrangement will avoid the temptation to use high-priced materials outside the bounds of legal regulations. It may also avoid the ambiguity over content ownership rights associated with completely free-access models for scholarly publishing.

Further Development of the Very-low-cost Model
The task before us is to begin to develop academic publishing projects based on the VLC model. As noted above, some tools to begin such projects now exist and more will surely be developed. We anticipate a number of lines of activity for future development work, including better tools for editorial operations and tools to integrate additional services into academic publishing operations.

Automated Editorial Tools
Thus far, improvements in communications and computing technologies have done little to reduce the cost of core editorial office activities such as the review of submissions and the refinement of content. Creating tools to increase the efficiency of editorial operations is a logical next step on the road to reducing the costs of academic publishing. Such tools might provide assistance to editors in the initial screening of manuscripts through the analysis of text. More-structured manuscript preparation requirements might be coupled with online analysis options that allow editors to check on different aspects of manuscript structure. Specialized tools might also be created to assist in the vetting of analysis and reporting techniques common to certain fields of work.

Additional Services to Readers at Modest Fees
Although the jury is still out on the question of how much readers will pay for content online, including academic content, there is the potential of offering additional services, including research and educational services, for additional fees to subscribers of academic journals. Determining the services to be offered and how to position specific journals to offer them is an important task for the short-term future. Equally important is the development of online platforms that facilitate the integration of publishing and other services to enhance the manageability of diverse services.

Conclusion
The advent of new communications and computing technologies has begun to transform both academic work and the scholarly communication process. The changes that have occurred over the past decade have been substantial, but those likely in the next decade may be even greater. Finding the appropriate model to sustain serious and compelling academic publishing projects will ensure that scholarly communications processes move forward and share fully in the new opportunities that cut across all sectors.

Notes

1. P. Berger and S. P. Huntington, *Many Globalizations: Cultural Diversity in the Contemporary World* (New York: Oxford University Pr., 2003).

2. W. T. Anderson, *All Connected Now: Life in the First Global Civilization* (Boulder, Colo.: Westview Pr., 2001).

3. F. J. Lechner and J. Boli, *The Globalization Reader* (Oxford, Eng.: Blackwell, 2003).

4. A. Schiffrin, *The Business of Books: How International Conglomerates Took Over Publishing and Changed the Way We Read* (New York: Verso, 2000).

5. B. Kahin and H. R. Varian, *Internet Publishing and Beyond: The Economics of Digital Information and Intellectual Property* (Cambridge, Mass.: The MIT Pr., 2000).

6. K. Hunter, "Adding Value by Adding Links," *Journal of Electronic Publishing* 3, no. 5 (1997). Available online from http://www.press.umich.edu/jep/03-03/hunter.html.

7. J. Willinsky, "Proposing a Knowledge Exchange Model for Scholarly Publishing," *Current Issues in Education* 3, no. 6 (Sept. 13, 2000). Available online from http://cie.ed.asu.edu/volume3/number6/.

8. A. Odlyzko, "The Economics of Electronic Journals," *First Monday* 2, no. 8 (1997). Available online from http://www.firstmonday.dk/issues/issue2_8/odlyzko.

9. M. Bot, J. Burgemeester, and H. Roes, "The Cost of Publishing an Electronic Journal," *D-Lib Magazine* (Nov. 1998). Available online from http://www.dlib.org/dlib/november98/11roes.html.

10. C. Candee, "Fat Cat Publishers Breaking the System," *Syllabus* (May 2004). Available online from http://www.syllabus.com/artricle.asp?id=9357.

11. G. Glass, "A New Day in How Scholars Communicate," *Current Issues in Education* 2, no. 4 (1999). Available online from http://cie.ed.asu.edu/volume2/number2/.

12. R. Kling, L. Spector, and G. McKim, "Locally Controlled Scholarly Publishing via the Internet: The Guild Model." *Journal of Electronic Publishing* 8, no. 1 (2002). Available online from http://www.press.umich.edu/jep/08-01/kling.html.

13. J. W. T. Smith, "The Deconstructed (or Distributed) Journal: An Emerging Model?" Paper presented at the Online Information 2004 Conference, London, Nov. 2004.

14. Public Knowledge Project, "Front Page News." 2004. Available online from http://www.pkp.ubc.ca/.

15. Frameworkers, "ContentWorks Publishing." 2004a. Available online from http://www.frameworkers.com/.

16. ———. "ContentWorks Evaluator." 2004b. Available online from http://www.frameworkers.com/.

17. J. Willinsky and L. Wolfson, "The Indexing of Scholarly Journals: A Tipping Point for Publishing Reform?" *Journal of Electronic Publishing* 7, no. 2 (2001). Available online from http://www.press.umich/edu/jep/07-02/willinsky.html.

18. For example, Open Archives Initiative, "Mission Statement." 2004. Available online from http://www.openarchives.org/organization/index.html.

19. L. Mongin, Y. Fu, and J. Mostafa, "Open Archives Data Service Prototype and Automated Subject Indexing Using D-Lib Archive Content as a Testbed." *D-Lib Magazine* 9, no. 12 (2003). Available online from http://dlib.org/dlilb/december03/mongin/12mongin.htgml.

20. D. Sullivan, "Google Scholar Offers Access to Academic Information." *SearchEngineWatch* (2004). Available online from http://searchenginewatch.com/searchday/article.php/3437471.

21. University of Michigan News Service, "U-M Expands Access to Hidden Electronic Resources with OAIster." 2004. Available online from http:///www.umich.edu/news/index.html?Releases/2004/Mar04/r031004.

22. G. Natriello and M. C. Rennick, "An Online Journal as a Virtual Learning Environment," in *International Handbook of Virtual Learning Environments,* ed. J. Weiss, J. Nolan, and P. Trifonas (New York: Springer, forthcoming).

Chapter 7

Knowledge Level of Postsecondary Educators Regarding Copyright and Copyright-related Issues

Jasmine R. Renner

Abstract

Knowledge of copyright is essential for educators in today's rapidly changing educational and technological environment. The study analyzed the knowledge levels of Ohio's postsecondary educators regarding copyright and copyright-related issues. A stratified random sample of 120 postsecondary educators who taught Web-based courses from public/state, private, religious, and two-year colleges participated in the study. The study utilized two instruments: the copyright questionnaire to assess the knowledge levels of educators regarding the Copyright Act and copyright ownership issues and a copyright follow-up survey to gather and evaluate educators' responses to issues related to copyright knowledge, ownership, and management in their current institutions.

Data collected from the questionnaire were subjected to several ANOVA tests, t- tests, and Turkey's post hoc test. Data from the survey were analyzed utilizing a modified version of Spradley's (1976) thematic content analysis. The study also utilized a legal research methodology to collect, review, and analyze state and federal case law relevant to a discussion on copyright ownership.

The results of the study reveal that postsecondary educators have some knowledge of the Copyright Act and copyright-related issues but, for the most part, were unaware about major provisions of the act. Two demographic variables had a significant effect on postsecondary knowledge of copyright law. Educators who taught graduate courses scored significantly lower than those who taught undergraduate and professional courses.

Additionally, educators who were aware of their institution's copyright policy scored higher than those who were not. Results from the follow-up survey revealed that most educators feel limited in their knowledge regarding copyright, are concerned about legal issues, and request ongoing in-services and workshops to remain informed. The study concluded that institutions of higher education must respond to copyright issues and provide ongoing education and access to copyright materials for faculty members.

Introduction

Institutions of higher education exist to advance and disseminate knowledge, and they accomplish these objectives through teaching, research, publication, and community service. Today's rapidly changing educational and technological environments bring new challenges to old practices. For example, traditionally, a university professor has been the sole author or copyright owner of most copyrighted works in higher education.[1] Today, some universities produce works that use an entire team of experts to bring a project to fruition.[2] Scholars have suggested that technological advancement in institutions of higher education is growing at a rapid and unprecedented rate.[3] Amid these developments, misunderstandings have arisen among faculty and the institutions they serve regarding intellectual property rights.[4]

Meanwhile, studies reveal that the knowledge levels of educators and administrators about the current Copyright Act of 1976 are ambivalent and, at best, low.[5, 6] Scholars who have studied the phenomena on copyright ownership of Web-based courses suggest that there are conflicting views with regard to ownership claims made by the university and faculty.[7]

The purpose of this study was twofold. First, the study assessed the knowledge levels of Ohio's postsecondary educators regarding copyright ownership by testing their knowledge of standard copyright questions drawn from the Copyright Act of 1976. In addition, several demographic factors were examined to determine a significant relationship to educators' knowledge base of the Copyright Act. The demographic factors were: number of years teaching, number of years using Web-based technology in an institutional setting for instructional purposes, faculty rank, full-time or part-time employment status, highest level of education, level of course taught, institution type, participation in copyright law–related conferences, and awareness of institutional copyright policy. Most of the variables in this study are those utilized by L. S. Shane in his doctoral dissertation, which analyzed the knowledge levels of K–12 educators regarding copyright ownership of their multimedia classroom projects.[8] Second, the study analyzed and reported data on educators' responses about knowledge of copyright law, the management of copyright-related information by university officials, and responses by participants regarding the best way of getting out copyright information to their respective institutions.

Overview of the Literature

The U.S. Constitution grants the power to Congress "to promote the progress of science and useful arts, by securing for limited times to authors and inventors the exclusive right to their respective writings and discoveries."[9] The first Copyright Law was passed on May 31, 1790, during the second session of Congress and granted authors the exclusive rights to any book, map, or chart they created for a renewable fourteen-year term.[10]

Knowledge of copyright is essential for educators in today's rapidly changing educational and technological environment. For hundreds of years, university professors have created courses, written lectures, and developed exams without concern about who owned them.[11] With the growth of distance education programs and the commercial potential for licensing successful courses, universities are seizing control of courses, mass-producing them in either World Wide Web or CD-ROM format, and selling the rights to other institutions.[12]

In the past, university officials and faculty have always regarded legal knowledge as simply a boundary in which administrators are free to exercise their professional prerogatives.[13] Such a view, though true, misrepresents the nature of the real purpose, importance, and responsibilities of university leaders to acquire a base of legal knowledge in their daily activities. Despite the widespread perception by many that understanding the law is entirely a technical skill, educators must be aware of rules, regulations, and judicial mandates—or at least know where to locate them.[14]

Viewing the law through this lens ignores its importance as one of the cornerstones of an ordered society and overlooks the value of a legal perspective in addressing university problems and opportunities.[15] Thus, the need for a sound base of knowledge for educational leaders cannot be overemphasized. Until recently, many educators had not considered the issue of intellectual property in the arena of copyright ownership. Yet, as more faculty members utilize the Internet and more institutions develop distance education courses, it is more important than ever that faculty and the institutions at which they work have a clear, legal understanding of intellectual property rights.

Because universities are fluid institutions,[16] many policy-making decisions often take place within a legal framework. Therefore, an understanding and recognition of the rationale of various laws regulating certain issues and what values guide the development of the laws is crucial. More crucial is the fact that educational leaders cannot afford to be misguided as to the proper actions to be pursuing because of lack of knowledge or information on legal concepts regulating various aspects of their work. For educational leaders to gain a robust legal perspective, there is a need to move beyond the directives and understand the various statutes that govern and regulate their daily instructional, administrative, and educational workloads. An understanding of legal regulations also can enhance the process of identifying problematic situations, anticipating alternative conclusions and their consequences, and seeking principles and data to support a conclusion.[17]

Scholars maintain that educators are not merely passive conduits of the law but do play an important role in interpreting and applying the law within their own jurisdictions.[18] They maintain that educators retain considerable discretion to make decisions and establish policies.[19] Knowledge of how the law works should lead to the realization that educators, not courts or legislatures, must determine what actions are reasonable and just in campus situations. Moreover, by understanding the evolution and current status of the law, educators can gain a context for contemplation of what the law should be in the future. Yet, many educators and university leaders do not feel ownership in directing the outcomes of the law. Rather, they view legal mandates as either affording more protections than they do or imposing unreasonable barriers.

The relationship between the practice and the knowledge base of educators has obvious implications for the programs in which they are prepared.

Currently, studies reveal that many educators lack knowledge about the law and how to apply it in practical situations.[20, 21] Preparation programs need to guide educators so that they become more aware of legal concerns and give more critical thought to legal responsibilities in their professional roles. Also, specific courses focusing on law and ethics may be useful in helping future academic leaders acquire skills in legal discourse. If university administrators and faculty are active participants in shaping their campus's laws, they have a relationship to what is known on matters that relate to legal knowledge. Through their deliberations and actions, university officials can contribute to this knowledge. Consequently, any purported knowledge for university leaders should represent itself as a resource for administrative and faculty action, rather than as a detriment to such action. It would seem that the purpose of having this knowledge base is to make it available to educators, the wide range of cultural, social, and intellectual materials that can help them understand the circumstances and opportunities that their work presents to them.

Population Sample

The study's population consisted of 120 randomly selected postsecondary educators in Ohio's public/state, private, and two-year community and technical colleges. The study had a 51 percent response rate. Postsecondary educators included full professors, associate professors, assistant professors, and instructors and lecturers of Web-based/online courses. The population frame was obtained from the *2001–2002 Ohio Board of Regents Directory.* The directory contains information and data generated by the *Higher Education Information Systems,* which lists the names of all colleges and universities in the state of Ohio as well as postsecondary educators instructing Web-based courses. Sample selection for the study also included the following criteria:

• The institution from which the participant was instructing a Web-based/online course must fit into one of the four classifications of institutions provided by the Ohio board of regents higher education classification system and must have a current policy on intellectual property.

• Distance education in the form of Web-based /online courses was offered.

• The participant was an instructor engaged in teaching Web-based/ online classes during at least one semester of the 2002 academic year.

Study's Objectives

The study addressed the following research questions:

1. What is the level of legal knowledge of Ohio's educators in public/state, private, and two-year institutions of higher education regarding the Copyright Act of 1976?

2. Do the following variables significantly affect the level of legal knowledge of postsecondary educators regarding copyright ownership of Web-based/online courses and materials?

    a. Number of years teaching in higher education

    b. Number of years using Web-based technology in an institutional setting for instructional purposes

    c. Faculty rank

    d. Employment status

    e. Highest level of education completed

    f. Education level taught

g. Institution type

h. Participation in law-related workshop on copyright law

i. Awareness of institutional copyright policy

3.   What is the knowledge base of educators regarding copyright owner-ship as stipulated in section 201 of the Copyright Act of 1976?

4.   What sources of law-related information are educators familiar with regarding copyright law and copyright ownership?

5.   Do educational institutions have copyright guidelines that address the issue of Web-based/online courses and materials created by its own fac-ulty?

Instrumentation

The study utilized two instruments: the copyright questionnaire (appendix A) to assess the knowledge levels of educators regarding the Copyright Act and copyright ownership issues and a copyright follow-up survey (appendix B) to gather and evaluate educators' responses to issues related to copyright knowledge, ownership, and management in their current institutions. The copyright questionnaire was slightly adapted from the copyright and mul-timedia questionnaire utilized by Shane in his doctoral dissertation.[22] The copyright questionnaire comprised three parts. Part one included seven ques-tions that asked factual questions about the U.S. Copyright Law of 1976. These questions were based on general provisions of the act. Part two of the questionnaire listed fourteen true-and-false question items about copyright ownership. The copyright ownership questions were drawn directly from the Copyright Act of 1976. Part three of the questionnaire contained nine demographic questions directed to participants of the study. The follow-up copyright survey comprised ten open-ended questions designed to gather and evaluate educators' responses to issues related to copyright knowledge, ownership, and management in their current institution.

Research Design and Data Analysis

This study combined quantitative, qualitative, and legal research methods to examine the knowledge levels of postsecondary educators regarding copyright and copyright ownership of Web-based courses and materials. Several one-way analyses of variance were conducted on the independent/demographic variables. The One-Way ANOVA procedure displayed multiple comparison statistics to evaluate the differences of knowledge levels between educators' groups based on each of the independent/demographic variables (number of years teaching, number of years of experience using Web-based technology for instruction in an institutional setting, faculty rank, employment status, highest level of education completed, level of courses taught, type of institution, participation in copyright law–related conferences, and awareness of institutional copyright policy).

This statistical technique examined the variability of sample values and examined observations within each group as well as how much the group means varies.[23] Based on these two estimates of variability, conclusions were drawn about the population means. The second half of the quantitative design was descriptive in nature. Utilizing the statistical analysis software, a frequency was run on all items and presented the mean scores and standard deviation of educators' knowledge levels of copyright law and copyright ownership. The data were analyzed using frequency and percentage tables and the following parametric tests: t-tests for the difference between means, and the one-way analysis of variance tests. The basic level of significance for the study was set at .05. This level of significance adequately guarded against Type I errors without being conservative to the point that meaningful differences were not found significant.

The qualitative methodology utilized in this study is the thematic content analysis, a modified version of Spradley's domain analysis procedure.[24] This research method was used to identify key themes related to the subject matter and to count the frequency of each theme across open-ended responses for the ten questions in the survey.

The legal research methodology used in this study is the case summarization method. The primary objective of the legal research was to collect, review, and analyze state and federal law relevant to a discussion on copyright ownership as it relates to joint authorship, the work-made-for-hire doctrine, and the teacher's exception rule. The cases analyzed and reviewed were collected through the traditional and online legal research method. Cases were accessed via the Lexis Nexis Academic and Congressional Universe, which yielded a total of ninety-eight hits of cases at the federal, state, and district levels.

Data collected from the copyright questionnaire were subjected to several analyses of variance tests (ANOVA), t- tests, and Tukey's post hoc test. Data from the copyright follow-up survey were analyzed utilizing a modified version of Spradley's thematic content analysis.[25] The study utilized data collected from the legal research methodology to review and analyze state federal a case law relevant to a discussion on copyright ownership.

Results

The results of the study suggest that postsecondary educators have some knowledge of copyright act and copyright-related issues but, for the most part, were unaware of major provisions of the act. Two demographic variables had a significant effect on postsecondary knowledge of copyright issues. Educators who taught graduate courses scored significantly lower than those who taught undergraduate and professional courses.

Additionally, educators who were aware of their institution's copyright policy scored higher than those who were not. Results from the follow-up survey revealed that most educators felt limited in their knowledge regarding copyright, are concerned about legal issues, and request ongoing in-services and workshops to remain informed. The copyright questionnaire consisted of twenty-one multiple-choice and true-and-false question items. The legal knowledge score of each participant was the raw score of items answered correctly out of twenty-one question items.

Prior studies assessing the knowledge levels of educators regarding copyright law and fair use have used a 75 percent score as indicating proficiency in the knowledge level of the subject matter.[26] Similarly, the present study utilized a 75 percent score to define proficiency in its subject matter. Based on this standard, the results of this study show that 12 percent of the participants (8 out of 62) achieved proficiency. Thirty-five individuals scored at least 50 percent on either part I or part II of the questionnaire.

Nineteen individuals scored below 50 percent on their overall scores. The number of correct responses from individual scores of participants ranged from 2 out of 21 (10%) to 18 out of 21 (86%). Overall, the grand mean score for the group was .569, with a standard deviation of 0.144.

The first research question in the present study was the following: What is the level of legal knowledge of Ohio's educators in public/state, private, and two-year institutions of higher education regarding the Copyright Act of 1976?

The overall mean score for the sample reveals that there is some level of legal knowledge among Ohio's postsecondary educators regarding copyright law and copyright ownership. The results reveal that although postsecondary educators have some knowledge, they are to a large extent unaware of major provisions of the act. Therefore, they may need some attention in the subject matter. A summary of the mean scores of each group of participants is presented in table 1.

Summary of Results from Collapsed Cells
After conducting an initial statistical test on the demographics (independent variables), it was necessary to collapse certain cells because of insufficient data in certain categories. First, the highest level of education completed was collapsed from five levels to four, combining participants with a bachelor's degree and those actively working on a master's degree.

Table 1. Educators' Knowledge of Copyright Law Group Mean Scores			
	Total Sample(n=62)		
Demographic Variable	N	Mean	SD
Number of years teaching			
0–2	10	0.524	0.143
3–5	9	0.583	0.157
6–10	22	0.556	0.159
11–15	10	0.584	0.120
Over 15 years	11	0.610	0.136
Number of years using web-based technology			
0–1	13	0.583	0.153
2	19	0.513	0.135
3	15	0.615	0.128
4	9	0.593	0.164
5 years or more	6	0.563	0.156
Professor	8	0.576	0.125
Associate Professor	20	0.557	0.191
Assistant Professor	15	0.586	0.132
Instructor/Lecturer	19	0.564	0.111
Employment status			
Part-time position	14	0.557	0.121
Full-time position	48	0.572	0.151
Highest level of education			
Bachelors	7	0.525	0.163
Actively working on master's degree	1	0.620	
Master's degree	16	0.624	0.101
Actively working on a doctoral degree	4	0.452	0.045
Doctoral Degree (JD, Ed.D. M.D. Ph.D.)	34	0.555	0.155

Table 1. Educators' Knowledge of Copyright Law Group Mean Scores (Cont.)			
	Total Sample(n=62)		
Demographic Variable	N	Mean	SD
Level of education courses taught			
Undergraduate	45	0.591	0.129
Graduate	11	0.450	0.165
Professional	6	0.620	0.120
Institution type			
Four-year public college or university	21	0.605	0.131
Two-year public college or university	9	0.576	0.099
Private/religious college or university	14	0.497	0.185
Two-year technical or community college	18	0.578	0.133
Bachelors	7	0.525	0.163
Actively working on master's degree	1	0.620	
Master's degree	16	0.624	0.101
Actively working on a doctoral degree	4	0.452	0.045
Doctoral Degree (JD, Ed.D. M.D. Ph.D.)	34	0.555	0.155
Level of education courses taught			
Undergraduate	45	0.591	0.129
Graduate	11	0.450	0.165
Professional	6	0.620	0.120
Institution type			
Four-year public college or university	21	0.605	0.131
Two-year public college or university	9	0.576	0.099
Private/religious college or university	14	0.497	0.185
Two-year technical or community college	18	0.578	0.133
Participation in law-related copyright workshops			
Yes	7	0.571	0.138
No	55	0.568	0.146

Table 1. Educators' Knowledge of Copyright Law Group Mean Scores (Cont.)			
	Total Sample(n=62)		
Demographic Variable	N	Mean	SD
Awareness of institutional copyright policy			
Yes	26	0.620	0.127
No	4	0.512	0.150
I don't know	32	0.534	0.148

Second, the existence of an institutional copyright policy was collapsed from three levels to two, combining participants who indicated that they were not aware of any institutional copyright policy in existence at the universities and those who indicated that they did not know whether such policy existed. The collapsed results of the mean score for participants in both categories are reported in tables 2 and 3.

Analysis of Variance

The study's second research question asked the following: Do the following variables significantly affect the level of legal knowledge of postsecondary educators regarding copyright ownership of Web-based /online courses and materials: (a) number of years teaching in higher education, (b) number of years using Web-based /Internet technology for instruction, (c) faculty rank (d), employment status, (e) highest level of education completed, (f) education level taught, (g) institution type, (h) participation in law-related workshops, and (i) existence of institutional copyright policy?

To examine the impact of these demographic variables on the legal knowledge of Ohio's postsecondary educators regarding copyright law and copyright ownership, several one-way analyses of variance were conducted.

Table 2: Educators' Knowledge of Copyright Law: Group Mean Scores Results from Collapsed Cells (highest level of education)			
	Total Sample(n = 62)		
Demographic Variable	N	Mean	SD
Highest level of education			
Bachelor's/Actively working on master's degree	8	0.537	0.155
Master's degree	16	0.624	0.101
Actively working on a doctoral degree	4	0.452	0.045
Doctoral Degree (JD, Ed.D., MD, Ph.D.)	34	0.555	0.155

Table 3: Educators' Knowledge of Copyright Law: Group Mean Scores Results from Collapsed Cells (awareness of the existence of an institutional copyright policy)			
	Total Sample(n=62)		
Demographic Variable	N	Mean	SD
Awareness of the institution's copyright policy			
Yes	26	0.620	0.127
No / I don't know	36	0.531	0.146

A summary of the results is presented in table 4. The results of the one-way ANOVA tests revealed that there was a significant main effect on the level of course taught on the level of knowledge of postsecondary educators regarding the Copyright Act (F [2,59] = 5.26, p = 0.0079). To determine where among the level of courses taught the significant differences lie, a post hoc test was conducted. Under Tukey's test for comparisons between pairs of means, postsecondary educators who taught graduate courses scored significantly lower than postsecondary educators who taught undergraduate or professional courses. Postsecondary educators who taught professional courses scored the highest. However, there was no significant difference between the total score of postsecondary educators who taught professional courses and those who taught undergraduate courses. The results of the post-hoc tests are presented in table 5.

Table 4: Analysis of Variance on Demographic Variables				
Variables	SS	df	Test Statistic F/T	P
Number of years teaching	0.046	4	0.54	0.7105
Number of years using Web-based technology	0.099	4	1.20	0.3204
Faculty rank	0.008	3	0.12	0.9454
Employment status	0.002	1	0.11	0.7459
Highest level of education completed	0.154	4	2.07	0.0965
Educational level taught the most	0.193	2	5.26	0.0079*
Institution type	0.102	3	1.68	0.1822
Participation in law-related workshop	0.000	1	0.00	0.9634
Institution copyright policy	0.119	1	6.09	0.0164*

* Significant at the alpha level of 0.05

Furthermore, the ANOVAs revealed that there also was a significant main effect on the awareness of an institutional copyright policy on the level of knowledge of postsecondary educators regarding copyright ownership $(T\ (1,\ 60)\ =\ 6.09,\ p$

Table 5: Tukey's Post Hoc Test Results for Level of Course Taught by Ohio's Postsecondary Educators	
Level Taught Comparisons	Difference Between Means
3 - 1	0.02867
3 - 2	0.17000***
1 - 2	0.14133***
***Comparisons significant at the 0.05 level. Level of course taught group description: 1=undergraduate, 2=graduate, 3=professional	

= .0164). Those who were aware of the existence of their institution's copyright policy scored significantly higher than those who either were unaware of a policy at their institutions or reported that their institution had no such policy. The ANOVAs reported no significant effects at the alpha level of .05 for the remaining independent variables (number of years teaching, number of years of experience using Web-based technology in an institutional setting, faculty rank, employment status, highest level of education completed, type of institution, and participation in copyright law–related conferences).

Copyright Follow-up Survey Results

Twenty-five participants out of the sixty-two indicated that they would be willing to complete the copyright follow-up survey. Twenty-one follow-up surveys were completed with an 84 percent return rate two weeks after the initial mailing. The qualitative methodology used in the present study is referred to as thematic content analysis, which is a modified version of Spradley's domain analysis procedure. This qualitative method is used to identify key themes related to the subject matter found in a survey, questionnaire, or interview and to count the frequency of each theme across open-ended responses.

The third question was the following: What is the knowledge level of educators regarding copyright ownership as stipulated in section 201 of the Copyright Act? Data from the copyright follow-up survey revealed the following. Five respondents (23%) maintained that the copyright questionnaire showed the limits of their knowledge on the topic. One respondent said, "I think the copyright questionnaire was thorough, but I know little about copyright laws or ownership issues, so the questions were difficult." Another said, "My knowledge is spotty at best." Yet another said, "I feel very limited in knowledge (lack of) copyright law and my questionnaire answers will prove it." A summary of the reported responses is presented in table 6.

Table 6: Frequency Table Coded Responses from Copyright Follow-up Survey				
		Total Sample(n=21)		
Question	Code	Response	N	%
Do you think that the original questionnaire you completed truly tested your knowledge level of copyright ownership? If so, how? If not, why not?	1	Yes	6	28.5%
	2	No	3	14.2%
	3	Yes, it seemed thorough	4	19%
	4	Yes, showed limit of my knowledge	5	23.8%
	5	Maybe, I felt inadequate in my knowledge	1	4.7%
	6	Yes, very comprehensive	2	9.2%

Question four of the study asked: What sources of law-related information are educators familiar with regarding copyright law and copyright ownership? The resource most frequently mentioned by respondents was the Web or the Internet. Six respondents (28%) selected this choice. The second most mentioned resource was the university's copyright policy; five respondents (23%) selected this choice. Other resources mentioned are access to library materials, university and intellectual property offices, and faculty handbooks. The least-mentioned resource was a text on copyright law; only one respondent offered this option. Another respondent mentioned consulting notes from a course taken at another university. A summary of the reported responses is presented in table 7.

The fifth and final question of the study asked: Do educational institutions have copyright guidelines that address the issue of Web-based/online courses and materials created by its own faculty? Six of the respondents (28%) said "I don't know," another five (23%) maintained they had specific guidelines, and four of the respondents reported uncertainty by saying "I don't think so, but not certain." A summary of the reported responses is presented in table 8.

In summation, the open-ended responses to key questions about copyright ownership, management, and the availability/nonavailability of copyright resources in their institutions provided by the respondents revealed educators' attitudes toward copyright management. Their responses ran the

Table 7: Frequency Table Coded Responses from Copyright Follow-up				
		Total Sample(n=21)		
Question	Code	Response	N	%
What sources of law-related information are educators most familiar with regarding copyright law and copyright ownership?	1	Internet/web	6	28.5%
	2	Access to library materials	3	14.2%
	3	Book on copyright	1	4.7%
	4	Through university & intellectual property office	3	14.2%
	5	Through university copyright policy	5	23.8%
	6	Faculty handbook	2	9.5%
	7	From a course taken at another university	1	4.7%

gamut from very positive ("I view this as an opportunity to be informed about my intellectual property rights") to not wanting to be bothered about copyright issues because "We knew when we took our appointment that we lost our intellectual property rights because of the work-for-hire doctrine," and responses that were shades in between.

Conclusion

As Web-based, electronic, and related delivery systems continue to increase, the complexity of access to and unawareness of copyright information may

Table 8: Frequency Table Coded Responses from Copyright Follow-up Survey				
		Total Sample(n = 21)		
Question	Code	Response	N	%
Does your institution have copyright guidelines specifically for Web-based online courses and materials produced by its own faculty?	1	Yes	5	23.8%
	2	No	5	23.8%
	3	I do not know	6	28.5%
	4	Don't think so	2	9.5%
	5	I think so, but not certain	2	9.5%
	6	Maybe	1	4.7%

escalate. Increased effort in providing for and making accessible information relating to copyright may be required to achieve a comprehensive knowledge base of legal information among educators. Institutions have a major responsibility to facilitate such a process. The demonstrated level of legal knowledge about copyright in this study warrants a holistic institutional approach to the issue of knowledge for its faculty. In this regard, it is recommended that universities and colleges review existing customs and dissemination practices with regard to copyright policies and management. Most educators indicated that they were unaware or do not seem to know where and how to access this information. In addition, most institutions are struggling to keep up policies and guidelines in this area. For the most part, policy consideration for copyright protection did not envision the rapid technological developments that distance education has posed. As a first and practical step, each institution must examine and review its current copyright custom and dissemination practices to ensure that educators are aware of, and have access to, this information.

Second, in the area of copyright ownership, institutions must have a clear strategy on how to address issues of ownership and management of Web-based intellectual property and to make such information available to educators. The difficulty from a policy point of view is that, for the most part, there is no clear established position from the law. The law itself is evolving and remains unclear. However, the issue most institutions are struggling with is whether Web-based courses and resources created by faculty qualify for copyright protection.

The problem is that at many universities, electronic courses do not fit into existing institutional policies for intellectual property.[27] Observers say that in some ways electronic courses are like inventions, in which case the universities usually own the patent rights to their professor's inventions and share with them the income from licenses on those patents.[28] In other ways, online materials are like textbooks. Universities rarely claim any rights to such works, leaving professors to deal independently with publishers. When trying to determine in which category to place electronic courses, observers say they can be classified as one, the other, or both.[29] To compound this problem, policy interpretation and formulation may vary from institution to institution based on current intellectual property needs. A clear strategy would enable institutions to assume leadership and direct effective initiatives to provide ample education and information to educators who create this type of intellectual property. As with any pedagogical change, successful implementation of an effective policy that provides for the continuing education of copyright law depends on faculty acceptance and participation. As a result, any purported knowledge base for educators should represent itself as a resource for administrative action and include a thorough understanding of educators' experiences in utilizing technology. The purpose of increasing the knowledge base of educators is not to supply additional legal information; rather, it is to make available the wide range of intellectual materials that can help them understand the circumstances and the opportunities that their work presents to them.

Most important, there is a need to provide a number of resource platforms for easy access to all information about copyright. Resource platforms may include in-services, preservices during orientation week for faculty, departmental workshops, and ongoing continuing education on this subject area. Institutions also can develop a direct system that is accessible to all for signaling updates on copyright information. Institutions of higher education should promote and provide opportunities for educators with responsibilities related to the legal utilization of Web-based technology to increase their knowledge of, and exposure to, copyright issues. Resources should be allocated to stimulate participation in law classes and workshops as well as to provide in-service meetings on the subject of copyright. In turn, postsecondary educators should seek opportunities to sustain and increase their awareness of, interest in, exposure to, and knowledge of copyright.

Notes

1. L. G. Lape, "Ownership of Copyrightable Works of University Professors: The Interplay between the Copyright Act and University Copyright Policies," *Villanova Law Review* 37 (1992): 223–71.

2. L. Guernsey and J. R. Young, "Who Owns On-line Courses?" *Chronicle of Higher Education* (June 5, 1998): A21–23.

3. A. Hill, "Professors Question Benefit of Using Course Cyber-notes at University of Illinois," *Colorado Daily U-Wire,* Sept. 28, 1999.

4. Guernsey and Young, "Who Owns On-line Courses?"

5. M. E. Chase, "An Analysis of the Knowledge Levels of Media Directors Concerning Relevant Copyright Issues in Higher Education (Ph.D. diss., Univ. of Pittsburgh, 1994).

6. A. F. James, "Educators Attitudes Concerning Copyright" (Ph.D. diss., Univ. of Arkansas, 1981).

7. L. N. Gasaway, "Impasse: Distant Learning and Copyright," 62 *Ohio State Law Journal* 783, 2001.

8. L. S. Shane, "An Analysis of the Knowledge Levels of California K–12 Teachers Concerning Copyright Issues Related to Classroom Multimedia Projects (Ph.D. diss., Pepperdine Univ., 1999), unpublished.

9. U.S. Const. Art I, § 8, cl.8.

10. J. K. Miller, *Applying the New Copyright Law: A Guide for Educators and Librarians* (Chicago: American Library Association, 1979).

11. W. R. Bobbitt, "Intellectual Property Conflicts between Universities and Faculty Members over Ownership of Electronic Courses" (Ph.D. diss., Bowling Green State Univ., 1998).

12. Guernsey and Young, "Who Owns On-line Courses?"

13. L. Bull and M. McCarthy, "Reflections on the Knowledge Base in Law and Ethics for Educational Leaders, *Educational Administration Quarterly* 54, no. 2 (1995): 613–16.

14. Ibid.

15. William J. Bennett, "Excessive Legalization in Education," *Chicago Daily Law,* Mar. 22, 1988.

16. R. Birnbaum, *How Colleges Work: The Cybernetics of Academic Organization and Leadership* (San Francisco, Calif.: Jossey-Bass, 1988.

17. Bull, L., and M. McCarthy. "Reflections on the Knowledge Base in Law and Ethics for Educational Leaders. *Educational Administration Quarterly* 54, no. 2 (1995): 613–16.

18. Ibid.

19. Ibid.

20. D. W. Chapman, G. P. Sorenson, and A. F. Lobosco, "Public School Administrators' Knowledge of Recent Supreme Court Decisions Affecting School Practice," *Educational Policy* 2 (1988): 11–28.

21. Goodlad, J. *Teachers for our Nation's Schools.* (San Francisco, Calif.: Jossey Bass, 1990)

22. Shane, "An Analysis of the Knowledge Levels of California K–12 Teachers Concerning Copyright Issues Related to Classroom Multimedia Projects."

23. M. J. Norusis, *SPSS 7.5 Guide to Data Analysis,* 1ˢᵗ ed. (Englewood Cliff, N.J.: Prentice-Hall, 1997).

24. J. Spradley, *The Ethnographic Interview* (New York: Holt, Rinehart, and Winston, 1979).

25. Ibid.

26. Shane, "An Analysis of the Knowledge Levels of California K–12 Teachers Concerning Copyright Issues Related to Classroom Multimedia Projects"; James, "Educators' Attitudes Concerning Copyright"; Chase, "An Analysis of the Knowledge Levels of Media Directors Concerning Relevant Copyright Issues in Higher Education"; S. L. Wertz, "Knowledge of the 1976 General Revision of the Copyright Law, pp. l94–533, by College and University Media Center Directors in the United States" (Ph.D. diss. Univ. of South Carolina, 1984), unpublished.

27. G. Blumenstyk, "Campuses in cyberspace," *Chronicle of Higher Education* (Dec 15, 1995): A-19.

28. W. R. Leibowitz, "Let's Settle This, Online," *National Law Journal* (1999): A20.

29. Guernsey and Young, "Who Owns On-line Courses?"

Appendix A. Copyright Questionnaire (Instrument I)
Copyright Questionnaire Adapted from Dr. Stephen Shane (1999)

PLEASE READ THE INSTRUCTIONS BEFORE RESPONDING TO THE QUESTIONS.

Instructions: Thank you for volunteering to participate in this study. Your responses to this questionnaire will be treated with utmost confidentiality. The questionnaire has no identifying numbers or marks on it. Please do not indicate your name or put any identifiers that can be traced back to you. *Place an "X" in the blank space to indicate the selected answer of your choice.* Please select only *one response* to each question.

PROVIDE RESPONSES TO ALL ITEMS OF THE QUESTIONNAIRE

PART I: COPYRIGHT QUESTIONS

CHECK THE "BEST " ANSWER

1. Copyright protection for a work begins when:
a. _____ the work is first created and put in some fixed form
b. _____ the work is first published
c. _____ the work is registered with the U.S. Copyright Office

2. Facts or ideas can be protected by copyright law:
a. _____ just like any creative works
b. _____ only if registered with the U.S. Copyright Office
c. _____ under no conditions

3. The owner of a copyright has the exclusive right to do, and to authorize others to do, some of the following. Which one of these is *not* included in the copyright holder's right?
a. _____ to reproduce the copyrighted work
b. _____ to prepare derivative works based on the copyrighted work
c. _____ to restrict distribution of the work and transfer of ownership
d. _____ to perform or display the copyrighted work publicly

4. The "fair-use" provision of the copyright law allows the reproduction of some copyrighted materials for several purposes without being an infringement of copyright. Which of the following purposes is *not* allowed under this provision?

a. _____ criticism
b. _____ news reporting
c. _____ teaching
d. _____ researching
e. _____ they are all covered under the provision

5.   When determining if a given use fits under the "fair-use" provision of the copyright law, four factors are examined. Which of the following is *not* one of the four factors?
a. _____ the purpose and character of the use
b. _____ the nature of the copyrighted work
c. _____ the amount and sustainability of the portion used
d. _____ the medium of the copyrighted work
e. _____ they are all factors to be considered

6.   The duration of the copyrighted protection of a work created by an individual under the Copyright Term Extension Act of 1998 is:
a. _____ 28 years
b. _____ 75 years
c. _____ the lifetime of the author
d. _____ the life of the author, plus 70 years

7.   A copyright notice that contains the copyright symbol ©, name of the copyright holder, and the date of copyright:
a. _____ must be on all copyrighted work
b. _____ if missing, is proof that the work is in the public domain and can be used by anyone, for anything.
c. _____ is not required any longer, but is still a good idea to put it on any published work
d. _____ is not required and is of no value

PART II: COPYRIGHT OWNERSHIP QUESTIONS

8. A work created by an educator utilizing Web resources is covered by copyright from the moment the work is placed in a fixed medium of expression.
a. _____ True
b. _____ False

9. Copyright can protect creative forms of expression; for example, books, articles, artworks, music, and software.
a. _____ True
b. _____ False

10. Generally, educators who integrate technology into their classroom instruction become the copyright owners with the exclusive right to control the material they create.
a. _____ True
b. _____ False

11. Ownership of a copyright, or of any of the exclusive rights under a copyright, is distinct from ownership of any material object in which the work is embodied.
a. _____ True
b. _____ False

12. The authors or creators of a joint work in a Wb-based/ online course are co-owners of copyright in the work created.
a. _____ True
b. _____ False

13. Copyright in a work protected under the Copyright Act vests initially in the author or authors of the
work.
a. _____True
b. _____ False

14. In the case of a work made for hire, the employer or other person for whom the work was prepared is considered the author of the copyright work.
a. _____ True
b. _____ False

15. Copyright in a separate contribution to a collective work resulting from Web-based instruction (e.g., a set of Web sites joined by hyperlinks) is distinct from copyright in the collective work as a whole.
a. _____ True
b. _____ False

16. When an individual author's ownership of a copyright has not previously been transferred voluntarily, a governmental body, official, or organization cannot take action to seize, transfer, or exercise rights of ownership with respect to the copyright
a. _____True
b. _____False

17. In the absence of an express transfer of the copyright, the owner of copyright in a collective work is presumed to have acquired only the privilege of reproducing and distributing the owner's contribution as part of that particular collective work.
a. _____True
b. _____False

18. Transfer of ownership of any material object (e.g., a compact disc) does not of itself convey any rights in the copyrighted works embodied in the object.
a. _____True
b. _____False

19. Transfer of copyright ownership may be completed by either verbal or written contract.
a. _____ True
b. _____ False

20. The ownership of a copyright may be bequeathed by will.
a. _____True
b. _____ False

21. Only the owner of copyright in a work has the right to prepare or to authorize someone else to create a new version of that work. Accordingly, you cannot claim copyright to another's work, no matter how much you change it, unless you have the owner's consent.
a. _____True
b. _____False

PART III: DEMOGRAPHIC QUESTIONS

22. How long have you been teaching in higher education?
a. _____ 0–2 years
b. _____ 3–5 years
c. _____ 6–10 years
d. _____ 11–15 years
e. _____ over 15 years

23. How long have you been using Web-based/Internet technology for instruction in an institutional setting?
a. _____ 0–1 year
b. _____ 2 years
c. _____ 3 years
d. _____ 4 years
e. _____ 5 years or more

24. What is your faculty rank in your current institution?
a. _____ Professor
b. _____ Assistant professor
c. _____ Associate professor
d. _____ Instructor/lecturer

25. What is your current employment status?
a. _____ Part-time position
b. _____ Full-time position

26. What is the highest level of education you have completed?
a. _____ Bachelor's degree
b. _____ Actively working on a master's degree
c. _____ Master's degree
d. _____ Actively working on a doctoral degree
e. _____ Doctoral degree (J.D., Ed.D., MD, Ph.D.)

27. In the past five years, which educational level have you taught the most?
a. _____ Undergraduate
b. _____ Graduate
c. _____ Professional

28. At which institution types are you currently teaching?
a. _____ Four-year public college or university
b. _____ Two-year public college or university
c. _____ Private/religious college or university
d. _____ Two-year technical or community college

29. Have you participated in a law-related workshop on copyright law?
a. _____ Yes
b. _____ No

30. Does your institution have a copyright policy?
a. _____ Yes
b. _____ No
c. _____ I don't know

Appendix B. Copyright Follow-up Survey (Instrument II)
Follow-up Copyright Survey

Instructions: Thank you for volunteering to participate in this part of the study. Your responses to this survey will be treated with utmost confidentiality. The survey has no identifying numbers or marks on it. Please do not indicate your name or put any identifiers that can be traced back to you.

1. Do you think that the original questionnaire you completed truly tested your knowledge level of copyright ownership? If so, how? If not, why not?

2. What sources of law-related information are educators most familiar with regarding copyright law and copyright ownership?

3. Where, or how, did you learn what you know about copyright law?

4. Has an institution official discussed copyright ownership issues for Web-based/online courses with you in a meeting or in-house session? If so, what professional role did the official play at your institution?

5. If you answered yes to item # 4, what issues did your institution address?

6. Do you think that educators should be knowledgeable about copyright when dealing with their students and their classroom? Why or why not?

7. Do you think that your colleagues are concern about copyright when dealing with Web-based online courses? Why or Why not?

8. What do you think is the best way to get this copyright information to educators in postsecondary institutions?

9. Does your institution have copyright guidelines specifically for Web/based/electronic/online courses and materials produced by its own faculty?

10. Does your institution have specific guidelines or procedures regarding copyright ownership of Web-based/online courses and materials when collaborating with other institutions?

Chapter 8

DRM: The Good, the Bad, and the Ugly

John T. Mitchell

Abstract

Digital rights management (DRM) technology is neither good nor evil, yet its uses can range from laudable to criminal. DRM can be used for lawful purposes, such as to protect copyrights from infringement and to encourage wider dissemination of works. Some positive uses can cause unintended injury that may be minimized by regulation. Other uses may serve no lawful purpose but, instead, enforce unlawful agreements in restraint of trade or evade statutory limits on the copyright. Using established analog case law, this paper offers a road map for discerning among uses of DRM that should be encouraged as "good," uses that may be "bad" (but tolerable if properly managed), and uses that are so "ugly" they should be prohibited and punished.

DRM has moved beyond mere acronym to become one of the newest words in the English language. Rather than being used to manage copyrights, however, it is often used to gain control over noninfringing uses of a copyrighted work regardless of whether the statutory rights of others are trampled.

It is not the DRM itself that is good, bad, or ugly but, rather, the uses to which it is placed. By analogy, a gate can be used for the "good" purpose of keeping out persons not entitled to enter the land, it can be "bad" when its use to protect the property from trespassers has the unintended consequence of preventing friends or emergency vehicles from entering, and the same gate can be downright ugly when used by private parties, acting without authorization, to charge the public a toll to enter public lands. This paper suggests that good DRM should be encouraged and refined, bad DRM should be examined using traditional antitrust principles under a "rule of reason" analysis to determine whether harms are outweighed by the benefits, and all ugly DRM should be condemned and prosecuted as vigorously as is copyright infringement.

There is excellent legal precedent for this approach. Copyright holders have been trying for nearly a century to gain unlawful control over downstream uses of their works. This paper will dust off the analog case law and apply it anew to the world of DRM, leaving a road map for discerning between uses of DRM that should be encouraged, monitored, or prosecuted.

The first section outlines copyright and competition principles. The second section reviews the changes brought about by the Digital Millennium Copyright Act (DMCA). It suggests a more conservative interpretation of the DMCA, consistent with basic copyright and competition principles. The third section distinguishes between the so-called good, bad, and ugly uses of DRM, arguing that good uses are those that operate within the copyright limits. Bad uses may not necessarily respect the limits of the copyright but further important public policy objectives, and may be tolerated because of their overall value. Finally, ugly uses have no redeeming social value and should be treated as illegal per se because they expand the scope of copyright and restrain lawful trade with no countervailing public benefits.

Back to the Basics of Copyright and Competition Law

Members of the Copyright Industry Organizations,[1] representing the major record companies, motion picture studios, and software publishers claim the general right to control "use" of their works.[2] But the rights granted by the United States Copyright Act, like the copyright laws of all other countries, are limited to certain specified rights and certainly do not extend to all uses. These limitations are of crucial importance to an understanding of how DRM can be used for good or abused for evil.

We begin with the purpose of copyright protection. It is not, as U.S. Federal Reserve Board Chairman Alan Greenspan maintains, to generate private profits that will drive trade:

> If our objective is to maximize economic growth, are we striking the right balance in our protection of intellectual

property rights? Are the protections sufficiently broad to encourage innovation but not so broad as to shut down follow-on innovation?[3]

It has never been the objective of copyright law to "maximize economic growth." Were that the case, actions by copyright owners that maximize economic growth by limiting access to copyrighted works to an elite segment of the population would be encouraged. But under the U.S. Constitution, the only purpose is "to promote the progress of science and the useful arts."[4] Economic benefits are only a means to encourage the creation and dissemination of more and better works of authorship for the public good.

This distinction between the true purpose of copyright laws, the promotion of science and art, and the purpose suggested by the major copyright-holding companies must be underscored anew in this digital age. Up until very recently, copyright owners had very few means of controlling noninfringing uses of their works. Today, however, it is not only possible, but increasingly likely, that copyright owners will use technological devices, such as DRM technology, to gain control not only over lawful, noninfringing uses of their works in hopes of thereby gaining greater revenues from them. Because restrictive DRM that prevents, controls, or otherwise limits noninfringing uses directly undermines the purpose of copyright law (even if the stock market responds favorably and the copyright holder profits thereby), it is in the public interest to ensure that use of such DRM not be allowed to forever expand the scope of the copyright holders' power to limit the progress of science and the useful arts.

With this proper perspective in mind, we can turn to an examination of the historic limits on the exclusive rights of the copyright owner.

Limitations by Exclusion

The Copyright Act "has never accorded the copyright owner complete control over all possible uses of his work" but has, instead, limited the holder to the enumerated statutory rights.[5] The Supreme Court had explained previously:

> The Copyright Act does not give a copyright holder control over all uses of his copyrighted work. Instead, [Section 106] of the Act enumerates several 'rights' that are made 'exclusive' to the holder of the copyright. If a person, without authorization from the copyright holder, puts a copyrighted work to a use within the scope of one of these 'exclusive rights,'

he infringes the copyright. If he puts the work to a use not enumerated in [Section 106], he does not infringe.[6]

Two of these limitations by exclusion warrant special attention:

Limited Performance Right

There is no exclusive right to perform a work, but only an exclusive right to perform a work "publicly." This is true under the laws of the United States,[7] and it is the international norm. The applicable international treaties limit the obligation of signatory parties to that of protecting a right to perform works publicly—never privately.[8]

Until recently, little attention was given to this limitation because copyright holders generally lacked the capacity to monitor or control private performances of their works. But many major copyright holders have begun to use modern DRM technology to infringe upon the public's nonexclusive right to perform works privately. As is discussed below, such uses of DRM technology serve to enlarge the scope of the copyright monopoly beyond the limits established by law and carry with them substantial antitrust implications.

Limited Distribution Right

The right to "distribute" a work is limited to the distribution of "copies and phonorecords" in which a work is fixed.[9] Section 101 of the United States Copyright Act specifies that they must be "material objects." Thus, although the industry often uses the term "distribution" to include the licensing of broadcast or other public performance rights, the distribution right it limited to the distribution of the physical media on which the works are reproduced. The physical property rights are distinct: "Ownership of a copyright, or of any of the exclusive rights under a copyright, is distinct from ownership of any material object in which the work is embodied."[10]

The popular press (and sometimes even courts and members of Congress) refers to peer-to-peer "distribution" when what they really mean is peer-to-peer reproduction. The person downloading a work is making a reproduction, whereas the person from whom the download is made, the so-called uploader, may be, at most, contributing to the reproduction by actively offering the file for reproduction.

Rights holders must look to specific rights, such as the right of distribution, public performance, reproduction, and so on, to determine the scope of their respective monopolies, and it is clear that there is no general right to control all forms of dissemination. Some rights pertaining to dissemination may not be exclusive at all. The right of the owner to convey a copy or phonorecord by private gift or lending, for example, trumps the distribution right of the copyright owner. But suppose a copyright holder grants a license to reproduce the work only to prospective licensees who first agree to waive their right to redistribute the licensed reproductions? Antitrust law principles come into play when one discrete exclusive right under copyright is used to leverage control over, or to suppress, transactions in which a work may be disseminated without implicating the exclusive rights of the copyright holder.

Finally, the distribution right may be exhausted. At the beginning of the twentieth century, the U.S. Supreme Court determined that the distribution right of the copyright holder did not extend so far as to empower the copyright holder to place restrictions on the terms and conditions of resale.[11] Following this decision, the U.S. Congress specifically provided for the exhaustion of the right of distribution following the first sale of the copy.[12] This came to be known as the "first-sale doctrine," a term that continues in use today even though the law has changed to entitle the owner of a copy or phonorecord to dispose of it without the consent of the copyright holder, whether or not the copy was ever sold by the copyright holder.

The exclusive right of distribution is limited by the countervailing entitlement of the owner of a lawfully made copy "to sell or otherwise dispose of the possession of that copy or phonorecord" without the consent of the copyright holder. For example, a copy lawfully made in a retail store or a private home by downloading it from the Internet under license from the copyright owner may be sold or rented without the copyright owner's permission.

The common principle underlying such public policy is that it is a bad idea to allow copyright holders to control the distribution of copies that they no longer own. Nearly one hundred years ago, the committee of the U.S. Congress that recommended codification of the judicially created first-sale doctrine stated that "it would be most unwise to permit the copyright proprietor to exercise any control whatever over the article which is the subject of copyright after said proprietor has made the first sale."[13]

In short, the public policy granting copyrights "excludes from it all that is not embraced" in the original copyrighted work and "equally forbids the use of the copyright to secure an exclusive right or limited monopoly" beyond the scope of the Copyright Act and which is "contrary to public policy to grant."[14]

Limitations by Exception
Other copyright limitations are derived from express restrictions imposed by law. In general, the statutory limitations are contained in sections 107 through

122 of the United States Copyright Act. Although there are others, sections 107 through 122 expressly limit the scope of the copyright at its inception. Section 106 of the Copyright Act, from which copyrights are derived, begins by specifying that the six individual rights[15] granted to authors are "subject to" the limitations set forth in sections 107 through 122.[16] Other limitations, such as section 1008 (allowing noncommercial copying of sound recordings), do not diminish the scope of the copyright itself but, rather, serve as a limit on the enforcement of the right. Two of the statutory limitations most important for this analysis are summarized below.

The Right to Make Fair Use of Copyrighted Works

Section 107 of the United States Copyright Act establishes a right to make "fair use" of copyrighted works.[17] This limitation on copyrights represents a codification of a limitation established by the courts, which was in large measure required to preserve fundamental values found in the First Amendment to the U.S. Constitution.[18] The fair-use limitation is important not only for education, news reporting, and similar uses expressly noted in section 107, but it also serves an important function in preserving competition. For example, one may make fair use of copyrighted works for purposes of comparative advertising[19] and for the purpose of directing consumers to the copyrighted work.[20] The right of fair use in U.S. law is consistent with international norms.[21]

The Rights of Owners of Lawfully Made Copies

Section 109(a) is often referred to as the first-sale doctrine, reflecting its roots in an early U.S. Supreme Court case that concluded that one "who has sold a copyrighted article, without restriction, has parted with all right to control the sale of it. The purchaser of a book, once sold by authority of the owner of the copyright, may sell it again, although he could not publish a new edition of it."[22] With minor exceptions, this prevents the copyright owner from exercising any rental right over copies owned by others.[23] Without exception, it prevents the copyright owner from controlling reselling, whether new or used, thereby preserving markets for second-hand copies, which further the copyright objective of increasing dissemination by making more works accessible to those who have not the will or the means to pay full price for a new copy. Our library system, gifts, informal lending, yard sales, and barter (e.g., something as simple as trading baseball cards) depend on the first-sale doctrine for their existence.

The right of owners to resell or rent motion pictures and other audiovisual works without the consent of the copyright owner gave rise to the worldwide video rental market and has ensured the lowest possible cost to consumers for purchases and rental of VHS and DVD copies of motion pictures. Had it not been for the U.S. first-sale doctrine, the home video market would most likely have evolved into a niche market similar to the old laser discs, targeted at consumers with high disposable income who could afford to pay more than fifty dollars per copy of a videocassette movie. Instead, the U.S. home video market grew into a market representing 62 percent of film revenues, while at the same time the cost of buying a movie has dropped to less than half the original price and access to watching a movie by rental has plummeted to an average of around three dollars.[24]

It is paradoxical, yet true, that the financial success of the home video market in generating the majority of Hollywood's revenue is due to *lack* of control by the studios that hold the copyrights.[25] More important than the substantial profits that have been generated is the fact that they are simply the by-product of a more important result. Lack of copyright holder control over redistribution of copies has led to much wider dissemination of creative works to the general public without harming copyright holders in the least. The freedom to sell used copies adds value to the original purchase. Even the freedom to give the copy away likely has some less tangible value that makes the consumer more willing to pay for it. And just as there are millions of people who cannot afford new cars but can drive if given access to a used car market, there are millions of consumers who cannot afford the price of a new DVD movie but can provide an evening of home entertainment with the inexpensive rental of a "previously viewed" movie. For this reason, substantial attention is given in this paper to DRM that interferes with the normal incidents of ownership of physical property.

Limitation by Complementary Law
When the precise scope of the copyright is determined, first by examining the grant and then by examining the limitations to which the grant is subject, other limitations required by complementary laws come into play. Two such limitations stand out: freedom of expression guaranteed by the First Amendment, and antitrust limitations.

First Amendment Limitations
The First Amendment to the U.S. Constitution provides that "Congress shall make no law . . . abridging the freedom of speech, or of the press." Although this prohibition is presented in absolute terms, the Constitution itself also authorizes Congress to enact copyright laws. Article I, Section 6, states that Congress shall have the power "To promote the Progress of Science and Use-

ful Arts, by securing for limited Times to Authors and Inventors the exclusive Right to their respective writings and discoveries." The courts have, therefore, been called on to determine the proper balance between Congress's power to grant exclusive rights for authors and the prohibition against Congress restricting freedom of speech, because every prohibition of copyright infringement abridges freedom of speech.

The normative approach to resolving this conflict is to consider the First Amendment interests in the context of a fair-use analysis.[26] Although the results of such an approach may not always be sound, the structure itself, when properly applied, tends to accommodate both interests. But the unrestrained expansion of copyright owner power over freedom of expression outside the bounds of copyright certainly could violate the First Amendment if it were enforced by the courts. Use of DRM technology to evade First Amendment limitations on copyrights, or to restrain freedom of speech not involving copyright infringement, should find no shelter in the law.[27]

Competition Law Limitations

The U.S. Congress also has the power to regulate commerce and hence the power to establish antimonopoly laws and other antitrust and fair competition laws.[28] Much has been written concerning the interplay between antitrust law prohibiting monopolies and unreasonable restraints of trade, on the one hand, and intellectual property law that confers legal monopolies, on the other,[29] but one thing is clear: No matter how lawful a statutory copyright monopoly may be, "A copyright owner may not enforce its copyright to violate the antitrust laws or indeed use it in any 'manner violative of the public policy embodied in the grant of a copyright.'"[30]

In short, when a copyright owner attempts to leverage the copyright into control over matters outside the individual copyright, whether over other copyrighted works, noninfringing uses of the copyrighted work, or markets beyond copyright, the law steps in to condemn it.[31]

Until only recently, copyright owners and their legal representatives tended to approach copyrights as extending to everything they could control, without limitation, because they generally had no reasonable expectation of preventing noninfringing uses. The advent of digital technology has changed all that. Today, DRM technology not only enables better control over conduct historically recognized as infringing but, with the same ease and for the first time in history, enables control over conduct that falls wholly outside the reach of the copyright monopoly and which has been, in some instances, specifically placed off-limits to copyright owner control.

The Digital Millennium Copyright Act and DRM

The Digital Millennium Copyright Act (DMCA) was enacted by the U.S. Congress in 1998 in large part to fulfill the U.S.'s obligations under two recent World Intellectual Property Organization (WIPO) treaties: the WIPO Copyright Treaty and the WIPO Performances and Phonograms Treaty. Just as innovations in digital technology made it easier to infringe copyrights, digital technology also promised to make it easier to protect copyrighted works from infringement.[32] To try to keep protective technology one step ahead of infringing technology, WIPO treaties obligate parties to provide "adequate legal protection and effective legal remedies against the circumvention of effective technological measures that are used by [copyright owners] *in connection with the exercise of their rights* . . . and that *restrict acts* . . . which are *not* authorized by the [copyright owners] concerned *or permitted by law*" (emphasis added).[33] The treaties do not require legal protection against circumvention of technological measures that restrict acts permitted by law, yet they opened an avenue for the major copyright-holding industries to forever alter the copyright landscape by converting a publicly designed structure (balancing private rights against public interests) into a regime in which copyright holders can employ modern technology to create their own rights without concern for the public interest.

The Copyright Industry Organizations claim the right to use DRM technology to nullify the public rights the U.S. Congress conferred upon the owners of lawfully made copies.[34] On the contrary, the obligation to protect DRM from circumvention is limited to circumvention for infringing uses.[35] The language of the agreement on Trade-Related Aspects of Intellectual Property (TRIPS) remains in full force and contains at least three provisions that demonstrate the international community's understanding that copyrights must serve the public interest and should not be abused. They are to be "to the mutual advantage of producers and users . . . in a manner conducive to social and economic welfare, and to a balance of rights and obligations.[36] Members are expected to "prevent the abuse of intellectual property rights by right holders or the resort to practices which unreasonably restrain trade."[37] Anti-competitive practices aided by intellectual property rights are to be guarded against.[38] Members are encouraged to consider means of redressing situations in which the copyright holder abridges the rights of members of the public to enjoy lawful, noninfringing uses.[39]

Against this backdrop, Congress enacted the DMCA, prohibiting the circumvention of "a technological measure that effectively controls access to a work protected" by copyright.[40] No doubt the U.S. Congress thought that, in enacting the DMCA, it was carrying out its obligations under the two new

WIPO treaties to provide "adequate legal protection and effective legal remedies against the circumvention of effective technological measures that are used by [copyright owners] *in connection with the exercise of their rights* . . . and that *restrict acts* . . . which are *not* authorized by the [copyright owners] concerned *or permitted by law.*" But the language of the DMCA has taken a different approach to achieving these objectives. Sections 1201(a) and 1201(b) of the United States Copyright Act omit the requirement that the use of technological measures be "in connection with the exercise of their rights" and also omits the words "or permitted by law," thereby leaving an open invitation to proponents of expanded copyright power to interpret this to mean that, *in addition* to laws protecting their copyrights from infringement, the DMCA added new *sui generis* laws protecting against the circumvention of their technological access controls even where they are designed and used with no connection to the exercise of their rights and solely to privately expand their control over noninfringing uses of their copyrighted works that are otherwise permitted by law.

One key provision of the DMCA, found at Section 1201(c) of the United States Copyright Act, expressly states that none of the entire panoply of lawful uses set forth in the act should be affected by the prohibition upon circumvention of access control technologies as set forth in the DMCA.[41] Clearly, Congress must have intended for the DMCA to further the constitutional objectives of the Copyright Act, which include both the rights granted in Section 106 and the limitations placed on those rights.

It should be noted, however, that the DRM technology at issue here is not the same as "a technological measure that effectively controls access to a work protected under this [Copyright] title." DRM technology can be much broader and would include such things as simple copy-protection technology (e.g., technology that does not control access to the work but may prevent its reproduction) and spying technology (e.g., technology that allows full access but monitors and reports usage). Thus, all uses of DRM technology may be analyzed under the principles set forth herein whether or not the specific DRM technology may lawfully be circumvented under the DMCA.

This discussion of the DMCA is for the purpose of stressing that (1) whether the technology is protected from circumvention by the DMCA is not determinative of whether the DRM use is good, bad, or ugly, and (2) the fact that a particular DRM technology may be protected from circumvention by the DMCA has no bearing on whether the DRM technology may lawfully be used in a particular way. The DMCA pertains to the legality of circumvention, not the legality of any given use of DRM technology.

Uses of DRM

The key to distinguishing between a good, a bad, or an ugly use of DRM is to examine what the DRM is used for rather than its technical capabilities. Just as it would make little sense to say all gates are good or all gates are bad, so it is with DRM. Identical gates, and identical DRM technologies, can be used for either end. The value or harm from any given DRM cannot be judged by its architecture alone but, instead, must be weighed against its use its purpose and effects—both intended and unintended.

The major Copyright Industry Organizations[42] are strong defenders of all DRM as "antipiracy" without regard to its uses, failing to acknowledge that some DRM antipiracy uses may cause such collateral damage as to be harmful and some may have nothing to do with copyright protection and everything to do with illegal activity. Similarly, there is a vocal anti-DRM chorus that believes "DRM is theft."[43] Although catchy, that short phrase fails to take into account that the evil of DRM is not in the DRM itself, but in how it is used. As we shall see, some identical DRM technology can have applications that are very good or very evil, depending on how the DRM technology is used.

Good Uses of DRM

As we begin our examination of DRM uses that are pure and positive, the characteristics of good uses of DRM will begin to emerge. Good uses of DRM further the objective of copyright law by either protecting the copyright from infringement or increasing dissemination of the work, and do so without enlarging the copyright or impairing noninfringing competition.

Good DRM also may be unrelated to copyright but nevertheless further some public good without also creating a public burden. To better understand what constitutes a good use of DRM, a few examples of applications meeting the above criteria are in order.

Perfecting Authorized Reproductions

Downloading copyrighted works from the Internet consists of making reproductions of the work into "copies or phonorecords," terms defined in the Copyright Act to mean any tangible medium, including a computer hard drive, onto which copyrighted works are recorded. Consider the simplest form of downloading for a fee. A popular DRM application involves some form of encryption that will be "unlocked" only after certain conditions take place, such as payment. If I agree to pay one dollar in exchange for the right to make a reproduction (a download) of the work, I will be reluctant to pay until I am sure the download is complete and accurate. The licensor (the entity with the right to authorize me to download it) is reluctant to allow the reproduction until it can be assured that I will make the payment. The solution is for the encrypted file to be reproduced and verified for accuracy before the payment is made and confirmed, at which time the file is unlocked to allow access. In such a case, the DRM serves as a "trustee" for the parties, automatically unlocking the file when a valid credit card account is given. Alternatively, the licensor may be willing to allow the person at my e-mail address to download the copy and may unlock it only upon confirmation that someone with my e-mail address replied to the licensor's e-mail.

In both of these examples, confirmation of payment and confirmation of the e-mail identity of the downloader, the DRM serves to confirm that the conditions precedent to the reproduction being licensed are fulfilled. It encourages and supports the purposes of the copyright because it makes it easier for the parties to the transaction to trust each other. It is no different than automating the analog counterpart. For example, if I am a publisher and the author of a book (the copyright owner, in this example) authorizes me to make 1,000 copies of the book in exchange for payment of $10 each, when I make the 1,000 copies I am presumptively licensed to do so even before I have made payment and would not be guilty of infringement. If, having run off 1,000 copies, I refuse to pay the agreed $10,000, the presumption of permission vanishes and I become an infringer. But if the author were to insist on advance payment, I, as publisher, may be reluctant to pay until I am assured that the manuscript provided by the author is in the agreed form. In this nondigital example, the law has long accommodated go-betweens—trustees, escrow agents, and the like who will overcome the lack of trust between the parties. The publisher can make payment to the trustee, who will not transfer the payment to the author until the publisher has received the agreed-upon manuscript and the 1,000 copies have been made.

Remote transactions over the Internet are no different. The DRM can easily take the place of the escrow agent, preventing access to the licensed reproduction until confirmation is made that the conditions on which the license was given have been met. Assuming that the underlying transaction is legitimate, such use of DRM is "good" because it facilitates the very kinds of transactions envisioned in the law. Indeed, when Congress passed the DMCA, it appears that it had precisely this type of DRM (or access control technology) in mind. As the House Judiciary Committee explained, "In order to protect the [copyright] owner, copyrighted works will most likely be encrypted and *made available to consumers once payment is made* for access to a copy of the work" (emphasis added).[44]

But Congress was not interested in creating new business opportunities by trampling on the Copyright Act's limitations. The objective was to protect copyrights, not "copywrongs."[45] The Report from the House Committee on the Judiciary goes on to explain Section 1201(a) of the DMCA as preventing "the electronic equivalent of breaking into a locked room in order to obtain a copy of a book," adding:

> Paragraph (a)(1) does not apply to the subsequent actions of a person once he or she has obtained authorized access to a copy of a work protected under Title 17, even if such actions involve circumvention of additional forms of technological protection measures. In a fact situation where the access is authorized, the traditional defenses to copyright infringement, including fair use, would be fully applicable. So, an individual would not be able to circumvent in order to gain unauthorized access to a work, but would be able to do so in order to make fair use of a work which he or she has acquired lawfully.[46]

The section-by-section analysis in the report further explains that the definition of "circumvent a technological protection measure" in Section 1201(a)(3), as used in paragraph (a), "covers protections against unauthorized *initial* access to a work" (emphasis added).[47]

In other words, Congress expected that DRM would be used to prevent people from downloading without paying, but after payment was made, the DRM would permit access without further restricting subsequent access. Such use furthers the interest of the copyright holder in protecting the work from infringement, furthers the public interest in facilitating broader dissemination of the work by removing barriers to the transaction, and goes no further than necessary to achieve those ends.

In like manner, there have always been intermediaries who use and facilitate access to the copyrighted works, but who own no copyrights in them. They, too, may need DRM to protect their interests. Theft-prevention technologies used in retail stores, particularly music and video stores, have become ubiquitous. (And, for the retailer, the interest in protecting against theft of an $18 copyrighted DVD movie is just as great as protecting against theft of an $18 public-domain DVD movie.) The occasional false alarm is an acceptable inconvenience because the reward of lower theft rates is lower prices. And just as the customer trying to walk out of a store with two copies of a DVD movie having paid for only one may rightfully be prevented from doing so by use of effective antitheft technology, so we should expect the person trying to reproduce two copies of a movie having paid for the right to download only one may rightfully be prevented from doing so by good DRM. Here again, if the charge for the right of reproduction is to pay for the cost of providing the service (not under copyright, but as a matter of private agreement), it makes little difference whether the "right of reproduction" given to make a down-loaded copy is granted by the copyright owner as a license of its exclusive right or granted by a facilitator who owns no copyright and perhaps offers only public-domain films.

Digital Ticket Taker

Another good use of DRM is as an automated ticket taker, equivalent to someone controlling access to a theater or museum. The person streaming or displaying the work over the Internet, whether they own the copyright or not, may wish to limit the audience to patrons who have paid the price to see it, those whose payments make the public performance or public display possible. Use of DRM to limit the audience only to those who have paid is as benign as posting a guard at the theater or museum door to check admission tickets. It is the equivalent of cable signal descramblers intended to limit the consumer's viewing to the channels paid for.

It warrants stressing that this use of DRM should have nothing to do with copyright per se.[48] It is never copyright infringement to sneak into a theater without paying, but it may nevertheless be trespass or illegal theft of services to do so, whether or not the movie being performed is in the public domain. DRM use that permits only paid subscribers to listen to a public performance over the Internet should be considered "good" insofar as it enables the person making the public performance to profitably finance the cost of it. It does so without enlarging the copyright because this use is equally helpful in encouraging more public performances whether the work being performed publicly is copyrighted or not.

Automated Accountant

In the physical world, a retailer may buy copies of a work at wholesale for resale to the public. The copyright owner needn't learn how many copies were actually sold to consumers as long as payment is received for all copies at the wholesale price. And, as we can recall from the earlier discussion of the first-sale doctrine, the copyright owner should have no control over whether the retailer sells the copies, at what price, or to whom. In the case of downloads, in contrast, the "lawfully made copy or phonorecord" does not come into existence until it is reproduced by the consumer. What is being sold is not technically a copy but, rather, a license to reproduce the work into a copy. Thus, in order for the retailer to "sell" the downloads to consumers, it must first obtain permission from the copyright owner.[49]

The copyright owner selling books at wholesale knows how many were sold. The copyright owner selling (to retailers) licenses to sublicense (to consumers) the right to reproduce the work into a copy must rely on the retailer to inform the copyright owner as to how many copies were actually reproduced by the retailer's customers. DRM can, in this case, serve an accounting function by "informing" the copyright owner every time a sublicensed reproduction is made. This can be done by means of a simple "reporting the numbers" function or, in a more complex scheme, having the copyright owner or its designee release the decryption key to the consumer when the retail transaction is complete.

Once again, this use of DRM does not hinge upon whether the work is copyrighted, as it could be used just the same for public-domain works. The consumer pays the retailer for the service of providing the work in pristine form (and making it easy to find and so on) and a license to reproduce it. If copyrighted, the retailer, with the authority of the copyright owner, licenses the reproduction and pays the copyright owner for the reproduction right based on the number of downloads accounted for. If not copyrighted, the retailer permits the reproduction and uses the accounting function for its own internal business control.

Without such DRM, copyright owners would be reluctant to allow any retailers to sublicense reproductions for fear that there would be no accountability and, whether copyrighted or not, retailers would be reluctant to allow unlimited downloads that tax their system and offer no remuneration. Unless the copyright owner could trust the retailer's word, the transactions might not take place at all. By using DRM, the copyright owner can trust the DRM where trust of its business partner may be lacking. Plus, even where trust is present, the automation of this function using DRM adds substantial efficiencies to the process. Thus, this use of DRM directly contributes to wider dissemination of the work relying on a larger number and broader variety of retailers, who can competitively seek out customers by offering the best price and quality of reproductions and support services.

Antitheft Device

Theft of copies of copyrighted works contributes to two problems adversely impacting availability. Theft of master copies, prerelease copies, sample copies, and so on often is the source from which infringing copies are made and distributed or made available on the Internet from where additional infringing copies can be made. Theft of copies at retail may not contribute as much to piracy, but the economic impact on the retailer results in a greater burden on public access to the works in the form of higher prices for the remaining copies. In both instances, normal product security measures may not be enough. Use of DRM to destroy stolen copies would lower the overhead associated with piracy and inventory shrinkage. Although there does not appear to be widespread application of DRM for such purposes, it may be only a matter of time before we see experiments with product "activation" at the checkout counter, such that a stolen copy could not be accessed or the use of tethering technologies to ensure that prerelease copies in the studio cannot be accessed on equipment outside the studio. To the degree that such uses only impair the private performance of stolen copies, the general purposes of copyright law are furthered. Although it is certainly true that the thief does not infringe the copyright by performing the work privately from the stolen copy, there is no serious harm to the public interest if thieves and their customers are prevented from doing so.

Theft of services is another antitheft application of DRM, such as cable television signal encryption. It infringes no copyright to decrypt a cable television broadcast without permission from the cable service provider, but the cable service nevertheless has a legitimate interest in ensuring that only subscribing customers will have access, whether or not the works being broadcast are copyrighted.[50]

Benign Supervisor

As is evident in the discussion of bad and ugly uses of DRM, the evils associated with harmful uses can be just as damaging when employed by third parties acting by agreement with the copyright owner. Whenever DRM is used by persons acting independently of the copyright owner, however, it is much more likely to be good, particularly where the third party has no particular legal power over access to the work that is DRM protected. An excellent example of good DRM used by third parties independently might be educational institutions and libraries that use DRM to facilitate lawful access up to the limits of the law, while protecting the institution and its patrons from claims of copyright infringement.

One example is DRM employed by an educational institution to implement the institution's rights under the TEACH Act while ensuring compliance with the law's requirements needed to qualify for the exemption.[51] The TEACH Act requires that the institution using the exemption provide informational materials to faculty, students, and staff that accurately describe and promote compliance with copyright law.[52] That requirement might be met by use of DRM that prevents access to works available electronically by disseminating such information before the first use and requiring the user to acknowledge receipt of such information before being given electronic access.

Similarly, the TEACH Act itself requires that, in the case of digital transmissions, the institution employ DRM to reasonably prevent retention of the work beyond the class session and to reasonably prevent unauthorized further dissemination of the work.[53] Such DRM is required by law. Consequently, its use is good even if the law might itself have room for improvement.

Although the use of DRM by third parties may be to protect the copyright from infringement (such as to protect the entity employing the DRM from liability for the conduct of others), such uses also may be for purely self-serving purposes. A few examples of the latter "benign supervisor" uses might be:

• An employer uses DRM to prevent employees from accessing certain sites from computers at work (whether or not such access is infringing).

• A law firm uses DRM to give its clients access to their files, but not to the confidential files of others.

• Medical personnel are given access to patient records on a need-to-know basis, using DRM to verify authorized users and to make inaccessible all unrelated patient records.

• Universities give each student access to his or her own electronic records using DRM to deny access to the records of others.

• Banks and financial institutions offer online banking services using robust DRM that verifies the identity of the customer before granting access to the appropriate account records.

• Parents unable to trust their children use DRM to prevent access to Internet sites of which the parent disapproves.

• An ATM machine—enough said.

These types of DRM uses are so positive that they are generally controversial only when they fail. Yet, Congress curiously chose not to include them in the DMCA's protection against circumvention unless the files or records being protected happen to be copyrighted.

Conceptually, the purpose and effect of "good" DRM is to manage rights that belong to the entity employing the DRM. In this regard, there is nothing significant about copyrights to distinguish them from other rights to which DRM may be applied. DRM can lawfully be employed for more than just copyright protection and good uses of DRM should be encouraged, even when they do not involve intellectual property rights.

This is not to say that good DRM can never cause harm. Just as an adult may trip over a child safety gate installed at the top of the stairs, perhaps the purists could come up with a hypothetical or anecdotal situation in which good DRM use has unintended consequences. But on the whole in the case of copyrighted works, the examples above have both the purpose and effect of facilitating the intended objectives of copyright protection by enabling access to works that might otherwise be unavailable. Certainly, there could be situations in which the accounting software malfunctions and incorrectly reports the number of downloads (authorized reproductions), but this is no greater evil than the book publisher miscounting the number of books reproduced. Or the ticket-taking DRM may refuse access to a streaming movie (a public performance) when the digital key was lost, just as the human ticket taker may refuse entry to a paid-up patron who lost the ticket. In all, however, any injury will tend to be of a type that can be redressed through ordinary customer service channels.

Bad Uses of DRM

Bad DRM ostensibly protects copyrights from infringement or facilitates greater access to copyrighted works, but its use carries with it a degree of "collateral damage" to rights belonging to the public. If the DRM is effective in protecting copyrights from infringement or facilitating greater access to copyrighted works and attempts to do no more than that, it may be tolerated as a necessary evil if the overall benefit to the public is positive. On the other hand, if furtherance of the copyright law's interests is slight in comparison to the damage to those interests, to competition, or to the general welfare, its use should be either prohibited or regulated so as to minimize the harmful effects.

This area is perhaps the most difficult one in which to apply legal rules for analysis because the outcome may depend on the intent of the user of the DRM technology, the balance of benefits and harms, and the availability of less restrictive alternatives. This paper proposes that courts borrow from the "rule-of-reason" analysis in antitrust law to evaluate the legality of such DRM use.

Most antitrust disputes are evaluated under a so-called rule-of-reason analysis. If the restraint is likely to have an anticompetitive effect (and is not a "naked" restraint of trade), the court will assess whether the claimed procompetitive benefits outweigh them and whether the restraint is reasonably necessary to achieve the stated benefits.[54] In the case of copyrights, we must look beyond restraint of trade, as such, and include expansion of the copyright reach beyond its statutory limits (and the counterpart, denial of rights, benefits, and entitlements reserved for the public under the Copyright Act) among the harms against which any purported benefits must be balanced.

Moreover, unlike antitrust, which looks to "procompetitive" benefits only, the copyright analysis should include benefits that further the objectives of copyright law.

"Ugly" uses of the kind discussed in the next subsection would be considered unlawful per se because, borrowing again from per se treatment under antitrust law; they are so plainly contrary to the purposes of copyright law or competition that no elaborate inquiry into positive effects is necessary.[55] The bad DRM, as described here, might be lawful or not depending on the totality of the circumstances, which could change over time or from one product line to another. The ugly uses of DRM described in the next subsection would be unlawful all the time.

For example, uses of DRM that only prevent noninfringing reproductions would serve no valid purpose and would be considered unlawful per se. DRM that is designed to prevent infringing reproductions, in contrast, serves the valid objective of protecting the copyright from infringement. Such DRM might, however, have the unintended consequence of suppressing noninfringing reproductions as well. If all available copies of a given work are locked down by anticopying DRM, it might fail a rule-of-reason analysis because the ability to make fair-use reproductions is an integral part of copyright law.[56] But if access for fair-use reproduction from some copies is widely available despite the application of anticopying technology to certain "high-risk" copies, courts may find that the increased public burden on fair-use copying is outweighed by a countervailing public benefit from reducing infringing reproductions.

It is not the intent of this paper to discern whether a given use of DRM would or should survive a rule-of-reason analysis. Similar factual situations may yield different results. Rather, the examples below suggest DRM uses that cannot be considered lawful (or laudable) under all circumstances, but neither should they be prohibited in every instance.

Timing Out for Public Good

A later section discusses "Timing Out for Private Gain: The Limited Download," explaining why certain uses of timing-out DRM are downright ugly. But there are at least three uses of timing out DRM that could well pass muster because their purpose and overall benefits weigh more heavily than the restraint.

One such use encourages transactions that result in an increased number of lawful copies through licensed reproduction (downloading). A second facilitates transfer of the possession of, not title to, a copy for the purpose of promoting the work, such as in so-called screeners of motion pictures. The third would allow timing out as a tool for mimicking physical distribution such as resales, rental, or lending, but to properly do so would need to be kept beyond the control of the copyright owner.

Try before You Buy

The first uses of timing-out technology appear to have been to encourage consumers to take a chance on software by offering a "trial" version. Unlike products that can be returned for a refund when satisfaction is guaranteed, the digital counterpart can be delivered as a download to a computer hard drive. Even if delivered on a tangible medium, most computer software so delivered is intended to be "installed" (i.e., reproduced) onto the hard drive of a computer (which then becomes a "copy or phonorecord" of the work) before it is performed.[57] When the hard drive becomes the lawful copy, it cannot be returned. Thus, timing-out technology offers a practical substitute for the return of the physical medium for a refund. A consumer dissatisfied with the product could decline to pay, with the understanding that the copy would be rendered inoperable after a reasonable trial term.

Under strict interpretation of the Copyright Act, a time-limited reproduction is a "lawfully made copy" and entitles the owner to dispose of possession of that copy. Arguably, the consumer who downloads the trial version to a CD is entitled to sell, lend, or give away that copy without regard to the copyright owner's wishes and the timing-out DRM would destroy that entitlement because the copy would become a useless piece of plastic. But the substance of the transaction is, in essence, to allow closer examination of the work before taking ownership. It is basically a delayed process of perfecting authorized reproductions discussed earlier. The copyright owner (directly or through licensees) offers the consumer the right to reproduce the work in exchange for payment. The consumer is reluctant to pay for a reproduction only to find out that the music is distasteful or that the computer program does not function as advertised. Thus, in a manner similar to the marriage annulment fiction, the parties can pretend the transaction never happened. "If you don't like the lawfully made copy, we can pretend you never made it. Your money will be refunded (or your payment obligation cancelled) and your lawfully made copy will be as though it had never been made." Such assurances will tend to oil the wheels of dissemination by removing a barrier comparable to a retail store posting a notice of its policy stating, "Buyer beware, all products sold on an as-is basis with no warranties express or implied. All sales are final. No exchanges, returns, or refunds."

To survive rule-of-reason analysis, the timed-out copy would almost certainly have to be at no cost. That is, the copy would be timed out only if the buyer of the license to reproduce it refuses to pay. If payment is made for a timed-out copy (or any other consideration, such as disclosure of valuable data unnecessary for the transaction or receipt of advertising), the reproduction should be viewed as licensed and paid for, and unless refunded, the timing out would be deemed to restrain trade in the aftermarket and unlawfully expand the copyright owner's control over performances to include private ones.[58]

Retention of Ownership

The second type of timing-out DRM could be used to ensure return (or its virtual equivalent) of copies that are owned by the copyright owner. Suppose a motion picture studio wants to allow critics to review a film before its release, or let video stores see a "screener" to encourage buying decisions long before the "street date" of the DVD, or allow the more than 5,000 members of the Academy of Motion Picture Arts and Sciences to see the film in order to vote for the Academy Awards (the Oscars) without ever taking title to a copy or having the opportunity to place it into the stream of commerce where someone could use it as a master for infringing reproductions.

This past year, the Motion Picture Association of America (MPAA) suffered a major embarrassment when its ban on distribution of screeners to academy voters was overturned by a federal judge, citing antitrust violations.[59] The purported reason for the ban was to prevent these screeners owned by the studios from being reproduced, particularly if they were in high demand in piracy channels because they had not yet been released on DVD.[60] But timing-out technology is readily available to render a DVD inoperable a few hours after viewing, and as long as the studio distributing them at no cost to academy voters retains ownership, the studio is free to render its own copies unplayable. Plus, to the degree that the MPAA may have had some valid antipiracy objective, it would make perfect sense to facilitate use of timing-out technology for any copyright holder of a nominated film who desired it.

Space Shifting

The question has been around in popular discourse ever since e-mail, Is it copyright infringement if I forward a copy to a friend and delete the original? Only a few years ago, the only way to lend, trade, or give away one's copies was to transfer possession of the physical medium on which the work was recorded. Digital technology has, in effect, freed these transactions from their physical limitations. It is the equivalent of magically transferring the ink from my book to a friend's blank pages in another state. My friend now can read the book (while I am left with blank pages), but the copyright owner remains whole because no *additional* copies have been made. The fundamental question is not so much what constitutes copyright infringement as whether certain activities never before available should be considered infringing, whether the ability to "move the bits (or 'content') around" should not be legally limited by a requirement that they remain on the same physical medium.

The idea of moving the "content" around as opposed to the physical medium certainly has an appeal. It is generally perceived as more efficient for all concerned. The tension comes over the question whether consumers are free to select their own technology for doing so or whether such "space shifting" should belong within the grant of copyright and under the exclusive control of the copyright owner.

Copyright owners do not appear fundamentally opposed to the idea of space shifting,[61] provided that they can control it. They feel they must be able to prevent it (otherwise they would be unable to control it or profit from it), they must be able to police it to guard against cheating (for example, policing whether the original was, in fact, deleted and no other copies were retained), and they must be able to authorize it (recognizing that if a consumer demand is not being met, some revenue might be derived from permitting the prohibited conduct).

To the degree that space shifting might be infringing, DRM that prevents it might be considered good. But if certain forms of space shifting might not be infringing, DRM that prevents noninfringing space shifting would logically be an ugly use of DRM, akin to placing a private fence around public land. The ability to use DRM to control compliance with space-shifting "permission" could lead to an ability to control a vast new market outside traditional copyright. The possibilities seemed endless: mining the data on who forwards what to whom, perhaps charging extra for the privilege of doing so; using consumers to market to other consumers otherwise unreachable by the copyright owner; reducing digital deliver costs by using consumers' own resources to deliver the "content." But if space shifting is lawful, what right does the copyright owner have to profit from giving permission to perform a noninfringing act?

If called on to draw a line between space-shifting activities that are lawful and those that are not, courts may well draw it much more favorably to the public than copyright owners might hope. For this reason, copyright owners may be best advised to move beyond the debate over legality and, instead, use DRM to facilitate "secure" space shifting that does not result in any additional copies, even if it means giving up the opportunity to leverage copyrights into greater control over space-shifting activities.

Under a secure "forward-and-delete" approach, the owner of a lawful reproduction of a song, for example, could e-mail it to a friend along with the DRM access key. The original is not deleted but is rendered inaccessible until the friend returns the access key, thereby preventing that person's access. In a more sophisticated variation on the same concept, it has been suggested that if there was a license to reproduce one digital copy, it does not matter how many actual replicas are made as long as only one can be accessed at any time. The definition of "copy" requires that it be accessible in some way in order to implicate the right of reproduction.[62] If DRM can be deployed to prevent the multiplication of accessible copies, copyright owners would be better served by facilitating the use of such DRM so that the public can transfer the "content" from one person to another with the same freedom and anonymity with which they currently transfer possession of tangible copies and phonorecords.

But who gets to decide? The ability to move the copy from one medium to another is considered by some to be a consumer right. Ever since the Betamax ruling, it has become common practice to make fair use of a broadcast television program by "time shifting" (reproducing the broadcast work for viewing at a more convenient time).[63] Advocates of a similar space-shifting fair-use right insist that if a consumer has, for example, paid for a reproduction onto medium A, the owner of that lawful copy should be able to move the copy to a more convenient medium.[64] It is often left unclear whether proponents believe that the original should be deleted.[65]

The concept certainly has some appeal. Imagine a public library allowing patrons to check out electronic copies of works as long as one library copy is rendered inaccessible until checked back in. Or suppose I want to let someone "borrow" a new song I downloaded? I could check it out to them and ask that they check it back in to me by the next day, and in my communication to them I could recommend they go to the same site I did to download their own copy. Or suppose a video store bought licenses to reproduce twenty copies of a movie and could allow its patrons to check out (download) the movie and charge them during the period it is checked out. For each movie checked out, one less movie would be available until the movie is checked back in. In that manner, we could duplicate the vigorous competition that has made video rental such a consumer bargain.

But is it legal? For a copyright law purist, the quick answer would be "not unless the copyright owner consented," because an unauthorized reproduction is made before the original is deleted.[66] Complicating this is the catch-22 that if the copyright owner consents to the reproduction, it becomes a "lawfully made" reproduction and therefore the copyright owner should not interfere with the perpetual private performance or redistribution of it.[67] Others might argue that although an unauthorized reproduction may have occurred, it falls within the fair-use exception because at the end of the transaction, there is still just one copy left, that it is the digital equivalent of giving your copy to someone else. Also, a persuasive case can be made that an inaccessible copy does not infringe the right of reproduction if it cannot be perceived, reproduced, or otherwise communicated.

In an attempt to remove any doubt about the legitimacy of the "forward-and-delete" method of space shifting, Congressman Rick Boucher introduced legislation during the 105th Congress that would have legalized the reproduction of a copyrighted work from one medium to another as long as the original was deleted. Section 4 of the "Digital Era Copyright Enhancement Act," House Resolution 3048, provided that Section 109(a) (i.e., the entitlement of owners of lawfully made copies to transfer possession of them without the consent of the copyright owner)

> applies where the owner of a particular copy or phonorecord in a digital format lawfully made under this title, or any person authorized by such owner, performs, displays or distributes the work by means of transmission to a single recipient, if that person erases or destroys his or her copy or phonorecord at substantially the same time. The reproduction of the work, to the extent necessary for such performance, display, distribution, is not an infringement.

The intent was to permit the owner of a lawfully made copy to do the equivalent of transferring possession even though the tangible medium itself would not change hands. As one advocate of the legislation explained:

> Copyrighted content can be delivered to consumers with digital rights management (DRM) systems that enable secure electronic transfers of possession or ownership, and that protect against unauthorized retention of the transferred copy. Through technological processes such as encryption, authentication, and password-protection, copyright owners can ensure that digitally downloaded copies and phonorecords are either deleted after being transferred or are disabled (such as by permanently transferring with the content the only copy of the decryption key).[68]

Congressman Boucher's proposal appeals to common sense. The single significant drawback is the inability to police compliance with the deletion requirement. Making a lawful copy or phonorecord by reproducing a work onto a tangible medium, for example, and then transferring possession or title to that tangible medium to another person is perfectly lawful. The legislation would have overcome the difficulty presented by tangible media such as a hard drive, which may contain many works and be impracticable to transfer to another person, by allowing the reproduction of the work onto the other person's media and deleting it from the original. At the end of the day, one person would own a lawful reproduction, just as before the transfer.[69]

Opposition to the measure was based principally on the fact that it would be virtually impossible to police compliance. The idea that consumers would simply say "Trust me, I deleted my copy after forwarding it to a friend" was too unnerving.[70] Yet, when opponents were asked whether their opposition would remain if technology was sufficiently secure to ensure that the deletion took place, their opposition appeared to lessen.[71]

Assuming, for a moment, that the DRM technology is sufficiently robust to lend reasonable confidence that the original will, in fact, be deleted when the copy is made by another (and practically any level of security is far greater than the security of an average music CD), what do we make of DRM used by the copyright holder to automate a process of forwarding to another and deleting the original, or using a keyed check-in/check-out mechanism to allow access by one person at a time? Certainly, all copies are lawfully made, even if the first are destroyed or made inaccessible (and incapable of being performed privately). With respect to the destroyed or inaccessible copies, the DRM serves to impair rights not belonging to the copyright owner (the Section 109 first-sale rights and the right of private performance), but, in exchange, the work is made available to a wider audience. And because the impairments with respect to the original are no worse than the impairment as a result of an outright transfer of the tangible medium itself, it is safe to say that such DRM could be implemented by the copyright owner in a way that withstands rule-of-reason scrutiny.

Nevertheless, even this technology could be abused. For example, if the copyright owner were to authorize and enable the use of such DRM to facilitate forward-and-delete or check-in/check-out models, one would anticipate a great temptation on the part of the copyright owner to charge for the privilege through cash payments, data mining, or the like. Perhaps, for example, the DRM would require that the identity of the sender and the recipient be disclosed to the copyright owner or its designee in order to function. In such case, rule-of-reason scrutiny might find the balance tipped the other way because the right is being leveraged into an entirely new market—the data-mining market.

But let's consider two other models, one in which a third party (a library or a retailer, for example) employs the DRM to imitate lawful transactions in the physical world and does so outside the control of the copyright holder, and another in which consumers employ "off-the-shelf" DRM to perform these automated tasks. Perhaps, for example, someone develops software that will automate the deletion after forwarding and keep an audit trail of proof. Or software is developed to ensure that one single decryption key is available to any one user no matter how many encrypted copies are reproduced. In such circumstances, there is no concern for enlargement of the copyright (because it is persons acting independently of the copyright owner who employ them), and any anticompetitive concerns are minimized by the fact that anyone else with a lawful copy may step in to supply a more positive consumer experience. In all, it might be safe to say that automated forward-and-delete or check-in/check-out DRM technology employed by persons other than the copyright holder could be considered good DRM, but for the possibility that the users of it might be guilty of copyright infringement.

I say "possibility" because it is not at all a certainty that such conduct would be infringing. The reason it has not been tested may have more to do with the high-stakes risk in the event a court disagrees, but courts in the United States and in Canada have ruled, in very analogous "analog" fact patterns, that transfer of the work from one medium to another using a technology that leaves only one copy at the end of the process is not a reproduction at all. That is, these courts did not base their holdings on any fair-use rights but, rather, on a finding that the processes used did not infringe the reproduction right in the first instance. In the United States, the defendant in *C.M. Paula Co. v. Logan*[72] had used "acrylic resin, emulsions, or similar compounds which act as the transfer medium to strip the printed indicia from the original surface on which it is printed, whereupon the image carrying film is applied to another article."[73] The court concluded that "such process is not a 'reproduction or duplication.'"[74]

> Each ceramic plaque sold by defendant with a Paula print affixed thereto requires the purchase and use of an individual piece of artwork marketed by the plaintiff. For example, should defendant desire to make one hundred ceramic plaques using the identical Paula print, defendant would be required to purchase one hundred separate Paula prints. The

Court finds that the process here in question does not constitute copying.[75]

The *C.M. Paula* court may well be on to something. The Copyright Act itself defines "copies" as "material objects, other than phonorecords, in which a work is fixed by any method now known or later developed, *and from which the work can be perceived, reproduced, or otherwise communicated*, either directly or with the aid of a machine or device" (emphasis added).[76] By definition, therefore, an inaccessible copy is not a "copy." Moreover, because the exclusive right of reproduction is limited to the right "to reproduce the copyrighted work in copies or phonorecords," it is not unreasonable to conclude that an alleged "reproduction" that cannot be "perceived, reproduced, or otherwise communicated" is not a reproduction at all under the meaning of the Copyright Act. That is, one can reasonably conclude that the act of reproducing a work into copies and phonorecords must, by definition, result in at least one additional perceivable, reproducible, or otherwise communicable copy.

The Supreme Court of Canada has also adopted this view. In *Théberge v. Galerie d'Art du Petit Champlain, Inc.*,[77] it arrived at the same legal conclusion as did the *C.M. Paula* court, on very similar facts and using a logic that is entirely consistent with the United States Copyright Act. In that case, the court concluded that by transferring authorized reproductions from a paper support to a canvas support for purposes of resale did not involve making a copy of the work infringing the right of reproduction.

> They purchased lawfully reproduced posters of his paintings and used a chemical process that allowed them to lift the ink layer from the paper (leaving it blank) and to display it on canvas. They were within their rights to do so as owners of the physical posters (which lawfully incorporated the copyrighted expression). At the end of the day, no new reproductions of the respondent's works were brought into existence. Nor, in my view, was there production (or reproduction) of a new artistic work "in any material form" within the meaning of s. 3(1) of the [Canadian] *Copyright Act*. What began as a poster, authorized by the respondent, remained a poster.[78]

It may be but a matter of time before courts in the United States and Canada are faced with a claim for infringement of the right of reproduction through the use of a technology that takes the bits from one digital medium ("leaving it blank") and places them on another medium or "backing." If, at the end of the day, no additional copy exists, it seems reasonable to believe that the courts could follow these nondigital precedents and conclude that consumers are free to use software that "transfers the bits to a new tangible medium" without infringing the right of reproduction because a single copy remains.

> As we would expect from the very word "*copy*right", "reproduction" is usually defined as the act of producing *additional* or *new* copies of the work in *any material form*. Multiplication of the copies would be a necessary consequence of this physical concept of "reproduction."[79]

Before that day comes, copyright holders may be wise to allow retailers, libraries, consumers, and any other independent intermediary to unleash competition in the transfer of the bits from one medium to another in a manner imitating the characteristics of redistribution authorized by Section 109(a), using robust DRM technology that is reasonably immune from abuse. If they fail to allow even robust DRM to be used in this positive way, they may learn the hard way that the courts are prepared to find noninfringement when less secure methods are used to achieve the same outcome.

To summarize this rather lengthy discourse, space-shifting technology allows for the "content" to be moved from one medium to another:

• If such conduct constitutes copyright infringement, copyright owners may authorize it.

  o Like any authorized reproduction, DRM technology that enforces lawful limitations on the license to reproduce the copy or phonorecord may be used.

  o But because the original and the second copy are both authorized, they are both lawfully made, and the provisions of Section 109 (and the first-sale doctrine in general) might apply.

  o Similarly, because the right to perform a work privately does not belong to the copyright owner, rendering one copy inaccessible would enlarge the copyright.

  o Accordingly, whether the copyright owner's use of DRM to permit reproduction on a second medium provided that the first reproduction is destroyed or rendered inaccessible necessarily burdens trade and enlarges the copyright. It is, therefore, necessary to assess whether these burdens are outweighed by the benefits of DRM-enabled space shifting.

• If space shifting is not infringing because no "new" copy is made, then the owners of the original copy may freely use DRM technology to enable such conduct.[80]

o Copyright owners who use the DRM to facilitate such noninfringing use would be providing a public service, but those who use DRM to prevent or burden such noninfringing use might be guilty of unilaterally enlarging their copyright monopoly beyond its scope, or worse, entering into agreements in unreasonable restraint of trade.

o Persons other than the copyright owners who use such space-shifting DRM technology for noninfringing purposes would be furthering the public policy objectives of copyright law. To the degree that any of them used it in a way that burdened redistribution, others could be expected to step forward and provide a more competitive and less burdensome service.

Because copyright owners will be limited in what they can do to restrict space shifting, and because the jury is still out on whether narrow space shifting may be beyond their control as a matter of law, copyright holders would be better served by encouraging libraries, retailers, and even consumers to freely employ robust space-shifting DRM technologies that are easy and transparent for the users while preventing abuses wherein copies are, in fact, multiplied.

Pure Copyright Protection

Several methods have been used to prevent unlawful reproductions of copyrighted works. Even when the sole purpose of the DRM is to prevent "unauthorized" reproductions, the problem is that reproductions that are unauthorized by the copyright owner may nevertheless be authorized by law. Such is the case of a reproduction made for fair use,[81] ephemeral recordings,[82] certain reproductions of computer programs,[83] or reproductions for the vision impaired.[84] Because DRM technology is generally not sufficiently sophisticated to distinguish whether a particular reproduction attempt is authorized by law, we can assume that copy-protection technology will, in general, impair the ability to make lawful reproductions authorized by law. Courts have yet to deal with this issue, but if we apply the rule of reason to the impairment of reproduction rights reserved to the public, it may be possible to determine whether the impairment is tolerable in light of other benefits to be gained by copy-protection DRM.

One of the first examples of copy-protection technology was the Serial Copy Management System,[85] which must be incorporated into certain new audio recording technology pursuant to the Audio Home Recording Rights Act. Because digital reproduction is virtually identical to the original, there was fear that multiple-generation copies would proliferate much faster than for analog reproductions (which degrade with each generation of copying), thereby impairing the right of reproduction. In imposing DRM technology by statute to prevent serial copying, Congress was careful to preserve the ability of the public to make noninfringing reproductions.[86] The Serial Copy Management System applied only to digital reproductions and did not interfere with the ability to make the first reproduction. Moreover, even infringing reproductions of sound recordings would be immune from prosecution,[87] as the act provided a means of compensation to the copyright owners to offset the anticipated economic impact from lost sales.[88] Thus, rather than impose a DRM to prevent all reproductions, the act provided that the DRM would prevent only certain types of reproductions and provided a safety valve to ensure that other reproductions could be made even more easily.[89] The act is, therefore, self-balancing.

Another example of copy-control technology that could pass muster here is the Macrovision encryption of certain motion pictures. Although it cannot properly be called DRM when applied only to analog (e.g., videocassette) copies, it is also used in the digital environment. Macrovision is intended to degrade the picture quality when a second-generation reproduction is made, yet it does not interfere with the consumer's ability to record over-the-air analog broadcasts of audiovisual works.[90] And as long as reproductions without degradation are readily available, the ability to make fair use of the work is generally preserved, impacting perhaps only a few very specialized applications. The content scrambling system (CSS) used on DVDs through agreement with the hardware manufacturers prevents reproductions, but it is more of a speed bump than a technology that would prevent fair use or other reproductions authorized by law because movies are typically available in other usable formats.[91] Although there may be disagreement as to how balanced such a DRM use is, the primary purpose is to prevent infringing copies of DVDs from being made and sold, and its impact on other lawful uses has, so far, been rather miniscule.

More recently, record companies have begun experimenting with new copy-protection technology to prevent CD-quality reproductions. There has been some controversy concerning the legality of preventing the very reproductions for which copyright owners are receiving royalties via taxes on hardware and blank media, but the response of the music industry has been to experiment with multiple reproductions on a single medium, enabling, for example, the reproduction of a compressed version while impairing the reproduction of the uncompressed version.[92]

Implementation of Legitimate License Terms
Copyright owners do have certain exclusive rights and are entitled to license them to others. Use of DRM to facilitate the licensing could generally be considered good, but we can treat as bad those uses of DRM that go further

than necessary to implement the copyright license by seeking agreement to (or simply enforcing) terms that may be anticompetitive or impose restrictions beyond the scope of the copyright.

An example from the early days of digital downloading is Universal Music Group's failed Blue Matter venture. Before being permitted to exercise the licensed right of reproduction to download a UMG song, consumers had to agree to an end-user license agreement (EULA) in which they promised never to exercise their statutory right to sell the copies legally made under UMG's license.[93] It purported to create a "right to use" the downloaded music[94] and prohibited the user from allowing others to play the legally made copies (phonorecords), even upon the licensee's death. Curiously, in the course of trying to prevent certain uses by agreement, the UMG license also expressly granted the right to make several copies, albeit subject to an agreement not to transfer possession to anyone else. Had UMG remained silent, a consumer making a reproduction and then selling it could have been prosecuted for copyright infringement. As a result of the UMG license, however, the consumer was authorized to make two MP3 copies and two copies onto CDs. These copies, having been lawfully made, could be distributed without the consent of the copyright owner pursuant to section 109 of the Copyright Act. UMG's DRM-required EULA purported to require relinquishment of a federal entitlement as condition of obtaining the license to reproduce the work, thereby enlarging the copyright holder's control. The consumer was free to sell the legal copies without risk of copyright infringement liability but might have had to argue (in defense of a breach of contract claim) that the EULA provisions were void as against public policy.[95]

This is but one example of myriad possible iterations of DRM technology through which the copyright owner may intend to protect its copyrights while carrying out legitimate licensing agreements that help further disseminate the work but fail, in that process, to respect the countervailing rights outside the copyright—rights reserved to the public. Here again, if the DRM (or EULA to which the DRM requires agreement) serves to enlarge the copyright power beyond its statutory limits, to infringe upon nonexclusive rights reserved to the public, or to restrain trade, it is incumbent upon courts and law enforcement officials to weigh whether such harms are outweighed by resulting benefits and to determine whether the harms are no greater than necessary to achieve the identified benefits.

DRM to Enable New Business Models

The major copyright-holding companies often refer to new business models they wish to develop using DRM. These models typically involve copyright expansionism and restraints of trade discussed below, reverse infringement by use of DRM technology to enlarge the reach of the copyright and suppress competition in aftermarkets. When it comes to reproduction and distribution of copies to the masses, systems controlled by the copyright owner are likely to pale in comparison to competitive offerings. For example, in the music industry, major retailers were ready, willing, and able to offer downloads before Napster ever came along to fill the demand with a nonmonetized, peer-to-peer delivery system. These retailers complained that the record companies would not license to them the reproduction rights they needed to offer these downloads or, if they did, the licenses came with restrictions beyond simply naming a wholesale price and requiring accountability and some level of security.[96]

At the time the record companies were refusing to allow music retailers to compete, they were entering into joint ventures with each other, tied to two brands of media players (one camp supporting Microsoft's player and the other RealNetworks' player). These services were based on distorting copyrights by licensing a reproduction at no charge, but charging for noninfringing private performances of the lawful reproductions. This so-called subscription service is equivalent to a book publisher charging people for the right to read books they own. Although DRM-controlled new business models run by joint ventures of major copyright-holding companies may be anticompetitive for a number of reasons, that is not to say that individual copyright owners could not, acting independently, make creative and lawful uses of DRM that would result in new positive business models. And if third parties are offered licenses to sublicense works in competition with each other and on a nondiscriminatory basis, we could expect unlimited innovation. Any speculation in this paper as to all possible models would certainly fail to predict many new types of business ventures that could be created by relying on DRM technology that facilitates competitive offerings rather than suffocating innovation by keeping vertical control within a copyright holder's clenched fist. But a quick glimpse at the future may nevertheless be useful.

DRM would, for example, be helpful in facilitating any number of creative ways of fighting to gain and keep customers: guaranteed quality of downloads, buy two downloads and get the third free, buy a pizza and download a movie at half price, hear music you like at the record store and have it waiting for you on your home hard drive by the time you get home, switch from a competitor's media player to ours and get ten downloads free or get a free top-of-the-line media player after ten downloads, come to retailer A because it offers a turnkey system good for people who know little about computers or come to retailer B because it is designed for those who want to mix and match the operating systems, codecs (compression/decompression algorithms), media players, rippers and file organizers of their choice.

Some business models might even push copyright law to its limits or require clarifying litigation or enabling legislation to facilitate. The point is not to cover every future business model but, rather, to underscore that for most of them to be viable, some form of DRM technology will probably be essential. It may be as simple as recognizing the source of your file (such as digital "watermarking") so that the person who complains that the download contained imperfections can prove that it came from source A rather than source B or that the person getting the third download free actually paid for the first two. Whether DRM used to enable these new business models is good, bad, or ugly is going to depend more on the character of the business model itself than on the structure of the DRM code. Most important, however, is the principle that DRM use will tend to be best if it enables the development of competing business models in which independent businesses compete (i.e., competing channels, each populated by independent competitors). At the ugliest extreme would be joint ventures among copyright-holding companies with a narrow selection of business models in which there is no real competition.[97]

Ugly Uses of DRM

Some uses of DRM have the sole purpose and effect of expanding the scope of the copyright, through technology, to give the copyright owner control over noninfringing uses. Ugly DRM is the kind that has little to do with managing or protecting copyrights, as its primary purpose is to unlawfully extend the scope of the copyright holder's control beyond the limits of copyright.

Examples of ugly DRM are technologies that tether legal copies to specific hardware or a specific user so that the market for lawful redistribution of those copies is eliminated. DRM that enables copyright holders to extend their copyright monopoly into control over the markets for codecs and media players is also very ugly, as there is absolutely no valid reason why copyright holders must condition the licensing of a reproduction or public performance on the use of any specific technology among many technologies that protect copyrights from infringement equally well. Another example is that of the timed-out copy (also known as the limited download) that has the sole purpose of preventing the continued lawful, noninfringing private performance of a work, like printing books in disappearing ink so that they cannot be reread or sold in the used book market. Because copyright owners have no exclusive right to perform any of their works privately (including stolen or pirated copies), any DRM that gives them control over private performances from lawful copies is downright ugly and should result in criminal penalties.

There are three broad categories of ugly uses of DRM. First, DRM may leverage the strength of the copyright to gain control over markets outside the copyright. Examples of this might be use of the copyright as a tool for data mining (requiring the disclosure of private consumer data, in addition to cash, as a condition of allowing access to the work); monitoring lawful noninfringing activity, such as reporting back the number of private performances made of the work; or using the copyright to give a competitive advantage with respect to another product, such as a media player, operating system, or proprietary compression format. I will address examples under the heading of copyright tying, not in the narrow antitrust sense, but in a broader sense peculiar to copyrights and recognized by the Supreme Court sixty years ago.

The second category includes DRM uses that seek to gain control over a right not belonging to the copyright owner, such as gaining control over the right to perform the work privately, a right that, as noted earlier, is excluded from the copyright. This category is discussed under the heading of limited download.

Finally, there are those uses of DRM that simply constitute bare restraints on trade by eliminating all legitimate competition in the sale and rental of lawful copies. The heading for this discussion is simply "Eliminating Competition." The limited download also has this effect, so these two categories should not be considered in isolation.

Copyright Tying

In the 1940s, the U.S. Supreme Court in *United States v. Paramount Pictures*[98] struck down the "block-booking" practices of motion picture studios. By refusing to license one or more copyrighted movies unless another undesired copyrighted movie was accepted, they sought to leverage the copyright in the desirable movie into power in the market for the less desirable. The court's reasoning should apply equally well to efforts to leverage the copyright into control over any matter outside the copyright. That is, if it is illegal to use the copyright in one work to tie in acceptance of an undesired second copyrighted work, it should be no less illegal to use the copyrights in several works to tie in acceptance of an undesired computer operating system, codec software, or media player. The court found the practice analogous to unlawful "tying" under pure antitrust analysis, but because the tying works were copyrighted, there was no need to perform a full antitrust analysis. Rather, the leveraging of a lawful copyright monopoly in this manner was sufficient to condemn it. The court stated:

> Where a high quality film greatly desired is licensed only if an inferior one is taken, the latter borrows quality from the former and strengthens its monopoly by drawing on the other. The practice tends to equalize rather than differentiate the reward for the individual copyrights. Even where all the films included in the package are of equal quality, the requirement that all be taken if one is desired increases the market for some. Each stands not on its own footing but in whole or in part on the appeal which another film may have. As the District Court said, the result is to add to the monopoly of the copyright in violation of the principle of the patent cases involving tying clauses.[99]

In *United States v. Loew's, Inc.,*[100] the U.S. Supreme Court once again condemned block booking, this time in relation to the licensing of motion picture films for televised performances. And again, the ruling diverged from traditional antitrust analysis by giving special attention to the importance of keeping the copyright holder's competitive actions limited to the exercise of exclusive rights in each individual copyrighted work. The court simply saw that use of a copyright to gain an advantage in relation to transactions beyond the scope of the individual copyright is unlawful.

Pure antitrust law relates to competition alone, but a copyright holder's restraints on trade also must take into account the public policy concerns relating to copyrights. The Copyright Act conveys legal, but very limited, monopolies over certain activity in exchange for additional limitations that would not apply where a product is not copyrighted. Therefore, the tying of the copyright to something outside the copyright is a misuse of the lawful monopoly. It avoids the Copyright Act's limitations and results in both an expansion of the individual copyright and a restraint in the market for the product or service outside the copyright. Thus, any use of the copyright monopoly to exercise control beyond the bounds of the lawful monopoly must be unlawful.

For example, under the Copyright Act, the person who downloads a movie under license from the copyright owner owns that copy and has the right to give it away, sell it, or lend it. Are copyright holders free to nullify those rights by conditioning the license to download on waiver of the federal entitlement to redistribute the copy without the copyright holder's consent? Because the rights of owners are part of the Copyright Act, and part of the trade-off of being granted certain exclusive rights in exchange for certain limitations, it should be clear that copyright holders have no right to prevent the owners of lawfully made copies from disposing of them lawfully. Similarly, because the right to perform the work privately is beyond the scope of the copyright, conditioning a license of the right of reproduction upon the licensee's agreement to use only the tied operating system, codec, or media player in conjunction with the reproduction and private performance of the work would appear to be unlawful on its face.

The Supreme Court's long-standing disapproval of such copyright tying has its roots in similar patent tying. In 1917, it explored the issue of private enlargement of the patent from an intellectual property law premise rather than as a mere antitrust concern. In *Motion Picture Patents Co. v. Universal Film Mfg. Co.*,[101] it determined that the owner of a patented motion picture film projector could not lawfully use a licensing mechanism to obligate purchasers of the machine to use it solely with motion pictures licensed under another patent (an expired patent, no less) that the company also owned.

> A restriction which would give to the plaintiff such a potential power for evil over an industry which must be recognized as an important element in the amusement life of the nation, under the conclusions we have stated in this opinion, is plainly void, because wholly without the scope and purpose of our patent laws, and because, if sustained, it would be gravely injurious to that public interest, which we have seen is more a favorite of the law than is the promotion of private fortunes.[102]

Although the exercise of exclusive rights conferred by patent law could not be unlawful in themselves, the Supreme Court concluded that the exclusive right of use could not be employed as a tool to expand the scope of the patent and that "it is not competent for the owner of a patent, by notice attached to its machine, to, in effect, extend the scope of its patent monopoly by restricting the use of it to materials necessary in its operation, but which are no part of the patented invention, or to send its machines forth into the channels of trade of the country subject to conditions as to use."[103]

The relevance to copyrights of the Supreme Court's analysis in *Motion Picture Patents Co.* is inescapable. If it is unlawful to extend the statutory monopoly by limiting the use of a patented motion picture projector to products beyond the scope of the projector patent, it stands to reason that it is equally unlawful to condition the licensing of copyrighted works upon the consumer's use of the computer operating system, codec, or media player designated by the copyright owner or upon relinquishment of statutory rights of the licensee. By agreeing to license rights the legislature gave to the copyright owner, such as the right to perform a work publicly or to reproduce it into copies, only in conjunction with the licensee's agreement to use specified access controls, codecs, digital media players, or operating systems, the copyright owner is using the rights conferred by the legislature to bargain for rights denied to the copyright owner by the same legislature. In the process, the limited copyright monopoly is enlarged and competition in the related goods and services is diminished. This is particularly true when the owner of the copyrighted motion pictures also owns an interest, through either direct investment or a joint venture, in the exploitation of the intellectual property associated with the tied technologies.

But the law did not stand still in 1917. From this premise, the courts continued to develop a unique theory of misuse of intellectual property compatible with, but independent of, traditional antitrust law. In *Morton Salt Co. v G.S. Suppiger Co.*,[104] for example, the U.S. Supreme Court examined the appellate court's approval of the use of the patent monopoly in a machine for depositing salt tablets to force licensees to use only salt tablets manufactured by the patent holder. The appellate court had reasoned that, under traditional antitrust law, "it did not appear that the use of its patent substantially lessened competition or tended to create a monopoly in salt tablets."[105] The Supreme Court reversed on grounds of patent misuse and concluded that, having done so, it was unnecessary to decide whether the antitrust statute itself had also been violated.[106]

> [t]he public policy which includes inventions within the granted monopoly excludes from it all that is not embraced in the invention. It equally forbids the use of the patent to secure an exclusive right or limited monopoly not granted by the Patent Office and which it is contrary to public policy to grant.[107]

Thus, even though misuse of intellectual property rights is consistent with antitrust theory, the misuse claim was viewed as independent of the antitrust claim. And this line of reasoning is not limited to patents. The *Morton Salt* ruling noted with approval the application of this doctrine to copyrights.[108] In *Paramount Pictures*, the Supreme Court further explained the limitations on copyright power in the context of "block booking."[109] It approved of the lower court's reasoning, which was based not only on the illegality of the restraint as a matter of competition law, but also for reasons based squarely on the U.S. Constitution and Copyright Act:

> The District Court held it illegal for that [traditional antitrust law] reason and for the reason that it "adds to the monopoly of a single copyrighted picture that of another copyrighted picture which must be taken and exhibited in order to secure the first." That enlargement of the monopoly of the copyright was condemned below in reliance on the principle which forbids the owner of a patent to condition its use on the purchase or use of patented or unpatented materials.[110]

Based on these principles, the doctrine of copyright misuse has developed as both a violation of antitrust law and an affirmative defense against copyright infringement when the copyright holder, by means of an overreaching license or other method of control, tries "to secure an exclusive right or limited monopoly not granted by the [Copyright] Office and which it is contrary to public policy to grant."[111]

Although some have questioned whether a pure copyright misuse claim may be pled affirmatively, the U.S. Supreme Court has shown no such reluctance. *Paramount Pictures*[112] and *Loew's*[113] did not involve separate claims for copyright misuse but were antitrust cases. They arguably could have served to limit copyright misuse to just another label for a type of conduct unlawful under traditional antitrust law.[114] Nevertheless, they find copyright tying unlawful precisely because the tying products were copyrighted. As the Supreme Court later explained in the "Betamax"[115] case,

> The Court of Appeals' holding that respondents are entitled to enjoin the distribution of [video tape recorders], to collect royalties on the sale of such equipment, or to obtain other relief, if affirmed, would enlarge the scope of respondents' statutory monopolies to encompass control over an article of commerce that is not the subject of copyright protection. Such an expansion of the copyright privilege is beyond the limits of the grants authorized by Congress.[116]

If not even the Supreme Court could authorize such enlargement of the copyright monopoly as a remedy for instances of clear copyright infringement, certainly the copyright owner is not permitted to use the antipiracy veil as a reason to enlarge its own copyright power.

Moreover, it is not necessary to establish market power in the manner of ordinary products because "either uniqueness or consumer appeal" of the product is sufficient to establish unlawful tying.[117] "This is even more obviously true when the tying product is patented or copyrighted."[118] To viewers, "there is but one '*Gone With The Wind*,'"[119] and the use of it to force others to take a less desired film, to install and use an unwanted media player, to confer upon the copyright owner the power to meter out wholly private performances, or to relinquish a federal entitlement to sell or rent the downloaded copy, is unlawful precisely because the appeal of a copyrighted film is being used to enlarge the power and scope of the copyright in that film and gain control over market decisions pertaining to lawful noninfringing activity.

These legal foundations remain viable today and have been expanded beyond the tying of other copyrighted works. For example, in *MCA Television Ltd. v. Public Interest Corp.*,[120] the Eleventh Circuit relied on these cases where the copyright owner was not leveraging a copyrighted work to force a second work on an unwilling buyer, but instead, was using the copyrighted work to force certain economic terms on the *willing* buyer of the second work. Although the issue came to the court as an antitrust counterclaim in a contract dispute, the court's analysis was substantively one of pure copyright law, as it expanded the reach of the *Loew's* and *Paramount* cases beyond mere block booking to cover the conditioning of a license of desired works (various television programs) on accepting *another desired work (Harry and the Hendersons)* for partial payment in cash rather than barter.

The applicability of *MCA Television* to the use of DRM technology is inescapable. Indeed, if unwanted business terms in contractual agreements would not pass muster, DRM technologies that foist those terms upon the other party without any bargaining opportunity must be even more deficient. For example, competing retailers and consumers may desire all of the copyrighted works being offered and also may desire to use certain operating systems, media players, codecs, or "good" DRM technologies that compete with those to which the copyrighted works are tied.[121]

Finally, it should be noted that this is not a mere exercise in legal theory. Copyright holders (at least those who have aggregated a sufficiently large stable of copyrights to avoid being ignored) have already shown a propensity for using the power of the demand for their copyrighted works to dictate ties to products and services of their choice. Sony was one of the first to tie its music to its hardware and proprietary software, eschewing the popular MP3 format in favor of its own ATRAC3 format.[122] Individual record companies attempted to dictate the winners and losers in the digital delivery marketplace. Joint ventures among major record companies and movie studios have seen fit to eliminate competition among related products and services by dealing exclusively with persons who select their chosen operating systems, codecs, and media players.[123]

Although Apple gained initial notoriety by tying its music downloading service to its iPod hardware, Apple is not the copyright owner, so presumably it is not extending anyone's copyrights into the market for portable music players.[124] Until the major record companies begin allowing all traditional music retailers to compete with Apple by offering them the same "wholesale" prices for downloads and allowing each to decide which codecs, media players, and hardware systems to support, the public may never learn just how easy and inexpensive it can be to enjoy downloaded music.

Timing Out for Private Gain: The Limited Download
In the eyes of copyright law, a "limited download" is the same as a store-bought copy in every respect, except that it has not been distributed.[125] Yet, more sophisticated DRM can be used when allowing the consumer to re-produce the copies at home, one at a time, for a specific computer operating system and media player, than when it is being reproduced by the thousands or millions at a factory for distribution to people with different operating systems and media players. When hardware manufacturers must somehow be persuaded to inject complexities into the devices that will give copyright owners greater control over what consumers can do, extreme behavior is likely to be somewhat muted. But when "software-side" DRM can exploit features of a particular hardware or operating system platform, the countervailing interest of hardware manufacturers can be disregarded. The copyright owner's only limitations are the limits of its own ingenuity. Thus, DRM that is dependent only on computer software at the disposal of the copyright owner is likely to be used much more aggressively. It is also likely to be uglier.

Such has been the case in several efforts by copyright owners to gain control over the public right of private performance. The most recent has been through Microsoft Corporation's "Janus" DRM, a new version of its DRM for the Windows Media Player.[126] The new DRM would limit the length of time or number of times that the owner of a legally downloaded copy of a work could perform it privately (i.e., play the music, movie, or game, or read an electronic book). As explained above, no copyright owner has the exclusive right to perform a work privately. This DRM, both in purpose and in effect, would empower the copyright owner that uses it to claim that right by might.[127]

Microsoft has been skillfully spinning this limitation as just the opposite. Instead of acknowledging that the DRM would place limitations on the uses of lawfully downloaded works that Congress has entitled the public to exploit without limitation from the copyright owner, or admitting that what Microsoft is actually offering is greater monopoly power to the copyright owner to limit the uses to which the public is entitled by law, Microsoft is pitching this devastating blow to the public's statutory rights as "good for you." The Microsoft press release quotes a Disney executive calling it "a positive development in the continuing effort to provide consumers with more choices for enjoying legitimate entertainment content on emerging digital platforms." In reality, the DRM gives copyright owners more choices for gaining control over lawful noninfringing activity, such as private performances, rentals, gifts, sales, or lending.

One of the "new" freedoms is supposedly the ability to "rent" downloaded copies. The term "rental" has never meant having to pay for the freedom to enjoy your own property. This is the equivalent of letting copyright owners charge bookstore patrons for reading a book twice.

Copyright owners enjoy an exclusive right of public performance but do not have an exclusive right of private performance.[128]

> The Copyright Act does not give a copyright holder control over all uses of his copyrighted work. Instead, [Section 106] of the Act enumerates several "rights" that are made "exclusive" to the holder of the copyright. If a person, without authorization from the copyright holder, puts a copyrighted work to a use within the scope of one of these "exclusive rights," he infringes the copyright. If he puts the work to a use not enumerated in [Section 106], he does not infringe.[129]

Thanks to the Microsoft DRM, however, copyright owners can obtain for themselves an exclusive right of private performance over copies owned by those who legally downloaded them.[130]

Although Section 202 of the Copyright Act makes clear that the copyright holder's copyrights in the work are distinct from the owner's rights in lawful copies of the work, the new Microsoft DRM would enable copyright owners to pretend that ownership of the copy has no bearing. Ironically, this would run counter to the position, vigorously defended by copyright owners when it was to their benefit—a tax benefit—to do so. In testimony before Congress addressing the question of whether the delivery of content of e-commerce networks should be considered trade in goods or trade in services, or both, the MPAA insisted that downloaded copies be treated just like physical copies, giving this example:

> If a consumer were to place a telephone order for a DVD of the film "Finding Forrester" and have a copy of that DVD delivered to his house on a UPS truck, that is a "goods" transaction. Likewise, if the same consumer ordering a copy of the same DVD on his/her computer and had the same content delivered digitally and downloaded from his computer to a write-able DVD—that is still a "goods" transaction. The only difference is that a digital network instead of a delivery van provided the transportation from the retailer to the consumer.[131]

The MPAA maintains that the digital nature of the delivery does not change the character of what is, in substance, still a physical "goods" transaction, and rightly so. The only thing that has changed is the location of the manufacturing facility—from a large factory to an individual's home. Yet, with the advent of Microsoft's new tool for, in effect, sending an agent along with the delivery truck to prevent the owner from enjoying the work as Congress intended unless the copyright owner is paid again, at least two members of the Motion Picture Association—Disney and Time Warner—appear to have abandoned their principled position in exchange for one favoring exploitation of copyright expansionism enabled by use of Microsoft's new DRM technology.

To illustrate why copyright owners should not be permitted to gain control over private performances using Microsoft's new DRM for so-called rental business models, let's consider what would happen if the copyright owner were to engage in a true rental business model. The copyright owner would reproduce copies or phonorecords and rent them to consumers. All it would be doing is transferring possession of the disc (not ownership), with no transfer at all of any copyrights. Yet, the renter would be free to play the work as many times as desired, without any limitation other than the expiration of the rental period, at which time the return of the disc to its owner, the copyright owner, would make it impossible to continue performing the work. But if the renter fails to return the disc when due and continues to perform the work after the right of possession has expired, such private performances would infringe no copyright. The copyright owner's only recourse would be for late fees—a simple breach of the rental agreement. If we consider, in contrast, a downloaded copy, owned lock, stock, and barrel by the consumer, it is evident that, just as with the rental copy, the copyright owner has no claim under law to prevent the private performance of the work, and because no rental is involved, there is no obligation to return anything to the copyright owner (as the copyright owner has never even owned the copy in question). The public policy foundation of the Copyright Act is to encourage all uses short of infringement.[132] The use by the copyright owner of Microsoft's DRM to limit noninfringing use constitutes a major expansion of copyright power by technological fiat.

Finally, it would be shortsighted to focus solely on the copyright owners of the works to which the Microsoft DRM would be applied. What is in this for Microsoft? The payoff for agreeing to implement the restraints on secondary markets and expansion of the copyright into the realm of private performances is that Microsoft's Windows Media Player would be designated as the sole "supported" media player. In exchange for Microsoft assisting in the ugly DRM effort, the copyright owners force the consumer to use Microsoft's Windows Media Player. Consumers who wish lawfully to download copies of copyrighted works and perform them privately on a more competitive media player of their choice will find that they are unable to do so. They may be able to use any number of media players for some works but still have to use Microsoft's product to gain access to those works whose copyright owners chose to enter this agreement with Microsoft to restrain trade in secondhand products and extract payment for (or control over) noninfringing private performances.

Eliminating Competition
The first-sale doctrine is codified in section 109 of the Copyright Act, which states in 109(a) that notwithstanding the copyright owner's section 106(3) right of distribution, the owner of a lawfully made copy "is entitled, without the authority of the copyright owner, to sell or otherwise dispose of the possession of that copy." Section 202 establishes that the owner of the copy doesn't necessarily control the section 106 rights and the owner of the section 106 rights does not necessarily control the copy. The intellectual property interest and the physical property interest are separate (and, as we have seen above, the intellectual property interest does not extend to noninfringing uses, such as the always noninfringing private performance or display of a work). If, through use of DRM technology, however, the owner of the intellectual property interest can gain control over the tangible property interest, the copyright owner could nullify section 202's distinction, nullify section 109(a)'s entitlement to part with ownership or possession of the tangible me-

dium without the copyright owner's consent, and nullify the public's freedom to perform the work privately from any copy.

In the two previous sections, we have seen that it is unlawful to leverage the copyright monopoly into control over rights, products, or services that are not part of the copyright being leveraged and that it is improper to interfere with the public's right to perform works privately. Although it may be the case that such burdens are but unintended collateral damage in an effort to protect copyrights or enhance dissemination, when the purpose and effect of a given DRM is to eliminate lawful competition, the practice should be condemned per se. Unfortunately, the practice is becoming more widespread.

As we saw in reviewing use of DRM to "time out" access to works, thereby rendering them incapable of being performed privately, some such limitations might be positive, as when it facilitates and encourages more reproductions,[133] and other limitations may be tolerable under the right circumstances.[134] In some instances, in contrast, the sole purpose of using DRM technology to make a work inaccessible for private performances is to eliminate competition from the lawful secondary markets involving redistribution of the work. (The same purpose and result may be achieved by "tethering" a particular copy to a device, such that it is only accessible for private performance if it is present with the device, such that it cannot be fruitfully sold, lent, or given away apart from the hardware.)

May the monopoly power of copyright, however limited, be used to gain control over distribution of a work after the distribution right has been terminated by law? May the copyright holder use technological devices to destroy competition in the market for used copies of its works, including commerce by sale, rental, gift, or lending? As noted above,[135] the answer is straightforward: "A copyright owner may not enforce its copyright to violate the antitrust laws or indeed use it in any 'manner violative of the public policy embodied in the grant of a copyright.'"[136]

Some of the motion picture studios have made no secret of their desire to leverage copyright and market power into control over the distribution markets, particularly video rental stores. One could argue that if copyright holders are too restrictive, their sales will be impacted and they will make adjustments. But such a view ignores two basic principles.

First, copyrights are monopolies. There are no substitutes for the works in greatest demand. Competition in the delivery of copyrighted works occurs primarily at levels of distribution below the copyright owner. For example, if consumers are dissatisfied with terms and conditions imposed by the retail seller, they can look to competing retailers for satisfaction. Even though each retailer may pay the same wholesale price for copies of the work, they can compete on all terms and conditions of the sale to attract customers. If, however, the copyright owner can impose uniform terms and conditions that all retailers must honor, there would be no alternative source offering better terms and conditions for the same product.

To illustrate, if one retailer were to make each customer sign a EULA stating that they will not let anyone else watch the movie, read the book, or listen to the CD, or agreeing to destroy the copy after reading or playing it, a consumer who objects to those terms needs only go to a competing retailer. If, on the other hand, the copyright owner imposes those very same restrictions on a copy by use of technology or EULAs, every retailer will be forced to pass those restrictions on to the consumer and the competitive benefits the consumer might enjoy are lost. Moreover, because each copyrighted work is unique, there is not likely to be a satisfactory market substitute for the work. For example, even among popular films, a consumer wanting to watch *The Matrix Reloaded* is not likely to substitute *Spy Sorge* just because the price is better or because he or she does not like the restrictions the copyright owner placed on the film. Plus, if there is independent demand for *Spy Sorge* and *The Matrix Reloaded*, buying, renting, or watching one is not going to reduce the desire to buy, rent, or watch the other.

Second, because of the uniqueness of each copyrighted work, there is little true competition among the major motion picture studios for consumer loyalty. That is, they attempt to draw consumers to demand a particular movie title, but not to demand a particular movie studio. With few exceptions, consumers are oblivious to which studio owns the copyright in a motion picture. When a group of friends decides to watch a movie, they may discuss which genre of film they want to watch, which theater or video rental store they will go to, and which specific movie title they can agree on, but it would be very unusual to discuss which copyright owner's works to patronize. The same is true for books: A person walking into any bookstore may find books organized by author, by title, by genre, but rarely by publisher. Music stores organize CDs by artist or by genre, but not by record label. Movies, likewise, depend on independent aggregators who present them to consumers based on genre or title, not by copyright owner.

Precisely because of the second point, motion picture studios have been unsuccessful in their efforts to establish a studio-based retail presence. Warner announced it was shutting down its retail stores, and Disney is cutting back as well.[137] Consumers simply do not wish to shop studio by studio. The consumer interface for motion pictures requires the services of aggregators who will select the merchandise most likely to be in demand without regard to who owns the copyright. With independent retailers, it matters not whether a given studio has the greatest market share. If a retailer believes there will be consumer demand for a particular title from a small independent studio, that title will be given prominence based on its own merit and not based on the studio's size. The same is true for libraries, swap meets, flea markets, and yard sales.

Although physical constraints and distribution logistics made it difficult for copyright owners to exercise complete control over distribution in physically delivered copies, DRM controls are clearly intended to impact competition in the physical distribution of lawful copies. Consider the words of Walt Disney's former CEO, Michael Eisner, four years ago, as his company was viewing the Internet video-on-demand market and considering possible alliances with other major studios. He explained that he wanted to eliminate the middleman, which is to say, eliminate competition from retailers and distributors. "The studio would like to offer downloads directly from their own websites. ... It's like a $2.50 video rental but we keep all the money."[138] Warren Lieberfarb, who at the time was president of Warner Home Video, told investors that the very first "business goal" of Warner Home Video was to "Replace video rental business and create a higher margin alternative to VHS rental."[139] Mr. Lieberfarb explained: "It's almost a business imperative for studios to displace the rental market" with VOD (video on demand) where the studios are "in control of their own margins."[140]

To achieve such objectives, movie studios who own the copyrights must keep upward pressure on the price (particularly the rental price) of DVDs containing new release movies.[141] In Europe, for example, where the rental right is not limited to those copies owned by the copyright owner, movie studios can routinely set a much higher wholesale price for copies they "authorize" for rental, thereby suppressing the kind of price competition that exists in the United States between rentals and sales. The resulting higher rental prices relieve downward pressure on sales prices and will make what are now relatively expensive Movielink downloads appear more competitive.[142]

In the United States, where the rental right cannot be used to suppress price competition between rental and sales channels (including resales), these stated objectives are being pursued through the use of DRM technology aimed squarely at the elimination or suppression of competition from secondary markets. Disney, for example, is pursuing secondary market elimination on three fronts: Time-limited downloads, vanishing DVD movies, and, most recently, time-limited personal video recorder functions.

We have discussed time-limited downloads above. In Disney's case, it has recently joined the MovieLink joint venture to disseminate its works under a plan that licenses the reproduction by the consumer but employs DRM (through Microsoft's Media Player) so that it cannot be sold, rented, lent, or given away. [143]

The MovieLink joint venture goes far beyond the mere pooling of copyrighted assets, as the venture involves the joint use by the member studios of identical restraints upon lawful uses, restraints such as tethering and timing out that serve no purpose, but to extend control over copyrighted works beyond the limits of the copyright authority. Although use of such restraints is not protected from antitrust scrutiny,[144] particularly when used in concert by the major studios, the DMCA nevertheless protects them from being circumvented by the public.[145] This gives the major motion picture studios the power to license reproductions from the Internet into lawful copies, coupled with the suppression of all trade in those lawful copies and the unauthorized charging for private performances. In an interview with *Video Store Magazine*, Jim Ramo, CEO of Movielink, recently explained it this way:

> "[Consumers] will simply go to a web site, search and choose titles and be given suggestions. They'll click on the movie, click 'buy' and then download it," Ramo said. "The intent is to have a per-viewing capability and a price per view."[146]

In other words, the Movielink studios intend to charge for the right of reproduction (the download) and then usurp the right of private performance by charging the owner of the lawfully made copy on a per view basis. Indeed, the article goes on to explain that viewing these copies will be permitted during the "pay-per-view window," which is to say, consumers could get to privately perform the works from their own copies only during the period in which cable systems were licensed to make public performances of the works. (The cable pay-per-view service is simply another way that *licensees* can structure payment for *public* performances, as an alternative to cable subscription fees or selling of advertising time during free (to the public) broadcasts.[147]) And in case Movelink's plan to take control over private performances of lawfully made copies was not sufficiently clear, Ramo indicated a willingness to actually destroy the lawful copies belonging to others:

> "We definitely are going to have a fee-per-use basis," he said. "What will happen to the content on your hard drive, whether it self-destructs or sits there on your hard drive, will be in the software business rules."[148]

Of course, it would not really "*self*-destruct," as those "software business rules" would implement affirmative steps by Movielink, in cooperation with DRM software companies (Microsoft, in this case), to destroy or disable the lawfully made copies belonging to others and prevent those copies from being lawfully redistributed in competition with their new copies.

"The movie studios aren't about to give up their best product for VOD until they're absolutely satisfied they've gotten the best deal for themselves, which means exploring direct-distribution options like streaming video over the Internet; hammering out favorable revenue splits with operators; and possibly eliminating middlemen 'aggregators.'"[149] Warner Home Video's spokesperson was quoted along those same lines: "'The video rental and sales business has matured and now exhibits only marginal rates of growth,' [Warner Home Video President Warren] Lieberfarb said. 'Accordingly the opportunity growth for Hollywood comes . . . from the aggregation of VOD and DVD [sales].'"[150] The article notes that Lieberfarb "also suggested that the industry unify its VOD message under one brand," which appears to explain part of the rationale for the MovieLink joint venture. These comments echoed a similar statement by Yair Landau, president of Sony Pictures Entertainment, four years ago, as reported in *Daily Variety*: "Studios must work together and act swiftly or 'you're opening it up to someone else to aggregate the services.'"[151]

Large copyright-holding companies such as these are able to gain monopoly controls that are exponential in relation to the number of copyrighted works they control. In the words of the Register of Copyrights:

> Copyright has sometimes been said to be a monopoly. This is true in the sense that the copyright owner is given exclusive control over the market for his work. And if his control were unlimited, it could become an undue restraint on the dissemination of the work.
>
> On the other hand, any one work will ordinarily be competing in the market with many others. And copyright, by preventing mere duplication, tends to encourage the independent creation of competitive works. The real danger of monopoly might arise when many works of the same kind are pooled and controlled together.[152]

The restraints do not stop at joint ventures for movies downloaded over the Internet. Disney recently announced a new venture of its own, "Movie Beam," intended to allow consumers to reproduce copies at home but armed it with a DRM technology that destroys the copies in twenty-four hours.[153]

Restraints on the ability to redistribute lawfully reproduced copies may seem quaint considering that most applications at the moment involve re-productions onto hard drives or "personal video recorders" that are unlikely to be lent, traded, or resold for their content, but DRM technology is now available, and currently being test-marketed by Disney, to eliminate competition in the secondary market (resales, rentals, gifts, and lending) for ordinary store-bought DVD movies.

They take a standard DVD and go to the added time and expense of making it inoperable after a period of time. Despite the increased cost of manufacturing, the wholesale price will be much lower than the standard DVD that costs less to manufacture. The product itself will be less versatile. It will have a shelf life of only about a year unopened, but when removed from the package, it will last only forty-eight hours. The standard DVD is cheaper to manufacture, has a virtually unlimited life span, and will not degrade after opening. How can a copyright owner justify going to the added expense of making a product much less valuable and then selling it for a fraction of the cost of the more valuable product that was cheaper to make? At first glance, it would seem to be against the copyright owner's self-interest to do so. If the copyright owner expected to benefit from selling at a much lower wholesale price, one would think that the cheaper price could be offered more easily on an unaltered DVD because the manufacturing cost is lower and demand for a more versatile product (with a resale value) would be higher. The benefit to the copyright owner can only be derived from its theft of the public's rights and elimination of the lawful secondary markets.[154]

As seen above, the copyright owner has no right to control private performances. Even a thief can watch a stolen DVD without infringing the copyright. By taking away from the public the ability to perform works using lawful copies that are already in circulation, the copyright owner using the time-limiting technology apparently expects to sell more copies at greater total net profits, even if that means a lower number of viewers. To do so, the lowest-priced copies (such as by rental and resales) and free copies (such as from gifts or library lending) that are currently available would have to be suppressed. Those who are least advantaged economically, that is, those who depend on the cheapest rentals, used product markets, library borrowing, private lending and bartering, or gift economies (because they cannot afford anything more), are the most likely to be harmed, even as more copies are available at a cheaper price for those who can afford to buy new products.

Accordingly, the copyright owner's motive in deploying such DRM is profit, but it can only achieve those profits by eliminating competition from lawful secondary circulation. That is, a DVD that "vanishes" after forty-eight hours will only be attractive at a six- to seven-dollar retail price if used DVDs at that same price (with unlimited playback and resale value) are eliminated, if rentals available for two to four dollars are eliminated, and if library lending and free gifts of used DVDs are eliminated. Flexplay Technology's EZ-D DRM technology[155] being tested by Disney's Buena Vista Home Entertainment accomplishes all this.

Thus, Disney and other copyright owners who agree with Flexplay to suppress those secondary markets will be the only beneficiaries. They will make higher profits even as fewer people get to enjoy the movies and the public bears the cost of millions more discs being manufactured, sold, and tossed in a landfill. The unlimited life span of freely recirculating copies envisioned by Congress would be tossed in the dustheap of history.

When copyright owners use DRM technology to gain additional rights or additional control beyond the copyright, they circumvent the limitations the law has placed on their exclusive rights. The public policy granting copyrights "excludes from it all that is not embraced" in the original copyrighted work and "equally forbids the use of the copyright to secure an exclusive right or limited monopoly" beyond the scope of the Copyright Act and which is "contrary to public policy to grant."[156] In short, an agreement between a copyright owner and Flexplay to employ the EZ-D DRM technology is calculated to eliminate lawful trade-in, and repeat lawful performances of, noninfringing copies in violation of antitrust law and unlawful avoidance of the limitations imposed on copyrights. It is directly antagonistic to the purpose of copyright law in encouraging the widest possible dissemination of creative works and should be unlawful per se.

Conclusion

Before making use of a particular DRM technology, the copyright owner should first ask whether the technology serves to protect any of the six specific rights under copyright law or whether it serves to increase dissemination of the work. If the answer is no, such use should be abandoned because it serves no legitimate purpose. If the answer is yes, a determination should be made as to whether any negative impacts (enlargement of the copyright beyond its statutory scope, reduction in public access to and enjoyment of the work, reduction in competition for licensed reproductions, displays, or public performances) are minimized and are reasonable in light of the public benefits to be gained and no greater than necessary to achieve those public benefits.

Just as there is a "good" gate that I might install to prevent unauthorized access to my driveway, an "ugly" gate might be one I put up on your driveway, or on a public road, preventing access without my permission to property I do not own. Like good uses of gates, it makes sense that good uses of DRM should be encouraged and picking their locks should generally be prohibited. Like ugly uses of gates, ugly uses of DRM should be prohibited, as the installer of the gate or the DRM has no right to limit the access, the motives of the installer are unjust, and the burden on the public and on the rights of others is too great.

Somewhere in between is the "bad" gate used to protect my property, but that I installed in a way that partially blocks the public road or damages my neighbor's property. Just as it is not unreasonable for the government to prohibit private gates from swinging out into the roadway and just as my neighbor should have a cause of action for trespass if the hinge post of my gate is installed on my neighbor's property, so, too, should the government have freedom to require that DRM technology likely to have adverse effects upon the public or the rights of others be redesigned so as to avoid those effects.

DRM can, indeed, be used to manage rights of the copyright holder, and to the degree that it does it can serve a valuable purpose by encouraging the copyright holder to disseminate works with some comfort that the rights conferred by law will be respected. DRM can sometimes be used to manage rights for a positive end, but with unintended consequences. Technological limitations imposed with the sole intent of protecting the copyrights from infringement may have the effect of limiting lawful uses the copyright holder has no right to control. In those cases, a careful assessment of whether the end justifies the means is in order. Finally, DRM can be abused, by either automating and technologically enforcing what would ordinarily constitute an unlawful agreement in restraint of trade or using technology to trump statutory limits on the copyright or to diminish freedoms to which the public is entitled by law. Such uses of DRM must be challenged and changed.

Notes

1. See, e.g., Joint Reply Comments of Copyright Industry Organizations Report to Congress Pursuant to Section 104 of the Digital Millennium Copyright Act, dated September 5, 2000, submitted by the American Film Marketing Association, the Association of American Publishers, the Business Software Alliance, the Interactive Digital Software Association, the Motion Picture Association of America, the National Music Publishers' Association, and the Recording Industry Association of America.

2. The Business Software Alliance (BSA), for example, urges consumers to ignore the rules of law and adopt, instead, the rules of an end-user license agreement: "When you purchase software . . . you are purchasing the right to use the software under certain restrictions imposed by the copyright owner, typically the software publisher. The precise rules are described in the documentation accompanying the software—the license." Available online from http://www.bsa.org/usa/antipiracy/Why-a-License-Matters.cfm (accessed 9 May 2004). BSA member Adobe Systems, Inc., similarly attempts to "educate" the public on the extra-copyright notion that purchasing computer software does not entitle the owner to any of the rights set forth in the Copyright Act. "Unlike other things you purchase, the software applications and fonts you buy don't belong to you. Instead, you become a licensed user." Available online from http://www.adobe.com/aboutadobe/antipiracy/piracy.html (accessed 12 May 2003). The Copyright Act contains no exclusive "right to use" that can be licensed, and myriad uses are beyond the reach of the copyright.

3. Alan Greenspan, "Market Economics and Rule of Law," remarks given at the 2003 Financial Markets Conference of the Federal Reserve Bank of Atlanta, Sea Island, Georgia (via satellite), Apr. 4, 2003. Available online from http://www.federalreserve.gov/boarddocs/speeches/2003/20030404/default.htm.

4. U.S. Constitution, art. 1, sec. 8. The right to exploit a work is never granted just for the sake of economic growth.

5. *Sony Corp. of Am. v. Universal City Studios, Inc.*, 464 U.S. 417, 432 (1989). These rights are enumerated in Section 106 of the United States Copyright Act.

6. *Fortnightly Corp. v. United Artists Television, Inc.*, 392 U.S. 390, 393-95 (1968) (footnotes omitted, emphasis added).

7. See sec. 106(4) of the United States Copyright Act.

8. See, e.g., art. 11 of the Berne Convention; art. 14.1 of the Agreement on Trade-Related Aspects of Intellectual Property; art. 8 of the World Intellectual Property Organization Copyright Treaty; art. 6 of the WIPO Performances and Phonograms Treaty.

9. Sec. 106(3) of the United States Copyright Act grants the right, subject to the right of the owner of a lawfully made copy to redistribute it, "to distribute copies or phonorecords of the copyrighted work to the public by sale or other transfer of ownership, or by rental, lease, or lending."

10. 17 U.S.C. § 202.

11. See *Bobbs-Merrill Co. v. Straus*, 210 U.S. 339 (1908) (if copyright holders leverage their exclusive rights into control of future sales, it would give them a right not included in the copyright and, in effect, expand the operation and construction of the Copyright Act beyond its meaning).

12. The rights of owners of lawfully made copies (part of the first-sale doctrine) are discussed later in this chapter.

13.   H.R. Rep. No. 2222, 60th Cong., 2d Session (1909). The U.S. Congress first codified the first-sale doctrine in the Copyright Act of 1909. At that time, the House Committee on Patents stated that this codification was intended "to recognize the distinction, long established, between the material object and the right to produce copies thereof." Id. cf. sec. 27 of the Copyright Act of 1909 ("nothing in this title shall be deemed to forbid, prevent, or restrict the transfer of any copy of a copyrighted work the possession of which has been lawfully obtained").

14.   *Lasercomb America, Inc. v. Reynolds*, 911 F.2d 970, 977 (4th Cir. 1990) (quoting, with revisions, *Morton Salt Co. v. G.S. Suppiger Co.*, 314 U.S. 488, 492 (1942)) (brackets omitted).

15.   The six limited rights are: (1) to reproduce the copyrighted work in copies or phonorecords; (2) to prepare derivative works based on the copyrighted work; (3) to distribute copies or phonorecords of the copyrighted work to the public by sale or other transfer of ownership, or by rental, lease, or lending; (4) in the case of literary, musical, dramatic, and choreographic works, pantomimes, and motion pictures, and other audiovisual works, to perform the copyrighted work publicly; (5) in the case of literary, musical, dramatic, and choreographic works, pantomimes, and pictorial, graphic, or sculptural works, including the individual images of a motion picture or other audiovisual work, to display the copyrighted work publicly; and (6) in the case of sound recordings, to perform the copyrighted work publicly by means of a digital audio transmission.

16.   The Supreme Court drew attention to this important language in *Sony Corp. of America v. Universal City Studios*, 464 U.S. 417, 447 (1984).

17.   The fair-use the factors considered by the courts are (1) the "purpose and character" of the use, (2) the "nature of the work," (3) the "amount and substantiality of the portion used in relation to the copyrighted work as a whole," and (4) the "effect of the use upon the potential market for or value of the copyrighted work."

18.   *Eldred v. Ashcroft*, No. 01-618, slip op. at 29, 537 U.S. 186, ___, (Jan. 15, 2003) ("copyright law contains built-in First Amendment accommodations").

19.   *Triangle Publications, Inc. v. Knight-Ridder Newspapers, Inc.*, 626 F.2d 1171 (5th Cir. 1980) (fair-use right to show competitor's magazine cover to make comparison).

20.   *Ty, Inc. v. Publications Int'l Ltd.*, 292 F.3d 512 (7th Cir. 2002).

21.   Cf. Berne Convention for the Protection of Literary and Artistic Works, art. 10, 10bis, and 13; Agreement on Trade-Related Aspects of Intellectual Property Rights, art. 13; WIPO Copyright Treaty, art. 6 and 10; WIPO Performances and Phonograms Treaty, art. 8(2), 12(2), and 16.

22.   *Bobbs-Merrill Co. v. Straus*, 210 U.S. 339 (1908). The copyright owner was attempting to enforce a minimum resale price for its books on the basis of a purported agreement. Having determined that the copyright owner had no right to control the retail sales of books it had already sold at wholesale, the court concluded that it was

unnecessary to consider whether such minimum resale price agreement also violated antitrust law.

23.   Sec. 109(a) states: "Notwithstanding the provisions of [the exclusive right of distribution contained in] section 106(3), the owner of a particular copy or phonorecord lawfully made under this title, or any person authorized by such owner, is entitled, without the authority of the copyright owner, to sell or otherwise dispose of the possession of that copy or phonorecord." There are exceptions prohibiting rental of sound recordings and certain computer programs without the consent of the copyright owner, but no exceptions for motion pictures or other audiovisual works, books or writings, images, or most popular console video game software.

24.   Data from the Video Software Dealers Association.

25.   Hollywood feared this lack of control presented by home video recorders. Jack Valenti, president of the MPPA, likened it to being stalked by a serial killer known as "the Boston Strangler." He testified before the U.S. Congress: "I say to you that the VCR is to the American film producer and the American public as the Boston Strangler is to a woman alone." Testimony before the Subcommittee on Courts, Civil Liberties, and the Administration of Justice of the Committee on the Judiciary, House of Representatives, Ninety-seventh Congress, Hearing on Home Recording of Copyrighted Works, Apr. 12, 1982.

26.   *Eldred v. Ashcroft*, 537 U.S. 186 (2003) (copyright law safeguards freedom of speech by protecting expression, not ideas, and by accommodating fair use of copyrighted works).

27.   See, e.g., *Shelley v. Kraemer*, 334 U.S. 1 (1948) (private racially restrictive real estate covenant was not illegal but was nevertheless unenforceable in court).

28.   The U.S. Dept. of Justice and the FTC have overlapping authority to enforce many of the antitrust laws. The FTC has specific authority over unfair trade practices that might not be prohibited by general antitrust law. Private parties may enforce most antitrust laws when they suffer antitrust injury. In addition to federal antitrust law and prohibition of unfair trade practices, each individual state has the authority to enact antitrust and unfair competition laws regulating commerce within their own jurisdictions. This is in contrast to copyright law, which is purely federal and preempts any state regulation over the copyright subject matter.

29.   The U.S. Dept. of Justice and the FTC held a series of hearings on this issue, seeking input from a great number of experts in the area. See http://www.ftc.gov/opp/intellect/. It is unfortunate that these hearings focused primarily on patent law because there are so many ventures with a more immediate impact on consumers and the public interest that involve copyrights as opposed to patents. One of the few copyright-related submissions was made by this author on behalf of a trade association of motion picture video retailers based in the U.S. See John Mitchell, "Retailers of Intellectual Property: The Competitive Voice of Consumers," statement on behalf

of Video Software Dealers Association, Public Hearings on Intellectual Property Law and Policy in the Knowledge-Based Economy before the FTC and the Antitrust Division, U.S. Dept. of Justice, July 2002. Available online from http://www.ftc.gov/os/comments/intelpropertycomments/0207mitchell.pdf.

30. *Tricom, Inc. v. Electronic Data Systems Corp.*, 902 F. Supp. 741, 745 (E.D. Mich. 1995) (quoting *Lasercomb Am., Inc. v. Reynolds*, 911 F.2d 970, 978 (4th Cir. 1990)).

31. Greater consideration is given to the antitrust and other limitations on copyright expansionism later in this chapter.

32. Digital technology also makes it easier for copyright holders to extend control over their works beyond the limits of their copyrights.

33. Quoting from (emphasis added) WIPO Copyright Treaty, Article 11 ("Contracting Parties shall provide adequate legal protection and effective legal remedies against the circumvention of effective technological measures that are used by authors in connection with the exercise of their rights under this Treaty or the Berne Convention and that restrict acts, in respect of their works, which are not authorized by the authors concerned or permitted by law.") and WIPO Performances and Phonograms Treaty Article 18 ("Contracting Parties shall provide adequate legal protection and effective legal remedies against the circumvention of effective technological measures that are used by performers or producers of phonograms in connection with the exercise of their rights under this Treaty and that restrict acts, in respect of their performances or phonograms, which are not authorized by the performers or the producers of phonograms concerned or permitted by law").

34. For example, the Copyright Industry Organizations testified that the right of owners of lawfully made copies to redistribute them (under section 109 of the Copyright Act) would apply only "in the absence of licensing or technological restrictions to the contrary" imposed by the copyright owner. *Joint Reply Comments of Copyright Industry Organizations Report to Congress Pursuant to Section 104 of the Digital Millennium Copyright Act*, Sept. 5, 2000, p. 6 (submitted by the American Film Marketing Association, the Association of American Publishers, the BSA, the Interactive Digital Software Association, the MPAA, the National Music Publishers' Association, and the Recording Industry Association of America).

35. Cf. the *Digital Media Consumers' Rights Act of 2003*, H.R. 107, sec. 4, 108th Congress, which would bring the DMCA more in line with WIPO treaty obligations by providing that it is not a violation of the DMCA to circumvent an access-control DRM to make a noninfringing use of the work.

36. Art. 7 (objectives, emphasis added).

37. Art. 8, § 2 (principles, emphasis added).

38. Art. 40 (emphasis added).

39. Art. 48 (indemnification of the defendant). In the U.S., this principle has

been codified in the Copyright Act and emphasized by the Supreme Court. Ordinarily, a successful defendant in litigation in the U.S. has no recourse to compensate for legal expenses in defending against a failed lawsuit. Sec. 505 of the Copyright Act makes an exception to this general rule, however. It states in relevant part: "In any civil action under [the United States Copyright Act], the court in its discretion may allow the recovery of full costs by or against any party . . . [and] the court may also award a reasonable attorney's fee to the prevailing party as part of the costs." In *Fogerty v. Fantasy, Inc.*, 510 U.S. 517 (1994), the successful defendant had been denied an award of attorneys fees because the plaintiff had not sued in bad faith or made a frivolous claim. The court declared: "Because copyright law ultimately serves the purpose of enriching the general public through access to creative works, it is peculiarly important that the boundaries of copyright law be demarcated as clearly as possible. To that end, defendants who seek to advance a variety of meritorious copyright defenses should be encouraged to litigate them to the same extent that plaintiffs are encouraged to litigate meritorious claims of infringement." Id. at 527. Noting that lack of control by a copyright owner also may lead to the creation of additional works, the court added: "a successful defense of a copyright infringement action may further the policies of the Copyright Act every bit as much as a successful prosecution of an infringement claim by the holder of a copyright." Id.

40.   17 U.S.C. § 1201(a)(1)(A).

41.   Sec. 1201(c) provides: "(1) Nothing in this section shall affect rights, remedies, limitations, or defenses to copyright infringement, including fair use" under the Copyright Act. "(4) Nothing in this section shall enlarge or diminish any rights of free speech or the press for activities using consumer electronics, telecommunications, or computing products."

42.   Although calling it a copyright "industry" may sound derogatory to the ears of those who hold authorship in high esteem, it is a self-imposed label chosen by the trade associations representing the "industry" side of copyright. See note 1, above.

43.   E.g., New Yorkers for Fair Use (http://www.nyfairuse.org/) has prepared bumper stickers bearing that phrase. See http://www.cafeshops.com/nyfairuse.6856448.

44.   105th Cong., 2d sess., Rept. 105-551, House Committee on the Judiciary, May 22, 1998 (emphasis added).

45.   I had intended to attribute this play on words to Siva Vaidhyanathan, author of *Copyright and Copywrongs: The Rise of Intellectual Property and How It Threatens Creativity* (New York Press, 2003) but quickly found numerous "copy wrongs" or "copywrongs" takeoffs on copyright in the DRM context. There is even an organization named "copywrongs.org."

46.   105th Cong., 2d sess., Rept. 105-551, House Committee on the Judiciary, May 22, 1998.

47.   Id. Where *subsequent* access is controlled or prevented by the DRM, however, the use would be considered "ugly" and illegal.

48.   In this regard, Congress may have crafted the DMCA too narrowly by limiting its applicability to DRM that prevents access to copyrighted works without consent of the copyright owner, such that one who is not the copyright owner, or one who seeks to protect the public performance of a work in the public domain, gains no benefit. (Conversely, if protection solely of copyrighted works was the aim, Congress crafted the DMCA too broadly in that it bars access for noninfringing access). It is never copyright infringement to watch a cablecast movie, for example, but it may be theft of a cable signal to watch the program, copyrighted or not, by using a "black box" cable signal decoder to avoid paying for the premium or pay-per-view channel. But even though cable signal theft does not infringe any copyrights, it is nevertheless illegal under 18 U.S.C. § 2511 and 47 U.S.C. § 553. See § 553(a)(1) ("No person shall intercept or receive or assist in intercepting or receiving any communications service offered over a cable system, unless specifically authorized to do so by a cable operator or as may otherwise be specifically authorized by law").

49.   The MPAA has, however, argued that licenses to reproduce copies at the consumer level should indeed be treated as though they constituted sales of goods. See note 131.

50.   As noted in note 48, Congress recognized the legitimacy of this interest in protecting cable signals against theft by making it a federal offense to engage in signal theft. Notably, that provision has nothing whatsoever to do with copyright.

51.   Technology, Education, and Copyright Harmonization Act of 2002, 116 Stat. 1758, Pub. 107–273, Nov. 2, 2002, Tit. III-C, codified primarily at 17 U.S.C. § 110.

52.   17 U.S.C. § 110(2)(D)(i).

53.   17 U.S.C. § 110(2)(D)(ii).

54.   See, e.g., *Federal Trade Commission v. Indiana Federation of Dentists*, 476 U.S. 447 (1986); *Broadcast Music, Inc. v. Columbia Broadcasting System, Inc.*, 441 U.S. 1 (1979).

55.   See, e.g., *Federal Trade Commission v. Superior Trial Lawyers Association*, 493 U.S. 411 (1990); *National Society of Professional Engineers v. United States*, 435 U.S. 679 (1978).

56.   Because the right of reproduction is subject to the right of fair use, for example (see 17 U.S.C. §§ 106 introduction), and the right to make fair use is essential to accommodate copyright law to First Amendment liberties (see *Eldred v. Ashcroft*, 537 U.S. 186 (2003)), anticopying DRM must, by necessity, leave sufficient room for fair uses. The same would be true for other noninfringing uses.

57.   The Register of Copyrights has conceded that a computer hard drive containing a copy of a work is itself a "copy or phonorecord" as those terms are defined

in the Copyright Act, 17 U.S.C. § 101. See "Section 104 Report: A Report of the Register of Copyrights Pursuant to §104 of the Digital Millennium Copyright Act," U.S. Copyright Office, Aug. 2001 at 87 ("the copyright owner's reproduction right does not interfere at all with the ability of the owner of the physical copy to dispose of ownership or possession of that copy, since the first sale doctrine applies fully with respect to the tangible object (e.g., the user's hard drive) in which the work is embodied").

58.   See the later section titled "Timing Out for Private Gain: The Limited Download."

59.   See "Judge Blocks Ban on 'Screeners': Temporary Restraining Order Allows Indies to Send Out Tapes," MSNBC, Dec. 8, 2003. Available online from http://msnbc.msn.com/id/3660332/.

60.   The court was not impressed by this rationale because each studio was entirely free to make that choice independently. It could certainly serve no legitimate antipiracy purpose to require copyright holders to protect their copyrights in this way against their will. Opponents of the screener ban argued that it favored the major studios by raising barriers to the Oscar competition against smaller independent filmmakers.

61.   I use the term "space shifting" in a broad sense to include any variation on the theme of allowing only one accessible (perceivable, reproducible, or communicable) copy at any given time. Forward-and-delete is perhaps the most rudimentary form of space shifting, as it requires a separate action to delete the original and allows for a brief moment in which two copies might be accessible. So-called move technology that automates the process of reproducing the bits on the second medium concurrent with rendering the identical bits on the first medium inaccessible ensures that only one copy can be accessed at any given time. More complex variations include a check-out/check-in process that envisions access being passed to each authorized reproduction and returned to the original when no longer needed. An additional layer of sophistication might establish a parent–child relationship between reproductions, such that second-generation copies (copies of copies) are not permitted, but the master DRM from the original copy might allow for a predetermined number of accessible "child" copies. When the limit is reached, one "child" would have to be checked back in to the "parent" before another "child" could be made accessible. This latter model might be most appropriate in imitating a library or school lending process or a video store rental, whereas serial reproductions might imitate physical copies being passed along from one consumer to another by gift or resale. Sony designed such a model in 1999 for its portable players. See note 126.

62.   "Copies" and "phonorecords" must be capable of being "perceived, reproduced, or otherwise communicated." 17 U.S.C. § 101.

63.   *Sony Corp. of Am. v. Universal City Studios, Inc.*, 464 U.S. 417.

64. DigitalConsumer.org, for example, advocates a "Bill of Rights" giving consumers the right to "space-shift," ("the right to use your content in different places," such as copying to a portable player) and the "right to use legally acquired content on the platform of their choice." They do not seem concerned with limiting the proliferation of accessible copies, however. See http://digitalconsumer.org/bill.html.

65. Because the Audio Home Recording Rights Act prohibits filing infringement claims against persons reproducing sound recordings for "non-commercial" purposes, many believe that any noncommercial copying is noninfringing. A "buy one, get as many as I want free" policy may be allowed for certain types of noncommercial sound recording reproductions (17 U.S.C. § 1008), but presumably the affected copyright owners derive some revenue from the royalty on recording devices and media. However, that provision does not apply to literary works, visual works, or motion pictures or other audiovisual works for which there is not even a "personal use" exception.

66. The possibility of obtaining such consent from record companies appeared imminent a few years ago, albeit under a carefully controlled environment. As part of the Secure Digital Music Initiative (SDMI) led by the major record companies, efforts were made to obtain agreement from hardware and software manufacturers to create a "secure" digital environment operating under certain rules. Before failing, the organization issued specifications for portable devices that included concepts of "Move" (content "copied to its destination, and the original is made permanently unusable"), "Check-Out" ("the ability to render SDMI Protected Cont for Local Use is copied via the LCM [Licensed Compliant Module] to a single other location... and the number of permitted copies decremented by one"), and "Check-In" ("the ability to render SDMI Protected Content for Local Use is restored via the LCM to its original location . . . and the number of allowed copies is incremented by one. The Checked-Out copy shall then be rendered unusable.") "SDMI Portable Device Specification," Part 1, Version 1.0, July 8, 1999 Available online from http://www.sdmi.org/download/port_device_spec_part1.pdf.

67. See later sections titled "Timing Out for Private Gain: The Limited Download" and "Eliminating Competition."

68. Summary of testimony of Gary Klein, vice chairman, Home Recording Rights Coalition, Nov. 29, 2000. Public Hearing Filed in Response to 65 *Fed. Reg.* 63626 (Oct. 24, 2000), reprinted in *DMCA Section 104 Report*, U.S. Copyright Office, Aug. 2001, vol. 3, app. 8. (Admittedly, Mr. Klein's testimony falls into the common semantic errors by, for example, speaking of a "transferred copy." By definition, a copy is tangible and must be transferred physically. However, courts may avoid the semantics by simply concluding that the copy so created is not a "new" copy in that there is no multiplication of copies.)

69. It is for this very reason that Congressman Boucher's legislation may not even be necessary. That is, such actions may already be noninfringing.

70. The National Music Publishers Association, for example, noted "The impossibility of enforcing a mandate to delete one's own copy of a protected work when a copy of that work is forwarded to another" (id., app. 9, Panel 3, testimony of Susan Mann).

71. Mr. Bernard Sorkin, testifying for Time Warner, Inc., objected to the use of technology to enforce the intent of the legislation, saying, "I don't think the technology exists, to say nothing of the goodwill." But when pressed with the question whether "if indeed it is effective and comes about," he responded: "it sounds like something my company and perhaps others . . . would be willing to consider. We would have to be assured of its effectiveness on several levels." Id., app. 9, Panel 3.

72. 355 F. Supp. 189 (N.D. Tex. 1973).

73. Id. at 190.

74. Id. at 191.

75. Id. See, also, *Peker v. Masters Collection*, 96 F. Supp. 2d 216 (2000) (mere transfer of ink from oil painting replica to another medium is not a reproduction, but using the work on the new medium as a template to add brushstrokes imitating the original oil painting was infringement).

76. 17 U.S.C. § 101 (emphasis added). The term "phonorecords" contains identical accessibility requirements.

77. [2002] 2 S.C.R. 336, 2002 SCC 34.

78. Id. at ¶ 2.

79. Id. at ¶ 42 (emphasis by the court).

80. As noted, in the case of sound recordings, if more than one phonorecord becomes accessible, the legality may depend on whether the reproduction is immunized by the Audio Home Recording Rights Act. See 17 U.S.C. §§ 1001–1008.

81. 17 U.S.C. § 107.

82. 17 U.S.C. § 112.

83. 17 U.S.C. § 117.

84. 17 U.S.C. § 121.

85. 17 U.S.C. § 1002.

86. 17 U.S.C. § 1001(11) ("The term 'serial copying' means the duplication in a digital format of a copyrighted musical work or sound recording from a digital reproduction of a digital musical recording").

87. 17 U.S.C. § 1008.

88. 17 U.S.C. §§ 1003(c)(3) and 1004.

89. The Audio Home Recording Rights Act did not anticipate the phenomenon of peer-to-peer reproductions over the Internet. Record companies have been struggling with how to stop such reproductions without directly challenging the act of the

consumer in downloading a copy. To date, recording industry lawsuits have focused on the so-called uploading (not really uploading at all, as it simply leaves an existing file available from which others can make a reproduction), attempting to shut down the source for reproductions that would likely fall within the 17 U.S.C. § 1008 exemption, particularly if the reproduction is made directly to a "digital audio recording medium." It appears that in the beginning, the record companies were content to let music retailers bear the brunt of sales cannibalization from Section 1008 reproductions, expecting to receive greater revenue from the royalty structure than through lost sales. In hindsight, it appears that the record companies might have fared better if they had not brokered such a deal and, instead, helped music retailers compete on price, quality, and service against the so-called pirate reproductions. For example, in the home video industry, it is hard for professional pirates or casual consumers to compete with the convenience, quality, selection, and price of a cheap rental at the local video store. Wholesale prices of feature-length motion pictures are often lower than for a music CD because the competition among legitimate sales and rental channels is fierce and there is no subsidy for "free" noncommercial reproductions.

90. Macrovision uses "four-line colorstripe copy control technology." See 17 U.S.C. § 1201(k).

91. A more controversial feature of CSS is the provision for regional coding, which impairs the redistribution of lawful copies and tends to facilitate price discrimination. Although the motion picture industry defends it as an antipiracy tool, in reality it probably contributes to the proliferation of infringing copies, as legitimate retailers in one region are unable to meet the demand because the only copies available lawfully are coded for a different region. The pirates, who make their infringing copies without regional coding DRM limitations, are guaranteed exclusive access to the market.

92. The National Association of Recording Merchandisers issued a statement on Sept. 12, 2003, on release of the first copy-managed CD by BMG and Arista: "They have found a way to not only protect their content from piracy, but to recognize that some copying by consumers and retailers is legal and appropriate." (http://www.narm.com/Content/NavigationMenu/Media_Center/Press_Releases/20033/BMGArista.htm.) The copy-managed CD allows some copying intended to accommodate customary uses.

93. The UMG Blue Matter EULA is available at http://www.copyright.gov/reports/studies/dmca/sec-104-report-vol-3.pdf at page 491 (DMCA Section 104 Report, vol. 3, Appendix 9, Hearing Transcript Appendix 3).

94. There is no such general "right to use" a copyrighted work under the Copyright Act. As discussed, the right to play one's own music, to perform the work privately, is excluded from the copyright grant, such that playing music privately is never infringing and never within the right of the copyright holder to control.

95. See, e.g., *Softman Prods. v. Adobe Systems*, Inc., 171 F. Supp. 2d 1075, 1090 (C.D. Cal. 2001) (EULA purporting to diminish rights consumers enjoy under copyright law is inconsistent with the balance of rights established by Congress). The legal dynamics at issue here are discussed more fully under "ugly" uses of DRM in the section titled "Eliminating Competition." UMG's plan is somewhat more benign than a bare restraint in that it would be hard to enforce the EULA, and the accompanying license authorizes additional copies that can be placed in circulation, albeit in breach of the EULA.

96. See, e.g., Testimony of Mike Farrace, senior vice president, Digital Business, Towner Records, before the Senate Judiciary Committee, Apr. 3, 2001 ("Online Entertainment: Coming Soon to a Digital Device Near You"). (Tower's first online store began in 1995. Its attempts to grow were stifled not by piracy, but by the record companies, which required the equivalent of having "a different cash register for every distributor," inefficient steps in the downloading process, mining Tower's customers for private data, and "horrible" end-user license agreements that were not even available to customers until after they bought the copy. "OK. My suppliers have the right to get into retailing. Tower isn't afraid to compete with retailers. We think we're pretty good. But we don't think it's fair to let these companies use their power over us to steal our customers and ultimately steal our business. Retailers need rules that protect competition.")

97. During the heyday of its launch, the press*play* subscription music service joint venture of Sony Music and Universal Music Group purported to deliver the service through competing affiliates (MSN Music, Yahoo!, and Roxio). Consumers seeking to comparison shop would, however, find an identical selection, identical prices, and identical promotions at each of the three retail sites. For Tower records, Best Buy, or Joe's Music Store to participate in this new business model, they would have had to agree to offer the same prices and terms of service as each so-called competitor. All essential terms and conditions that could have bred vigorous competition were controlled horizontally and vertically by the joint venture copyright-owner partners.

98. 334 U.S. 131 (1948).

99. Id. at 158 (footnote omitted).

100. 371 U.S. 38 (1962).

101. 243 U.S. 502 (1917).

102. Id. at 519. This position was followed in *Carbice Corp. of Am. v. Am. Patents Dev. Corp.*, 283 U.S. 27 (1931) (owner of a patented package that used solid carbon dioxide could not obligate licensees to use its own solid carbon dioxide). In *Carbice*, the court noted that the law had already risen to prevent the unwarranted extension of other limited monopolies, such as trademarks and trade names, id. at 35, n.5 (characterizing this limitation as being "inherent" in the monopoly grant).

103.　243 U.S. at 516. "The patent law furnishes no warrant for such a practice and the cost, inconvenience and annoyance to the public which the opposite conclusion would occasion forbid it." Id.

104.　314 U.S. 488 (1942).

105.　Id. at 490.

106.　Id. at 494.

107.　Id. at 492.

108.　Id. at 494.

109.　Block booking is "the practice of licensing, or offering for license, one feature or group of features on condition that the exhibitor will also license another feature or group of features released by the distributors during a given period." 334 U.S. at 156.

110.　Id. at 157 (quoting the lower court, citations omitted). See, also, *In re Napster*, 2004 U.S. Dist. LEXIS 7236 at *39–40 (Feb. 22, 2004) ("Under the 'public policy' approach, copyright misuse exists when plaintiff expands the statutory copyright monopoly in order to gain control over areas outside the scope of the monopoly. . . . The test is whether plaintiff's use of his or her copyright violates the public policy embodied in the grant of a copyright, not whether the use is anti-competitive. However, as a practical matter, this test is often difficult to apply and inevitably requires courts to rely on antitrust principles or language to some degree") (citations omitted).

111.　*Lasercomb Am., Inc. v. Reynolds*, 911 F.2d 970, 976 (4th Cir. 1990), quoting from *Morton Salt*, 314 U.S. at 491. Moreover, copyright misuse is such a violation of public policy that some courts will not require that the person against whom the misuse is directed be a party to the litigation. "[T]he fact that appellants here were not parties to one of Lasercomb's standard license agreements is inapposite to their copyright misuse defense." *Lasercomb*, 911 F.2d at 979.

112.　334 U.S. 131, 156-159 (1948).

113.　371 U.S. 38 (1962).

114.　See *Paramount Pictures*, 334 U.S. at 159 (referencing the public policy of antitrust laws). The discussion of copyright misuse was under the heading "Restraint of Trade," id. at 141. "The antitrust laws do not permit a compounding of the statutorily conferred monopoly." *Loew's*, 371 U.S. at 52. See, also, *Eastman Kodak Co. v. Image Technical Services, Inc.*, 504 U.S. 451, 4808 n. 29 (1992) ("The Court has held many times that power gained through some natural and legal advantage such as a patent, copyright, or business acumen can give rise to liability if 'a seller exploits his dominant position in one market to expand his empire into the next'" (citations omitted)).

115.　*Sony Corp. of Am. v. Universal City Studios, Inc.*, 464 U.S. 417 (1984).

116.　Id. at 421.

117.　*Loew's*, 371 U.S. at 45 and n.4. See also id., at 48 and n.5

118. Id. at 45, n.4.

119. Id. at 48, n.6. *Gone With The Wind* was ranked fourth among the "top 100 films of all time" by the American Film Institute.

120. 171 F.3d 1265, 1277 and n.13 (11th Cir. 1999).

121. They also may rather not have to "pay with the right of private performance" or "pay with first sale rights" rather than just paying with cash.

122. See Yoshiko Hara, "Sony Puts Memory Stick into Latest Walkman," *EETIMES*, Sept. 23, 1999 (available online from http://www.eetimes.com/story/OEG19990923S0025). "The scheme accepts audio CD data and MP3 files distributed on networks, but Sony has prepared a proprietary environment and new data compression technology to handle the data." "OpenMG application software resident on a personal computer accepts digital data, encrypts it with an OpenMG key, and converts the data for ATRAC3 to store on the PC's hard disk. (ATRAC3 is an encoder/decoder that Sony has developed for the Memory Stick)."

123. For example, MusicNet, a music "limited download" joint venture of Bertlesmann, Time Warner, EMI Group, and Real Networks, required subscribers to use Real Networks' Real Player; *press*Play, a music "limited download" joint venture of Sony Music and Universal Music Group (though they sold their controlling interests as the Department of Justice was investigating the ventures), which required users to patronize Microsoft software. Movielink, a movie "limited download" joint venture of Time Warner, MGM Studios, Sony Pictures Entertainment, Paramount, and Universal Studios, to which the movie collections of Disney and Arista were added, required subscribers to exclusively use a Microsoft operating system supporting Windows Media Player 8 or higher. Each of these joint ventures obligated consumers to keep paying for the "right" to privately perform copies and phonorecords they had lawfully made using these services, using "ugly" DRM to enforce those terms.

124. It is certainly conceivable that a hardware manufacturer could enter into an agreement with the major record companies to give them a share of the revenue from the sales of the hardware, in which case the same anticompetitive and copyright-enlarging evils would come into play.

125. Under the authority of the copyright owner, the store-bought copy is reproduced at a factory (an exercise of the exclusive right of reproduction) and then distributed to wholesalers and retailers (an exercise of the exclusive right of distribution). When sold, however, Section 109 of the Copyright Act kicks in, exhausting most of the distribution right over those copies. In contrast, under the authority of the copyright owner, the downloaded copy is reproduced in a home and is not distributed. The copyright owner has only exercised the right of reproduction. Section 109 nevertheless exhausts the distribution right because it applies whenever someone other than the copyright owner owns the copy or phonorecord. Because the consumer owns the tangible medium on which the download is reproduced, the consumer

owns the resulting copy or phonorecord and the Section 109 rights of such owner trump most of the distribution rights of the copyright owner.

126.   "Microsoft Announces New Version of Windows Media Digital Rights Management Software" (hereafter "Microsoft DRM Press Release"), press release by Microsoft Corporation, May 2, 2004, available at http://www.microsoft.com/presspass/press/2004/may04/05-03DigitalRightsManagementTechnologyPR.asp. See, also, John P. Mello Jr., "Microsoft Updates DRM, Code-Named Janus," *Eommerce Times*, May 4, 2004, available at http://www.ecommercetimes.com/story/security/33626.html ("Janus will offer other pricing opportunities, such as renting music," according to one of its supporters.)

127.   Moreover, the new Microsoft DRM could effectively eliminate competition in the secondary markets for lawful copies. The fact that Section 109 of the Copyright Act entitles the owner of a lawfully downloaded copy of a copyrighted work to sell or transfer possession of it without the consent of the copyright owner is not in dispute. Even the major copyright holding companies agree. See, e.g., *Joint Reply Comments of Copyright Industry Organizations Report to Congress Pursuant to Section 104 of the Digital Millennium Copyright Act*, dated Sept. 5, 2000, submitted by the American Film Marketing Association, the Association of American Publishers, the BSA, the Interactive Digital Software Association, the MPAA, the National Music Publishers' Association, and the Recording Industry Association of America; *Hearing Before the Copyright Office and the National Telecommunications and Information Administration on a Joint Study on 17 U.S.C. Section 109 and 117* (Nov. 29, 2000) (statement of Cary Sherman on behalf of the Recording Industry Association of America, Inc., p. 298).

128.   Section 106(4). "No license is required by the Copyright Act, for example, to sing a copyrighted lyric in the shower." *Twentieth Century Music Corp. v. Aiken*, 422 U.S. 151, 155 (1975). Of course, those who own lawfully made copies and phonorecords should not be relegated to singing in the shower but have the right to play them in the car or the living room as well.

129.   *Fortnightly Corp. v. United Artists Television, Inc.*, 392 U.S. 390, 393-95 (1968) (footnotes omitted).

130.   It warrants noting that private performances do not constitute infringement regardless whether the person rendering the private performance owns a copy (or phonorecord) of the work.

131.   "Impediments to Digital Trade": Hearing before the Subcommittee on Commerce, Trade and Consumer Protection of the House Committee on Energy and Commerce, 107th Cong., Serial No. 107-36 (May 22, 2001) at 21 (statement of Bonnie J.K. Richardson, vice president for Trade & Federal Affairs for the MPAA).

132.   *Fortnightly*, 392 U.S. at 393, n.8 (citing Benjamin Kaplan, *An Unhurried View of Copyright* [New York: Columbia University Press, 1967], 57).

133.   See section titled "Perfecting Authorized Reproductions."

134.   See section titled "Timing Out for Public Good."

135. See earlier discussion of competition law limitations upon copyrights, generally.

136. *Tricom, Inc. v. Electronic Data Systems Corp.*, 902 F. Supp. 741, 745 (E.D. Mich. 1995) (quoting *Lasercomb Am., Inc. v. Reynolds*, 911 F.2d 970, 978 (4th Cir. 1990)).

137. "That's All Folks," ICv2 July 9, 2001. Available online from http://www.icv2.com/articles/news/528.html.

138. Paul Sweeting, "Digital Could Break Chains That Bind Studio Profits," *Variety*, Apr. 10, 2000.

139. Paul Sweeting, "VB in Depth: Lieberfarb Talks Rent Control," *Video Business*, Nov. 4, 2002.

140. Id.

141. Id.

142. Unfortunately, video retailers in Europe are also finding that the artificially higher retail (sales and rental) prices lend themselves to a more attractive market for professional pirates. They, too, benefit from less price competition.

143. See Holly J. Wagner, "Buena Vista PPV Inks Deal with Movielink," *Video Store* Online, posted July 23, 2003, available online from http://www.hive4media.com/index.cfm?sec_id=2&newsid=5109; Alex Veiga, "Disney, Movielink Ink Deal to Make Movies Available Online," *Miami Herald, Herald.com*, June 23, 2003, available online from http://www.miami.com/mld/miamiherald/business/6369515.htm.

144. The Department of Justice has already raised concerns about the effects of pooling where the pool includes nonessential patents. "Inclusion in the pool of one of the patents, which the pool would convey along with the essential patents, could in certain cases unreasonably foreclose the competing patents from use by manufacturers; because the manufacturers would obtain a license to the one patent with the pool, they might choose not to license any of the competing patents, even if they otherwise would regard the competitive patents as superior." Letter from Joel I. Klein to Garrard R. Beoney, Esq., Dec. 16, 1998. (At the time, Mr. Klein was assistant attorney general, Antitrust Division, United States Department of Justice.) It stands to reason that this concern would be just as valid where pooled copyrighted works were made available only on condition that certain nonessential technologies or business models were employed, thereby foreclosing competition in competing and possibly superior technologies and business models.

145. It is conceivable that courts will refuse to enforce the DMCA where it is being used to protect the use of technologies to unlawfully expand copyrights beyond their lawful limits, but this possibility has not yet been tested in U.S. courts.

146. Holly Wagner, "UPDATE: Movielink's New CEO Talks Business," *Video Store* Magazine, Feb. 1, 2002. Available online from www.hive4media.com/news//htnl/industry_article.cfm?article_id=2539. As noted, copyright law does not authorize copyright owners to charge "per view" for private performances.

147. The copyright holder has the right to authorize the public performance, but the decision whether to cover the cost of the license and earn a profit from the public performance by selling advertising on "free" television broadcasts, charge for cable subscriptions, or charge cable subscribers an additional "per-view" fee is *not* within the exclusive rights of the copyright holder. See, e.g., *United States v. Paramount Pictures, Inc.*, 334 U.S. 131, 142 (1948) (license to publicly perform a motion picture does not entitle the copyright owner to set minimum theater admission prices).

148. Wagner, "UPDATE: Movielink's New CEO Talks Business."

149. Charles Paikert, "Oh VOD, Where Art Thou?," *Cablevision* (Apr. 9, 2001, In Focus, p. 8).

150. R. Thomas Umstead, "Warner Video Chief Bullish on VOD," *Multichannel News* (Mar. 26, 2001, Top Stories, p. 3).

151. Scott Hetrick, "Bishop Fast-forwards MGM Video-on-demand," *Daily Variety* (Dec. 8, 2000, p. 8 [quoting Yair Landau]).

152. *Register's Report on the General Revision of the U.S. Copyright Law* (1961), at 5.

153. See Erik Gruenwedel, "Disney to Expand Movie Beam as DVD Sales Push Q2 Net," May 12, 2004. Disney CEO Michael Eisner "said Disney remains encouraged by the 'technological opportunity' represented by Movie Beam, a TiVo-like video-on-demand subscription service launched last year . . . . Movie Beam allows consumers to download up to 100 films (at $4 per new release; $2.50 per catalog release) into a set-top box via over-the-air TV broadcast spectrums. Each film can be viewed repeatedly over a 24-hour period."

154. Admittedly, the rental market need not be eliminated completely, but simply made less competitive or more profitable to the copyright owner. If the cheap 48-hour DVD were to take off, one would expect copyright owners to simply price the unlimited play DVD much higher, knowing the rental stores will have no choice, but to buy the unlimited play version. This is exactly what is occurring in Europe, where the "rental right" (instead of the DRM technology) enables the copyright owner to prevent price competition between sales and rentals.

155. The EZ-D DRM technology is the DRM technology currently being market-tested by Buena Vista Home Entertainment. It is a product of Flexplay Technologies, Inc. See http://flexplay.com for a description of Flexplay and the EZ-D technology and http://video.movies.go.com/ez-d/ for Buena Vista Home Entertainment's implementation of it.

156. *Lasercomb America, Inc. v. Reynolds*, 911 F.2d 970, 977 (4th Cir. 1990) (quoting with revisions from *Morton Salt Co. v. G.S. Suppiger Co.*, 314 U.S. 488, 492 (1942)) (brackets omitted).

Chapter 9

The Future of Fair Use: Fair? Futuristic? Usable?

Kathleen Wallman and Albert A. Gonzalez

Abstract

The Fair Use Doctrine, articulated in Section 107 of the Copyright Act, has been widely interpreted by users and by the courts over many years. But recent developments in law and technology have made brittle the doctrine's long-standing elasticity. This paper addresses the research question, How will technology and authors' assertions of their rights threaten the future of the fair-use doctrine, and, in the face of such challenges, what future protections will be required to ensure that the fair-use doctrine remains viable and available?

Lawrence Lessig's work, *Code and Other Laws of Cyberspace,* reflects both concern and optimism that the burgeoning of digital rights management (DRM) technology will staunch the loss of control that creators now have over the use of their work.[1] His optimism is premised on the arrival of an age when DRM will have achieved enormous scale such that consumption and exchange of copyrighted materials occurs exclusively within the domain governed by DRM. This will be the digital antidote to the digital copying nightmare that rights holders, particularly the music industry, have shivered about for more than a decade. This pervasive DRM architecture is still a long way off, even by the estimates of the most enthusiastic futurists but is well defined enough to give Lessig concern. His concern is premised on the power that DRM will give creators to unbundle their various rights and make them available for sale or rent individually. For example, the right to read a book might be priced differently from the right to print out a copy, or the right to have a digital copy of a book for a limited period of time might be priced differently from the right to have it indefinitely and to e-mail it to a friend.

But in a world dominated by DRM and unbundled rights, the creator may be able to thwart fair use by declining to make portions of the work available digitally and forcing those who wish to quote from it or make other fair use to buy either the whole work or a greater bundle of rights than would be strictly necessary to effectuate the desired fair use.

Such limitations might be a minor inconvenience for book reviewers and scholars who wish to make passing reference to a protected work or its ideas. Access for such purposes might be accomplished through library volumes, although the accession process might be too slow for some projects. The impact would be much more significant for classroom and research uses, however, with large ramifications for the way instructors and researchers incorporate diverse materials into their teaching and research projects.

This paper explores whether DRM, even when implemented at scale, is likely to impose an airtight stranglehold on fair use. It incorporates empirical and survey data about fair use in the university setting. In the face of challenges to fair use, this paper argues that the doctrine of fair use has an equally formidable constitutional foundation, as does the copyright law itself, rooted in both the copyright clause and the first amendment. The paper then examines, to the extent that DRM is deemed likely to impose a significant burden on fair use, what protections could effectively preserve fair use in the future to make sure that fair use remains fair and usable for the future.

A Short History of Fair Use
The Amorphous Nature of Fair Use
The doctrine of fair use allows the use and reproduction of copyrighted works for purposes that include criticism, comment, news reporting, teaching, scholarship, and research. Section 107 of the Copyright Code provides:

> Notwithstanding the provisions of sections 106 and 106A, the fair use of a copyrighted work, including such use by reproduction in copies or phonorecords or by any other means specified in that section, for purposes such as criti-

cism, comment, news reporting, teaching (including multiple copies for classroom use), scholarship, or research, is not an infringement of copyright. In determining whether the use made of a work in any particular case is a fair use the factors to be considered shall include—

1. The purpose and character of the use, including whether such use is of a commercial nature or is for nonprofit educational purposes;
2. The nature of the copyrighted work;
3. The amount and substantiality of the portion used in relation to the copyrighted work as a whole; and
4. The effect of the use upon the potential market for or value of the copyrighted work.

The fact that a work is unpublished shall not itself bar a finding of fair use if such finding is made upon consideration of all the above factors.

The doctrine has evolved over years with new imperatives that tip the balance it seeks to hold between content creators' rights and the public interest to use their works for narrow, but important, purposes. Fair use has survived, principally, because it fulfills the need to reconcile the two constitutional mandates that weigh this balance: the allowance of copyright restrictions, and the constraint of government interference with free expression.[2] DRM technology once again puts fair use to the test as the room for fair use of copyrighted works becomes smaller.

Although this paper discusses challenges for fair use in education, application of the doctrine in other settings points to its availability to varied interpretation. As reproduced above, Congress specified a four-part test for courts to determine whether any specific use of a copyrighted work is a fair use. These are: (1) the purpose and character of the use, including whether such use is of a commercial nature or is for nonprofit educational purposes; (2) the nature of the copyrighted work; (3) the amount and substantiality of the portion used in relation to the copyrighted work as a whole; and (4) the effect of the use upon the potential market for or value of the copyrighted work. Ruling use of copyrighted work as fair use is inherently a case-specific chore. Courts must measure whether or to what extent the use of copyrighted work influences criteria of the four-part test such that it should be deemed fair use.

In each case, authors' rights are pitted against the "breathing room" needed for society to promote the "progress of science and useful arts" by the use of others' works. In *Campbell v. Acuff-Rose Music, Inc.,* the Supreme Court held the rap music group 2 Live Crew's unauthorized use of a copyrighted song, Roy Orbison's "Pretty Woman," was fair use as the purpose was parody. The benefit to society of comment and criticism outweighed the minimal cost to the copyright holder in light of the four-part test, the Supreme Court held. The court also declined to treat the parodists' request for prior permission to use the song, which was denied by the copyright holder, as inconsistent with the parodists' later invocation of the fair-use defense. Significantly, the court also opined that the for-profit nature of the parodists' use of "Pretty Woman" was not fatal to the fair-use defense. In contrast to this result, in other cases, social benefit is unapparent and the use of copyrighted work for commercial profit nullifies the defense of fair use. For example, in *American Geophysical Union v. Texico, Inc.,* the act of copying articles from a journal by Texaco scientists failed to create a transformative work whose nature was favored by the four-part test. The court weighed heavily the commercial nature of the Texaco researchers' use of the articles, which were copied in their entirety, not for purposes of creating another work but, rather, for archival purposes that would allow the researchers to have them at hand in the future as desired.

With the vagaries of judicial interpretation, it is remarkable in some sense that the fair-use doctrine works at all in the digital environment. Even though the doctrine is no longer a creature of common law but has long been codified into law, it still requires a substantial amount of interpretive finesse on the part of the courts. Over the years, the courts have rendered the following decisions that have become as famous for the useful insights they afford into what the courts think fair use means as they have for the curious technicalities upon which they seem to rely.

For example, in *Basic Books, Inc. v. Kinko's Graphics Corp.,* 758 F.Supp. 1522 (S.D.N.Y. 1991), the court ruled that Kinko's had infringed the copyrights involved in that case by making copies of so-called coursepacks. Coursepacks entail copied material compiled from various copyrighted sources, then sold to students as course texts. The court weighed heavily Kinko's nature as a commercial entity, which, it concluded, rendered the purpose commercial rather than educational. Here, though the nature of the copied work may have been educational, the court ruled against Kinko's because of its for-profit purpose of use.

In *Princeton University Press v. Michigan Document Services, Inc.,* 99 F.3d 1381 (6th Cir. 1996), the copying entity likewise was adjudged guilty of infringement, largely on the same rationale as Basic Books, that is, that a commercial entity cannot execute an educational purpose. But neither Princeton nor Basic Books gave clear guidance on what percentage of the copyrighted work tripped the wire with respect to the "amount" factor, influencing the nature of the transformative work including its effect on the potential market for or value of the copyrighted work. Princeton involved copying of more than five percent of the work, and Basic Books involved copying more than 25 percent.

Some institutions have attempted to provide concrete guidance about how to apply the fair-use factors. The ALA issued its "Model Policy Concerning College and University Photocopying for Classroom, Research and Library Reserve."[3] In succinct understatement, the model policy introduces its discussion of the boundaries of fair use by observing that "[f]air use cannot always be expressed in numbers—either the number of pages copied or the number of copies distributed." The model policy indicates that copying without the permission of the rights holder is acceptable for classroom use under four conditions:

1. the distribution of the same photocopied material does not occur every semester;
2. only one copy is distributed for each student which copy must become the student's property;
3. the material includes a copyright notice on the first page of the portion of material photocopied;
4. the students are not assessed any fee beyond the actual cost of the photocopying

The model policy also requires adherence to brevity standards. Thus, "a prose work may be reproduced in its entirety if it is less than 2,500 words in length. If the work exceeds such length, the excerpt reproduced may not exceed 1,000 words, or 10% of the work, whichever is less. In the case of poetry, 250 words is the maximum permitted."

Other types of copying that do not meet the four conditions require the publisher's permission, according to the model policy. These include repetitive copying, semester after semester, of consumable works such as workbooks or exercise books and copying of coursepacks. The Copyright Clearance Center is authorized to grant permission on behalf of many publishers—and to collect fees for copying beyond the parameters of fair use when such copying is self-reported.

Many universities and colleges have adopted policies on the use and copying of copyrighted works. Generally, these embrace the basic principles of the model policy but vary as to the procedures recommended or required for assembling coursepacks or obtaining permission, where required, for example.[4]

But the most interesting point is this: although the model policy pointedly refers to the "right" of fair use, the language and tone of most of the policies is defensive in the sense of defining conservatively what is permissible copying. It is this fundamental conception of fair use as a leftover of the core copyright protections that rights holders reluctantly share only because it is difficult to protect that which must change if fair use is to survive into a useful future.

The Threat of Digital Rights Management Systems to Fair Use
Digital Rights Management Systems

The National Institute of Standards and Technology defines DRM as a "system of information technology (IT) components and services, along with corresponding law, policies and business models, which strive to distribute and control intellectual property and its rights." Enforced by the Digital Millennium Copyright Act (DMCA), which bans circumvention of DRM technologies, DRM seeks to ensure content creators their constitutional protection of copyright in the digital age. The objective is worthwhile and needed. However, the scope of DRM technology used to achieve this end limits the amount of copyrighted materials accessible for fair use available to content consumers.

DRM technologies are a responsive tool for content creators to ensure their rights as copyright holders. The need for this emerges where the creation of digital content, wherein the fiftieth duplicate of a work is of the same, high quality as the first, and its immediate proliferation over the Internet meet to challenge traditional forms of copyright protection. In this regime for digital content distribution, DRM enables creators to control how much of their content is seen, for what period and, perhaps most important, at what cost to consumers. Public interest groups such as the Electronic Frontier Foundation note these tools also "erode capabilities that had previously been permitted to the public by copyright law under the 'fair use' doctrine."[5] The unbundling of rights coded for in DRM technology affords content creators the ability to decline making a whole work available or to make select portions available with discretionary regard for fair use. In the process, promoting the "progress of science and useful arts" becomes a function of content creators' will rather than an effective, assured balance to the Constitution's allowance for copyright.

Circumventing DRM technologies for the purpose of fair use is hardly an option for the average content consumer. Nor is it legal in light of the DMCA. Bargaining power, through technological code and legal enforcement, therefore shifts into the hands of the content creator. This paper asserts that if fair use has any future, a defining and critical characteristic of the doctrine must be maintained: fairness. The reality of DRM technologies calls this into question.

The Reality of the Threat

It is reasonable to wonder whether Lessig's vision of DRM will be a real problem at all. The future exchange of DRM-protected copyrighted materials may never reach the scale foreseen in Lessig's vision. However, as DRM continues to grow in scale and sophistication, the future of fair use becomes increasingly uncertain. This is because the rules of the game have changed. Interpretations of what is fair use of copyrighted materials have been largely based on answering the question, What is the nature of the transformative work? DRM presents a technological bottleneck to encountering that important question to begin with; a filter is placed on the basic access to effectuate a desired fair use of copyrighted materials. As digital content becomes more cheaply produced and widely distributed, the effect of legal responses such as the DMCA has enforced the curtailing of content available for fair use.

As a *de facto* regulator of what copyrighted materials may be subject to fair use, the myriad implications for the university setting are still being realized. As observed by Georgetown law professor Julie E. Cohen, content providers using DRM can "prohibit fair-use commentary simply by implementing access and disclosure restrictions that bind the entire public."[6] For those in the university setting, this is cause for concern. The stark possibly that the room for fair use of copyrighted materials, especially toward the use of diverse and many sources in teaching, will become smaller as DRM grows in scale is not as far off as Lessig's vision. Academics are not only the source of much published "content," but also a major conduit and consumer of the content produced by others.[7] It behooves the commercial and academic consumer alike to ensure that fair use is just as fair and useful after—as before—the emergence of DRM and the proliferation of digital content.

This paper argues that DRM puts at risk the flexibility that has enabled fair use to remain adaptable in new settings and technology. The usefulness of fair use in the digital age is prescribed by the availability—or unavailability—of content. Things are changing, even if slowly, in how users consume content. The e-books of half a decade ago were gadgets at best and paperweights at worst when they decided, as if on their own, not to work at all. But downloadable content at sites like Amazon.com and freeculture.com are making on-screen reading more viable.

Fair Use in the Classroom and in Research Projects
The Survey

To achieve insight into how DRM might impact fair use in university and college research and teaching, we launched a survey aimed at university and college teachers and researchers. We used the tools and functionality available at www.surveymonkey.com to design and launch the survey, and although we originally planned to use the software suite Software Package for the Social Sciences to analyze the results, we found the analytical tools available in the Survey Monkey package well suited to our purposes.

Purpose, Concept, and Design

The survey design aims to collect data about current practices and habits regarding fair use of copyrighted materials in the classroom and research. We posed questions to ensure voluntary responses and that each respondent was actively involved with university or college research or teaching. We did not collect demographic data apart from asking how long the respondent had been in his or her current research or teaching role. We omitted such questions because we did not view other demographic data as being valuable, informative, or predictive with regard to the research question we identified.

We identified survey participants in a nonrandomized fashion from among groups likely to have an interest in the issue and to be willing to participate in a short survey. For instance, we contacted participants in the University of Maryland University College Center for Intellectual Property conference at which we presented this paper to the extent that such participants provided valid e-mail addresses. We also contacted students, faculty, and alumni associated with Georgetown University's Communication Culture and Technology Program and invited them both to take the survey and to forward the survey link to others whom they believed might be willing to take the survey. Because of the nonrandomized selection process and our openness to participation by persons whom we did not contact directly, we are unable to say exactly how large the population of persons contacted to inquire about their interest in the survey was. We estimate that the number contacted was at least two hundred.

We used survey and analysis tools available online through a subscription service called Survey Monkey (www.surveymonkey.com). Participants were invited to take the survey via a link embedded in an e-mail that we sent them. We then captured and analyzed that data to produce the results offered here.

The core questions of the survey, in addition to collecting data about current patterns and practices regarding use of copyrighted materials in teaching and research, posed hypotheticals designed to test how researchers and teachers might adjust their use of copyrighted works subject to DRM restrictions on copying, printing, and e-mailing. For example, respondents were asked,

> *If a text that you desired to use in your research or teaching were available in electronic form or in print, but the electronic version could not be printed, copied, or e-mailed, in whole or*

in part, to another user once you purchased it, what would you likely do?

Answer choices:

- Buy the electronic version: Inability to print or share would not deter me
- Buy the print version: I value being able to copy and share what I read
- Buy the electronic version: But only if it were much less expensive than print

Likewise, respondents were asked:

If a text that you desired to use in the classroom or in your research were available only in electronic form and could not be copied or e-mailed, in part or in whole, after purchase, what would you likely do?

Answer choices:

- Buy it and use it, and leave it up to students or research colleagues to obtain their own copies
- Drop the text from the syllabus or research project
- Make the text optional for the syllabus or project, not required
- My reaction would depend upon the price of the electronic text

As is evident, these questions aimed to test, in a preliminary way that can be expanded in a separate survey and study, researchers' and teachers' price sensitivity to DRM restrictions. Within the confines of a sub-twenty-questions survey, it was not possible to develop this topic. Further, price sensitivity is probably better explored among a universe of confirmed users of DRM-protected material, which was not possible to establish within the confines of this study.

Summary and Analysis of Results[8]
The survey produced eighty-two responses from persons who confirmed that they were enrolled in or employed by universities. For the reasons stated above, it is not possible to provide the total number of persons contacted

to inquire about their willingness to take the survey. Fifty-one respondents provided descriptions of their university roles as follows:

Mostly teach	0%
Mostly research	7.8%
Teach and research	15.7%
Administrator	23.5%
Student, with teaching or research role	52.9%

Ninety-four percent of respondents said that they used copyrighted materials in their work at least "on occasion." Ninety-two percent said that they were at least "somewhat" familiar with the doctrine of fair use; analysis of the data subset of those respondents who said that they were not familiar with the doctrine revealed that even most of those respondents disclosed at least occasional use of copyrighted materials in their work.

The most frequent response to the question, "Are you familiar with digital rights management (DRM) technology?" was no, with 42 percent of respondents offering this reply. Survey participants were then asked three hypothetical questions about their willingness to use electronic versions of copyrighted works that bore DRM limitations. The questions and breakouts of responses are as follows:

> *If a text that you desired to use in your research or teaching were available in electronic form or in print, but the electronic version could not be printed, copied, or e-mailed, in whole or in part, to another user once you purchased it, what would you likely do?*

- Buy the electronic version: Inability to print or share would not deter me
- Buy the print version: I value being able to copy and share what I read
- Buy the electronic version: But only if it were much less expensive than print

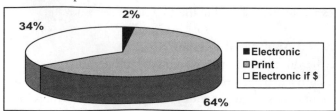

If a text that you desired to use in the classroom or in your research were available only in electronic form and could not be copied or e-mailed, in part or in whole, after purchase, what would you likely do?

- Buy it and use it, and leave it up to students or research colleagues to obtain their own copies
- Drop the text from the syllabus or research project
- Make the text optional for the syllabus or project, not required
- My reaction would depend upon the price of the electronic text

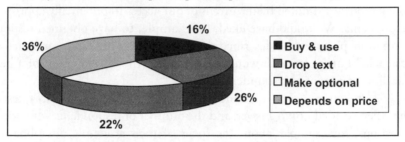

If a nonrequired text that you desired to use in the classroom or in your research were available only in electronic form and could not be copied or e-mailed, in part or in whole, after purchase, what would you likely do?

- Buy it and use it, and leave it up to students or research colleagues to obtain their own copies
- Drop the text from the syllabus or research project
- My reaction would depend upon the price of the electronic text

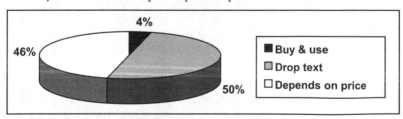

Conclusions Suggested by Results

Respondents' answers suggest that DRM limitations would deter research and teaching use of electronic copyrighted materials. Respondents largely would prefer to use print copies with the additional copying and sharing properties the print format affords. Only a minority of respondents would press ahead to use required or even nonrequired texts as planned if there were DRM restrictions on copying and sharing.

Significantly, a large percentage of respondents would at least consider using DRM-restricted copyrighted materials if the price were right, that is, reduced to compensate for the restrictions. This suggests an interesting market solution to preserve the viability of fair use—for a price.

Limitations of Research Method and Results

Two limitations of the research method likely impose limits on the extent to which extrapolation from these findings is appropriate.

First, the size of the survey sample was limited, and the targeting of our solicitations was limited by the extent of our access to potentially appropriate respondents. We would have liked, for example, to have obtained responses from more persons who described their roles as "mostly teach" or "teach and research." Future research would benefit from the development of a better database of potential respondents.

Second, our survey instrument allowed respondents to skip questions that they decided not to answer, and the number of respondents who skipped questions, for example, about the focus of their academic discipline (e.g., social sciences, humanities) suggests that some respondents found the answer choices ill suited to their circumstances. Additionally, numerous respondents skipped one or more of the core questions posed about how they use copyrighted materials in their work, again suggesting discomfort with the answer choices offered. Alternatively, it may be that asking pointed questions about the use of copyrighted materials—an issue that may have legal consequences—raised general discomfort about self-disclosure. Future survey instruments might pose more questions as hypotheticals in order to obtain greater participation.

Fair Protection for Fair Use

Like most tensions that technology creates between content creators and content consumers, there are several possible solutions from various disciplines. Each of these solution sets requires a fundamental reconceptualization of fair use as a right accorded to users, a notion not so strongly supported by the legislative history of the Copyright Act as the model policy suggests, but endorsed by logic itself. If the Copyright Act is a congressional construction of the Copyright Clause, it is apportioning and balancing no more and no less than the set of rights defined by the clause.[9]

One solution is from the discipline of law. In an approach obverse to the now familiar one in which content providers petition courts and legislators for broader definitions of what is protected and prohibited, users might persuade Congress to enact a law forbidding content providers from requiring a waiver of fair use. Fair use could become, in this way, a nonwaivable right in addition to an affirmative defense. Congress has been motivated to creative interpretations of the Copyright Clause in the past, but only on behalf of content providers.[10] It is not clear what kind of movement would have to coalesce among users to persuade Congress to act on their behalf.

Another possible solution is economic. The right of fair use could become waivable only upon compensation from the content provider to the content user in the form of added benefits, for example, bonus content, or reduced price. This latter possibility, reduced price, is suggested by the survey results. It is not clear currently what incentive content providers might require in order make such an offer; striking such a deal between providers and users might require years of trial and error in the bargaining process. But the introduction and success of services such as Rhapsody and iTunes in the music space give some reason for optimism.

Another variety of economic solution would be a boycott. Users could discipline providers by refusing to purchase content if an actual or de facto waiver of fair use is required.

Another possible solution could come from technology. If the real impetus behind DRM is to protect content providers from wholesale copying or hijacking of their works in amounts and substantiality that exceed fair-use parameters, smart DRM systems could limit users to copying or printing portions that would be within fair-use parameters. Watermarks in the content could keep track of how much of the work has been copied or printed over what period of time and allow or disallow additional printing or copying within the confines of fair-use parameters. The elements of such a system already exist, but, again, the back and forth between providers and users will need to evolve substantially before either party buys in to a system so pervasive.

Conclusion

The future of fair use depends on the vitality of the two main defining characteristics suggested by its very name: fairness and usefulness.

The concept of fairness entails a balance of interests between the creator's interest and the user's interest. A system that, by law or in practice, puts all of the bargaining power into the hands of the creator will not capture this sense of fairness.

Such a system also will fail to be useful to scholars and instructors. The inability to make fair use of works published in the future will contract the availability of such sources to refresh syllabi or to spontaneously supplement syllabi with timely content. Updating syllabi from semester to semester with fair-use-proof material will require students to purchase additional texts, increasing at the margin the already formidable financial commitment required for undergraduate or graduate studies. At the margin, faculty may decide to omit the text rather than create such additional burdens.

There is one final attribute that scholars and instructors can reasonably expect of the fair-use doctrine—that like the Constitution from which it is derived, it maintains a flexibility that enables it to remain futuristic, that is, adaptable to future, unforeseen circumstances. If the fourth amendment of the Constitution can be relevant not just when the King's men break down the front door, but when police use handheld thermography devices to detect in-home marijuana cultivation, it is not too much to expect the same flexibility of the Copyright Clause.[11]

Notes

1. Lawrence Lessig, *Code and Other Laws of Cyberspace* (New York: Basic, 1999).

2. D. Burke and J. Cohen, "Fair Use Infrastructure for Rights Management Systems," *Harvard Journal of Law and Technology* 15, no. 1 (2001): 43.

3. Available online from http://www.cni.org/docs/infopols/ALA.html#mpup.

4. Available online from http://fairuse.stanford.edu/Copyright_and_Fair_Use_Overview/chapter7/7-a.ht; http://library.bowdoin.edu/reference/copyright.shtml.

5. F. von Lohmann, *Fair Use and Digital Rights Management: Preliminary Thoughts on the (Irreconcilable?) Tension between Them* (San Francisco: Electronic Frontier Foundation, 2002).

6. J. Cohen, "Call It the Digital Millennium Censorship Act," *New Republic,* May 21, 2000.

7. S. Vaidhyanathan, "Copyright as Cudgel," *Chronicle of Higher Education,* August 2, 2002.

8. A detailed report of the survey results is available online from http://www.surveymonkey.com/DisplaySummary.asp?SID=491111.

9. The final conference report on the DMCA refers to fair use as one of the "existing limitations on the rights of copyright owners." Available online from http://www.ari.net/hrrc/H.R._2281-_conf._report.pdf. However, the house report on the 1976 Copyright Act, where the doctrine of fair use was first codified, studiously avoids calling fair use itself a right and endorses the letter agreement between universities and publishers in which both sides acknowledged that the types of copying identified as permitted under their agreement could change to the benefit or detriment of one side or the other. See http://www.title17.com/contentLegMat/houseReport/chpt01/sec107.html. That is not normally the way in which a "right" is defined.

10. *Eldred v. Ashcroft,* 537 U.S. 186 (2003).

11. The fourth amendment to the U.S. Constitution protects citizens against unreasonable searches and seizures. At the time of its adoption, searches and seizures involved physical intrusion into a citizen's premises. Over time, technological developments have made it possible to conduct searches and seizures without physical intrusion into a citizen's premises by means of wiretapping, aircraft overflight surveillance, or the use of thermographic devices to detect excess heat emanating from a building, which might be suggestive of marijuana growing. Accordingly, the courts have reinterpreted the fourth amendment in this modern context to explain which law enforcement tools and methods are unreasonable and what types of activities citizens may safely regard as private. *See Kyllo v. United States,* 533 U.S.27 (2001).

References

Burk, D., and Cohen, J. 2001. "Fair Use Infrastructure for Rights Management Systems." *Harvard Journal of Law & Technology* 15, no. 1: 42–83.

Cohen, J. 2000 (May 21). "Call It the Digital Millennium Censorship Act," *New Republic Online.* Available at http://www.tnr.com/index.mhtml.

Vaidhyanathan, S. 2002 (August 2). "Copyright as Cudgel." *Chronicle of Higher Education* 48, no. 47: B7.

von Lohmann, F. 2002. *Fair Use and Digital Rights Management: Preliminary Thoughts on the (Irreconcilable?) Tension between Them* (San Francisco: Electronic Frontier Foundation).

Contributors

Donna L. Ferullo

Donna L. Ferullo, JD, is director of the Purdue University Copyright Office. The office was established in July 2000 and is charged with providing advice and guidance to faculty and staff on copyright issues. Prior to joining Purdue University, Ms. Ferullo had a solo law practice in Boston, specializing in copyright law. She holds a BA from Boston College, a master's in library science from the University of Maryland, and a JD from Suffolk University Law School. Moreover, she is a member of the ACRL Copyright Committee and serves as Purdue's representative on the Digital Library Initiatives Overview Committee for the Big Ten Committee on Institutional Cooperation. Ms. Ferullo also serves on the copyright committee of the Indiana Partnership for Statewide Education (IPSE).

Albert A. Gonzalez

Albert A. Gonzalez is an MA Candidate, May 2004, Georgetown University, in Communication, Culture and Technology. Mr. Gonzalez is a graduate student and honors candidate in the Landegger Program in International Business Diplomacy at Georgetown's School of Foreign Service. In addition to communications, his current research centers on developing country competitiveness in attracting foreign direct investment. He is a former Riordan Fellow at the Anderson School of Business Management at UCLA and also a graduate of UCLA, B.A.

Abby Goodrum

Abby Goodrum is an assistant professor in the School of Information Studies at Syracuse University. She was formerly at Drexel University where she taught courses in visual information retrieval, knowledge management, and information architecture. Prior to beginning her academic career, she was a librarian for Cable News Network. Ms. Goodrum received her Ph.D. in information science from the University of North Texas, a master's degree in library science, and a bachelor's degree in radio, television, and film from the University of Texas. Abby's general research interests include information seeking and retrieval in multimedia environments, and the development of Web-based environments for the production and dissemination of still and moving images as well as the social, political, and economic impact of new media technology. An active ASIS&T member since 1991, she currently serves on the board of directors.

James Howison

James Howison is a Ph.D. student at the School of Information Studies at Syracuse University. His research focuses on P2P networking, distributed resource sharing on wireless grids, and effective practices in Open Source software communities, in addition to having an active interest in the work flow of academics. In 2000, he was invited to present at the first O'Reilly conference on P2P. Before coming to the United States, he studied computer science at the University of New South Wales and economics and politics at the University of Sydney.

Marcia W. Keyser

Marcia W. Keyser is coordinator of information services at Cowles Library, Drake University. Her duties include the management of e-reserves for the campus, serving as the library copyright expert, coordinating a virtual reference collaborative, and teaching information literacy. She came to Cowles Library in January of 2002 from the Texas A&M University-Kingsville's Jernigan Library, where she served as a reference librarian for eight years. She earned her MLS degree from the University of Missouri in 1993. Prior to becoming a librarian, she earned an MA degree in English and worked as an adjunct professor.

Clifford Lynch

Clifford Lynch is presently executive director of the Coalition for Networked Information (CNI). He has been director of CNI since July 1997. Prior to joining CNI, Dr. Lynch spent eighteen years at the University of California Office of the President, the last ten as director of library automation. Internationally known for his development of Melvyl, an information system that serves all of the campuses of the University of California, he has played a key role in the development of information standards. Especially noteworthy is his work on Z39.50, which addresses the need for interoperability among information retrieval systems. Dr. Lynch, who holds a Ph.D. in computer science from the University of California, Berkeley, is an adjunct professor at Berkeley's School of Information Management and Systems.

John T. Mitchell

John T. Mitchell of Interaction Law brings together his passion for protecting First Amendment freedom, maintaining a balanced approach to copyright law, developing sound public policy concerning digital media and electronic commerce, and strengthening the consumer and retail competition focus of antitrust law. For more than fourteen years, he has been representing trade associations, primarily those involved in retailing expressive materials, on antirust issues and a wide array of association issues. He is experienced in federal and nationwide litigation, legislative and administrative advocacy on matters of electronic commerce, First Amendment rights, copyright law, unfair trade practices, and antitrust law. Pro bono legislative work has included representation of illegal aliens, restoration of democracy in Haiti, representation of Chinese nationals following the Tiananmen Square massacre, and defense of the information commons. Mr. Mitchell received his JD degree magna cum laude from the University of Louisville Brandeis School of Law in 1987. In addition to a BA in philosophy and religion, he holds degrees in social work (MSSW) and in religious education (MRE).

Gary Natriello

Gary Natriello is professor of sociology and education at Teachers College, Columbia University. He is executive editor of *Teachers College Record,* a peer-reviewed academic journal with print and online audiences. Professor Natriello is also the interim director of the Gottesman Libraries at Teachers College and has served as chair of the Publications Committee of the American Educational Research Association and editor of the *American Educational Research Journal.* The author of numerous articles and books, he is a recognized expert in the social organization of schools, the evaluation of student and teacher performance, and the education of at-risk youth.

Allyson Polsky McCabe

Allyson Polsky McCabe teaches humanities in the College of Letters at Wesleyan University and English at Yale University. She is particularly interested in writing across the curriculum, and her courses have guided students' understanding of the ways that disciplinary knowledge is produced, organized, and managed and how to effectively use online tools for academic research.

Jasmine R. Renner

Jasmine R. Renner is currently an Assistant Professor in the Department of Education Leadership and Policy Analysis at East Tennessee State University. She currently instructs courses in Higher Education Law and Finance, School Law, and Law for Organizational Leaders. She is holder of a Law degree (LL. B Hons) from the University of Sierra Leone, Law School, an LL.M (Masters of Law) from the University of Georgia, School of Law, and an Ed.D. in Education Leadership and Policy Analysis from Bowling Green State University. She is also actively involved in research on copyright law in higher education.

Michael Rennick

Michael Rennick is director of online publishing for the *Teachers College Record* and the designer of numerous online learning venues, including course platforms, publishing platforms, editorial office management software, and research and development center sites. Together with Gary Natriello, he founded Frameworkers, LLC, a firm specializing in the development of tools for online publishing.

Kathleen Wallman

Kathleen Wallman is visiting research professor in communication, culture, and technology at Georgetown University. Professor Wallman is former deputy counsel to the president, White House Counsel's Office, and former deputy assistant for economic policy in the Clinton administration. She is a graduate of Catholic University, BA summa cum laude, and Georgetown University, MS in foreign service, with honors, and JD, magna cum laude. A selection of publications is available at http://www.wallman.com.